D0385965

READING AND THINKING

Using Supplementary Books in the Classroom

READING AND THINKING
Using Supplementary Books in the Classroom

MAURICE J. EASH

Hunter College

WITH SPECIAL CHAPTERS BY

RICHARD J. NICHOLS

Newark State College

MARILYN CARROL

Hunter College

GLADYS S. KLEINMAN

Rutgers—The State University

ANNE S. GROSSMAN

Hunter College

DOUBLEDAY & COMPANY, INC.

GARDEN CITY, NEW YORK

1967

Library of Congress Catalog Card Number 67–18665

Copyright © 1967 by Doubleday & Company, Inc.

All Rights Reserved

Printed in the United States of America

First Edition

Grateful acknowledgment is made for the use of excerpts from the following books:

"Blood Royal" by Montgomery A. Atwater. Reprinted by permission of the author and his agent, August Lenniger.

California Indian Days by Helen Bauer, copyright © 1963 by Helen Bauer; and *California Rancho Days* by Helen Bauer, copyright 1953 by Helen Bauer. Reprinted by permission of Doubleday & Company, Inc.

Choo Choo by Virginia Lee Burton, copyright 1937 by Houghton Mifflin Company. Reprinted by permission of the publisher.

Crusaders for Freedom by Henry Steele Commager, copyright © 1962 by Henry Steele Commager. Reprinted by permission of the author.

Yonie Wondernose by Marguerite de Angeli, copyright 1944 by Marguerite de Angeli. Reprinted by permission of Doubleday & Company, Inc.

Benjamin Franklin, copyright 1950 by Doubleday & Company, Inc.; *Buffalo Bill*, copyright 1952 by Doubleday & Company, Inc.; and *Leif the Lucky*, copyright 1941 by Doubleday & Company, Inc., all by Ingri and Edgar Parin d'Aulaire. Reprinted by permission of Doubleday & Company, Inc.

"The Cupboard" from *Collected Poems 1901–1918* by Walter de la Mare, copyright 1920 by Henry Holt and Company, copyright 1948 by Walter de la Mare. Reprinted by permission of The Literary Trustees of Walter de la Mare and The Society of Authors as their representative.

A Chipmunk Lives Here by Irmengarde Eberle, copyright © 1966 by Irmengarde Eberle Koehler. Reprinted by permission of Doubleday & Company, Inc.

The Lollypop Factory and Lots of Others by Mary Elting and Margaret Gossett, copyright 1946 by Doubleday & Company, Inc. Reprinted by permission of the publisher.

The Secret of the Simple Code by Nancy Faulkner, copyright © 1965 by Anne I. Faulkner, and *Small Clown* by Nancy Faulkner, copyright © 1960 by Anne I. Faulkner. Reprinted by permission of Doubleday & Company, Inc.

Tales from Silver Lands by Charles J. Finger (Newbery Award Winner, 1925), copyright 1924 by Doubleday & Company, Inc. Reprinted by permission of the Charles J. Finger Estate.

A Summer to Remember by Ann Finlayson, copyright © 1964 by Doubleday & Company, Inc. Reprinted by permission of the publisher.

The Wonderful World of the Air by James Fisher, copyright © 1958 by James Fisher and Adprint Limited. Reprinted by permission of Doubleday & Company, Inc.

The New Pet by Marjorie Flack, copyright 1943 by Marjorie Flack Benét. Reprinted by permission of Doubleday & Company, Inc.

The ABC's of Astronomy, copyright © 1962 by Doubleday & Company, Inc.; *Exploring Chemistry*, copyright © 1958 by Doubleday & Company, Inc.; *Exploring the Planets*, copyright © 1958 by Doubleday & Company, Inc.; *Exploring the Sun*, copyright © 1958 by Roy A. Gallant; and *Man's Reach into Space*, copyright © 1959, 1964 by Doubleday & Company, Inc., all by Roy Gallant. Reprinted by permission of Doubleday & Company, Inc.

Noah's Ark ABC by Willard Goodman. Reprinted by permission of Doubleday & Company, Inc.

Jets and Rockets and How They Work by William P. Gottlieb, copyright © 1959 by William P. Gottlieb, and *Space Flight and How It Works* by William P. Gottlieb, copyright © 1963 by William P. Gottlieb. Reprinted by permission of Doubleday & Company, Inc.

The Wonderful Story of How You Were Born by Sidonie Matsner Gruenberg. Copyright © 1952, 1953, 1959 by Doubleday & Company, Inc. Reprinted by permission of the publisher.

Pancho by Berta and Elmer Hader. Copyright 1942 by Berta Hader and Elmer Hader. Reprinted by permission of The Macmillan Company.

My Skyscraper City: A Child's View of New York, photographs by Katrina Thomas, verses by Penny Hamond, copyright © 1963 by Katrina Thomas and Jo Ann Hamond. Reprinted by permission of Doubleday & Company, Inc.

The Story of Illinois by Harry Hansen, copyright © 1956 by Harry Hansen. Reprinted by permission of Doubleday & Company, Inc.

The Quest of Archimedes by Tad Harvey. Copyright © 1962 by Doubleday & Company, Inc. Reprinted by permission of the publisher.

Stonehenge Decoded by Gerald S. Hawkins in collaboration with John B. White, copyright © 1965 by Gerald S. Hawkins and John B. White. Reprinted by permission of Doubleday & Company, Inc.

Fast Ball Pitcher by Jay Heavilin, copyright © 1965 by Doubleday & Company, Inc. Reprinted by permission of the publisher.

A Talent for Trouble by Jane Hinchman, copyright © 1966 by Jane Hinchman. Reprinted by permission of Doubleday & Company, Inc.

A Trip to the Pond by Melita Hofmann, copyright © 1966 by Melita Hofmann. Reprinted by permission of Doubleday & Company, Inc.

The Wonderful World of Mathematics by Lancelot Hogben. Reprinted by permission of Doubleday & Company, Inc.

Heroes of the Skies by Edwin P. Hoyt, copyright © 1963 by Doubleday & Company, Inc. Reprinted by permission of Doubleday & Company, Inc.

The Wonderful World of Life by Julian Huxley, copyright © 1958 by Julian Huxley and Adprint Limited. Reprinted by permission of Doubleday & Company, Inc.

Brown Cow Farm, copyright © 1959 by Dahlov Ipcar; *Stripes and Spots,* copyright © 1953, 1961 by Dahlov Ipcar; and *Wild and Tame Animals,* copyright © 1962 by Dahlov Ipcar, all by Dahlov Ipcar. Reprinted by permission of Doubleday & Company, Inc.

Profile of Kenya, copyright © 1963 by Leonard S. Kenworthy; and *Profile of Nigeria,* copyright © 1960 by Leonard S. Kenworthy, both by Leonard S. Kenworthy. Reprinted by permission of Doubleday & Company, Inc.

All Aboard the Train, copyright © 1964 by Ethel and Leonard Kessler, and *Big Red Bus,* copyright © 1957 by Ethel and Leonard Kessler, both by Ethel and Leonard Kessler. Reprinted by permission of Doubleday & Company, Inc.

"The White Seal," "Toomai of the Elephants," and "Mowgli's Brothers," all from *The Jungle Book* by Rudyard Kipling. Reprinted by permission of Mrs. George Bambridge, the Macmillan Company of Canada, Ltd., and Doubleday & Company, Inc.

The Wonderful World of Transportation by Laurie Lee and David Lambert, copyright © 1960 by Rathbone Books Limited. Reprinted by permission of Doubleday & Company, Inc.

The Quest of Louis Pasteur by Patricia Lauber, copyright © 1960 by Patricia Lauber. Reprinted by permission of Doubleday & Company, Inc.

"Buildings" from *Whispers and Other Poems* by Myra Cohn Livingston, copyright © 1958 by Myra Cohn Livingston. Reprinted by permission of Harcourt, Brace & World, Inc.

Myths Every Child Should Know by Hamilton Wright Mabie. Reprinted by permission of Doubleday & Company, Inc.

The Little Island by Golden MacDonald and Leonard Weisgard, copyright 1946 by Doubleday & Company, Inc. Reprinted by permission of the publisher.

The Winning of the West by Harold McCracken, copyright © 1955 by Harold McCracken. Reprinted by permission of Doubleday & Company, Inc.

Hailstones and Halibut Bones by Mary O'Neill, copyright © 1961 by Mary LeDuc O'Neill. Reprinted by permission of Doubleday & Company, Inc.

The Giant Nursery Book, copyright © 1957 by Tony Palazzo; *Goldilocks and the Three Bears,* copyright © 1959 by Doubleday & Company, Inc.; *The Three Little Kittens,* copyright © 1961 by Doubleday & Company, Inc.; and *The Little Red Hen,* copyright © 1958 by Doubleday & Company, Inc., all by Tony Palazzo. Reprinted by permission of Doubleday & Company, Inc.

Mystery on Telegraph Hill by Howard Pease, copyright © 1961 by Howard Pease. Reprinted by permission of Doubleday & Company, Inc.

Animals, Inc. by Roy Pinney, copyright © 1964 by Roy Pinney. Reprinted by permission of Doubleday & Company, Inc.

The Civil War by Fletcher Pratt, copyright © 1955 by Fletcher Pratt. Reprinted by permission of Doubleday & Company, Inc.

Partners: The United Nations and Youth by Eleanor Roosevelt and Helen Ferris, copyright 1950 by Eleanor Roosevelt and Helen Ferris Tibbets. Reprinted by permission of Doubleday & Company, Inc.

CONTENTS

PREFACE

This book was written for teachers, parents, librarians—anyone interested in the education of our young people. It was written out of a concern for improving teaching and learning through the tying of children's reading of trade books to the research findings about the way people think. Thus the first chapter describes a framework of areas of cognitive (thinking) abilities and relates them to development through use of written materials.

Chapters II through V show how content, as found in trade books in four specific subject areas, can be related to the framework of cognitive abilities. The authors believe that helping children to develop the cognitive skills with written materials is a good method of fostering the functional scholarship skills which are a significant part of all the advanced disciplines.

Chapters VI and VII look at some of the instructional issues that teachers face as they are confronted with a variety of instructional media.

It is the intent of the authors to write a book that will clarify complex research and promote its implementation in the classroom. The authors, having all been classroom teachers, are cognizant of the everyday problems teachers face: vast amounts of written material, children of widely varying reading levels, limited time for preparation and evaluation, to mention but a few. Consequently, in preparing the chapters using the framework on areas of cognitive abilities, many specific examples at varying levels of development are included.

Many of the examples, as well as the five areas of cognitive abilities, have been tested with classes of children. In the classroom demonstrations children reflected their individual levels of development as they responded to the suggested approaches. For this reason no strict grade level has been assigned to the examples, and a broad band of grading the examples —primary (Grades 1–3), middle (Grades 4–6), and upper (Grades 7–8)—has been used. The examples are, of course, only a start. As the teacher gains more experience with the framework and with materials, the range of potential use expands.

One of the most commonly agreed-upon goals in a reading program is the development of enjoyment of reading. I believe that assisting children in gaining command of more complex scholarship skills furthers this goal. Reading for enjoyment and development of functional scholarship skills are reciprocal and should proceed simultaneously. To paraphrase Alfred North Whitehead, education should be the communication of knowledge with enjoyment.

To begin to name all the people and sources which have been helpful in the formulation of the basic ideas and the writing of this book would entail compiling a lengthy list. The basic research and background material for the framework of areas of cognitive abilities described in Chapter I was drawn heavily from the pioneering work of Sir Frederic Bartlett, Donald E. Broadbent, David Ausubel, J. P. Guilford, Charles Osgood, Jean Piaget and the *Taxonomy of Educational Objectives Handbook I: Cognitive Domain,* Benjamin S. Bloom, Editor.

To others who have been especially helpful in reading, criticizing, and sharpening the manuscript at critical junctures, special acknowledgment is given to two esteemed professional colleagues, Dr. Robert Chasnoff of Newark State College, and Dr. Thomas G. Aylesworth, Senior Editor at Doubleday. And to my wife Cornelia, who has lent professional assistance and personal support at every point in the development of this manuscript, I owe infinite gratitude.

Maurice J. Eash

New York City
March, 1967

CHAPTER I

READING AND COGNITIVE ABILITIES

Three fourth graders were reading a lesson on local history. One read, "The streetcars were above the ground." Then came the following conversation:

"Do you think they were as high as the telephone lines?"

"How could they run up high without falling off?"

"Maybe they're like these new trains which hang underneath a track on poles?"

The last observation seemed to satisfy their curiosity and they returned to the story persuaded that monorails were at least fifty years old.

The story began, "A PICTURE OF Jefferson was hung in the White House." In the small reading group all the children slid over the words which were printed in capitals and then held the following conversation on the startling information they had just read.

Jess remarked, "I heard Lincoln was shot but I didn't know Jefferson was hung."

Donnie, extremely puzzled, picked up the thread and speculated on how bad a crime a President would have to commit in order to be hung. The conversation wandered far and wide. But none of the students checked back on the written context to discover if information had been skirted and the author's message distorted. No child suggested checking some outside evidence although several sources were readily available within the room.

These two stories demonstrate a phenomenon with which every classroom teacher is familiar. On the surface they are seen as typical children's misunderstandings, but analyzed in greater depth they are expressions of difficulty in thinking, or to use a more scientific term, cognition.

Educators have long stated their concern that there should be improvement in the teaching of thinking. Emerson's terse comment on what constitutes a scholar, "In the right state the scholar is man thinking," has, for most educators, acceptably described the relationship of scholarship and thinking. However, the specifics of thinking, or cognition as we shall call it in this book, have only recently been explored within a scientific framework and the evidences of these processes brought to light in such a manner that teachers can employ procedures to teach them directly in the classroom.

Identifying some of the basic areas of cognitive abilities from research findings, the following chapter describes and gives examples of how these areas can be cultivated through use of trade books in the classroom. Trade books have been selected as the illustrative instructional media not only on the grounds of their ready availability, but also because of the added feature that they can be pursued as independent activities within the classroom schedules.

Used as independent activities in the classroom, trade books afford students open-ended opportunities to explore meanings. In the exploration process students may be guided, through teacher assistance, to use several different kinds of cognitive abilities which help them plumb these meanings. Meanings hardly ever come directly and unassisted from written materials. And written materials form much of the basis for learning experiences in the classroom and pose their own special problems as well as special advantages.

In using written materials, the learner must bring an ability to decode meaning to the symbolic presentation, since words are symbols representing the reality of experience. In decoding meaning from symbols, the application of the kinds of cognitive abilities and the analysis of the written material may make the difference between useful knowledge and confusion. The development of the ability to use the various kinds of cognitive ability cannot be left to chance. As the opening examples in this chapter demonstrated, the students opted for misunderstanding because of the lack of command of sufficient cognitive skills. They could not apply proper procedures to the solution of a difficulty in understanding the author's message. In order to facilitate the use of cognitive skills it is first necessary to identify and isolate the main areas which have been suggested by research in cognition. In short, we need to know what we are talking about.

There have been scores of descriptions and complex classifications of cognitive abilities. Fortunately a combination of theoretical data and scientific investigations of cognition suggest that there is a simpler, broad framework of areas of cognitive abilities for which the classroom teacher can teach. Using this simpler framework of identified and defined areas of cognitive abilities, written materials can be selected to give students practice in each of the areas. These five areas of cognitive abilities are: *understanding, utilizing, discriminating, chaining,* and *judging.*

Understanding

Understanding is the ability to decode the author's meaning without infusing it with individual experiences or application. The learner apprehends the author's main idea without attaching any personal judgment to the message. In the understanding process, the learner is also able to select the author's main ideas and differentiate these from any subordinate ideas. Finally, the learner can reproduce a reasonably close meaning of the author's intended message. The use of the cognitive ability of understanding is essential as a base in order to use other cognitive abilities with written materials.

Central to the understanding process is the command of language and knowledge of vocabulary. Therefore, in the development of understanding, attention should be paid to vocabulary development. Especially important is the awareness of flexibility of meanings garnered from the sentence context. The teaching of flexibility of meanings as derived from context should be accompanied by urging the learner to understand the over-all message through acceptance of the author's ideas and themes on his—the author's—own grounds.

As a general method, the classroom teacher will want to stress obtaining the author's main idea. Entire stories or selected passages, such as the following examples, provide opportunities for students to build understanding abilities.

If you were asked to name some of the great women of history you would say Joan of Arc . . . and Queen Elizabeth . . . and Florence Nightingale . . . and Eleanor Roosevelt. . . . Certainly you would never say Harriet Tubman. You never even *heard* of her. Scarcely anybody has ever heard of her.

Yet she is one of the great women of history.

She was born a slave, on a Maryland plantation, and given the fancy name of Araminta, which she later changed to plain Harriet. She grew up as strong as any man, able to do a man's work plowing in the fields, or a woman's work cooking in the kitchen.

But she could never work hard enough for the brutal overseer who ran the plantation, and once in a fit of temper he threw an iron horseshoe at her and almost killed her. She got well, in time, but after that she was never quite the same: she would fall into a trance, she would go right out of this world and into another world of her imagination where she would see visions and hear voices—just like Joan of Arc.

When Harriet was twenty-five or thirty—it wasn't easy for slaves to keep track of their age—she ran away to nearby Pennsylvania. Good for her! But she wasn't content with that. In one of her visions God told her to go back to Maryland and find her father and mother, her brothers and sisters, and lead them to freedom. And she did.

That was her lifework, to go into the South and guide slaves back across the magic line to the land of freedom. Again and again she made her way deep into Maryland and Virginia—she had a kind of sixth sense about direction, and besides, so she always thought, God guided her. She was clever and shrewd, and could fool almost anyone. Who would ever suspect her of any mischief, this slave woman with a turban wound around her head, and a red bandana at her neck, shuffling along so simple and so innocent? If they *did* she knew how to throw them off the scent. She knew all the hiding places, all the woods and swamps and abandoned barns, in the whole countryside. In the winter months she worked up in Philadelphia, cooking and washing to make money. Then when spring came she was off to the South again. She brought out her parents, driving them herself in an ancient oxcart. She brought out whole families, eight and ten at a time. Sometimes she had to fight to get her slaves away and once—in New York of all places—she rescued a runaway slave from a mob and dragged him through the streets of the town to the riverbank where she pushed him into a boat that carried him off to safety.

Old John Brown—remember him in that poem "Old

John Brown, Osawatomie Brown"?—said that Harriet Tubman "was the most man that I ever met with." He ought to know. He was quite a man himself. He was the man who attacked Harper's Ferry—with just a handful of Negroes. He was the man whose body "lies a mould'ring in the grave—His soul goes marching on."

Harriet Tubman was the Moses of her people, leading them out of the wilderness and into the Promised Land.

Suppose you could save just one person, save one child from drowning, save one old lady from a burning house, give light to one man who was blind. Think how proud and happy you would be: it would be something to remember all your life.

Harriet Tubman saved three hundred lives. She led three hundred slaves across the magic line to freedom.

(Henry Steele Commager,
Crusaders for Freedom, pp. 77–79)

The above passage from a short essay on Harriet Tubman, because of the author's style and skill, is very useful in helping students develop understanding abilities. After reading the passage, the student can be asked to extract the sentence which is most nearly expressive of the author's main idea.

Or the student can write a summary sentence along with a single sentence on subordinate ideas used in support of the author's main idea. The supporting ideas in this instance are the reasons why the author selected Harriet Tubman as one of the great women of history.

The significant factor in all cases is to create a sensitivity in the learner to the necessity for remaining, as nearly as possible, within the intended meaning system of the author and to *differentiate the author's meaning from the learner's own interpretations*. The need for sharper differentiation of the meaning systems of reader and author when the author's meaning is removed from the original context is a fundamental step in understanding-development.

After the learner has done some initial exercises, the teacher can go over the results orally with the students by having them discuss the author's main idea and examine the reasons for any variance with each other or the author. These variances frequently are related to the students' intruding their own interpretation or focusing on only one segment of the generalization. In the initial phases of working on understanding, the use of trade books which have definable units, rather straightforward logic (such as in numerical approaches), avoids duality of meaning or assignment of several meanings to the same idea. An example of a passage which lends itself to early use of cognitive skills with younger children who are working on understanding is the following:

There was a little island in the ocean.
Around it the winds blew
And the birds flew
And the tides rose and fell on the shore.

Clouds passed over it
Fish swam around it
And the fog came in from the sea
and hid the little island
in a soft wet shadow.

(Golden MacDonald,
The Little Island, unpaged)

Following this example is a more difficult passage which can be used as students progress or with students who already have been using cognitive skills involved in understanding at a more advanced level.

What is a microscope?
The simplest answer is that it is an optical instrument for making small things look bigger. Yet "making things look bigger" does not fully express the

power of the microscope. Although a man-made object such as the point of a pin *does* look bigger under
the microscope, an object that has been part of a living
creature usually looks not only bigger but also far
more delicately elaborate than we could possibly have
imagined.

(M. D. Anderson, *Through the Microscope:
Man Looks at an Unseen World*, p. 11)

In both these examples the same principle still holds—
apprehend the main ideas of the author and keep
them from being reinterpreted or reshuffled in the
process.

There is considerable evidence that the closer to
an emotionally tinged area of the student's life the
material is, the greater the difficulty of developing accurate apprehension. Teachers may be alert for this, as
books contain passages about homes and the dynamics of family life. In developing the cognitive ability of
understanding, the use of trade books might very well
be graded for readers on this basis as well as on the
basis of the complexity of the author's ideas.

As an example, in the following passage on houses
in Kenya, teachers would want to be aware of distortion of understanding which creeps in because of the
emotional tonality of the subject, as well as students'
unfamiliarity with Kenya and its people.

Kenya's houses reflect the different ways of life of
her varied people.

As they move from place to place the nomads of the
north often carry the skeletons of their houses with
them. . . . Then, when they find a good place to stay
awhile, they erect poles and throw animal skins over
them to build makeshift dwellings.

Instead of taking their houses with them to each
new location where they settle for a few months or
years, the Masai make houses from earth. Their mud
houses are only three or four feet high, with one en-

trance through which they have to crawl. Inside are few belongings except for the grass mats or skins on which they sleep.

Most Africans, however, build more permanent houses. The Kikuyu, for example, build houses that are sturdy enough to last a long time. Often they are built in a day, with the help of members of family or friends. Materials are usually collected before the day of the "house-raising" with the men collecting the wood and women the grass which will be woven into the roof. Sugar cane juice or honey beer is sprinkled on the ground before the hut is begun, in order to keep evil spirits away. After the men have dug the postholes for the outer walls, the women take over and complete the work, weaving the grasses into a roof and making the mud walls.

(Leonard S. Kenworthy, *Profile of Kenya,* p. 35)

In short, the assimilation of the author's point of view unencumbered by the reader's personal meanings is the objective in this process.

Utilizing

An important part of learning—perhaps the most important part—is the ability to take an understanding from one context and to use it in another. Since it is rare, if ever, that the contexts of two situations are exact duplicates of each other, the learner must be able to abstract the main principle or idea and refashion it, keep its original validity, analyze the context of the second situation, and make the application. To be able to carry through this process is to demonstrate that the learning is truly functional.

A first step in utilizing is the ability to understand a principle or main idea. However, errors of understanding are not the same as errors of utilization. While it is helpful to make a distinction between the two, a teacher must check for errors of understanding in the teaching of utilization. The utilization of principles or ideas from one context to another is at the heart of the students' capabilities to transfer learning.

A high level of ability in the area of utilization promotes a flexibility which frees an individual from learning every bit of material in isolation and as a distinct entity. For example, a learner able to utilize the knowledge that an animal with a thick outside shell has different defenses against enemies than do other animals, is provided with a useful, flexible framework for viewing these animals and their habits.

Does the unfamiliar animal have a thick shell like some other known animal? If the answer is yes, then chances are its habits of defense are similar. And the learner does not need to investigate each animal as a distinct entity. Being able to contrast, compare, and build analogies is part of the skills involved in the area of utilization.

There is a need for teachers to be aware that students may confuse a fact with a generalization, or they may learn and apply separate facts. In this short passage from *Torpedo Run* the author provides the learner with a generalization which has broad utilization—speed can be used for defense purposes.

> *She was* nameless, with only a number given to her by the Navy, but her crew called her *Slewfoot*. She was 77 feet long, 20 feet wide and drew 4 feet of water. When her temperamental engines were right and her bottom was clean she could go 60 miles an hour, which, for a boat, is *very* fast. In the narrow waters around Bayonne, New Jersey, where she was built, she looked pretty big. On the vastness of the Pacific Ocean, going about her deadly business in the dark nights of war, she was a splinter.
>
> During World War II, *Slewfoot* and the rest of the PT boats were the smallest warships the Navy had.

Like many small things in Nature, *Slewfoot*'s life depended on her speed, for she had no protection against gunfire, torpedoes, bombs or strafing planes. Unlike the Navy's other ships, she had no armor; there was nothing for a man to hide behind when the tracers began to arc toward him, for *Slewfoot* was built of wood and mostly plywood at that.

She was designed to hit and—run. Designed to carry three engines with the combined ram of four thousand horsepower to get *Slewfoot* into position and—out again.

Seventy-seven feet of plywood carrying a wallop. On the forepeak there was a 37-millimeter cannon. On both bows were 20-millimeter cannon. Amidships forward were two rocket-launching racks. A little aft of them were two sets of twin .30-caliber machine guns. Farther aft, two on each side, were twin .50-caliber machine guns in turrets. On the stern there was a Bofors 40-millimeter cannon. Sometimes there were more guns than there were men to shoot them.

In addition to the guns, cannons and rockets, *Slewfoot* carried two flip-over torpedo racks each armed with two torpedoes capable of sinking any ship afloat.

And, against submarines, she had depth charges in racks on the stern.

Riding *Slewfoot* in battle was a little like riding a bomb. In her tanks she carried three thousand gallons of highly explosive aviation gasoline. When the PTs were hit they rarely sank in the slow and heartrending way of other ships. PTs simply vanished in one quick, awful flash of flame and smoke.

Compared with other warships, *Slewfoot* was manned by a bunch of kids. The oldest man aboard was the captain, an ancient twenty-one. The rest of them were nineteen, eighteen, even seventeen years old. There were usually a dozen men riding *Slewfoot* through the dark sea, their eyes straining for sight of the enemy, engines muffled, guns manned and ready.

There were motor machinist's mates—"motormacs" —to baby the three Packard engines; torpedomen for the "fish"; gunners. There was a quartermaster who watched over the charts and the movements of the ship; and a boatswain's mate—the bosun—to care for the boat itself. There was a radarman to watch the thin line going around and around; and, of course, the cook. There were two officers—the captain and the executive officer.

The men could sleep in the "dayroom" forward, just abaft the chain locker, in bunks along the sides. It was like sleeping in a crowded elevator that had broken loose and was falling to the bottom of the shaft over and over. But you got used to it just as you got used to standing forever with your knees loose and bent, and learned, many the hard way, what the man meant when he said, "One hand for you and one hand for the ship."

It took you only once to find out why they told you not to fall down on a PT boat. Standing up, holding on, your bent, loose knees absorbed the pounding of the hull against the sea, your body balanced with the astounding roll and pitch. If you fell down, when you tried to push yourself up, the deck dropped out from under you, then the boat came up as you came down. It was like trying to stand up on the bare back of the father of the Strawberry Roan.

One hand for you, one hand for *Slewfoot*.

(Robb White, *Torpedo Run*, pp. 1–3)

The learner would be asked to list the facts which support the generalization, that speed can be a defense, and would produce something like the following:

Facts
Could go 60 miles an hour
Designed to hit and run

Practice of this nature helps the learner see the basis for a generalization and gives him greater power in utilization. In this passage the author suggests that speed is a common defense. "Like many small things in Nature, *Slewfoot*'s life depended on her speed, for she had no protection against gunfire, torpedoes, bombs or strafing planes." For utilization practice the learner could be encouraged to read passages from such other trade books as *Animals, Inc.,* where the same generalization about speed as a defense is found in a different context.

The short passage from *The Wonderful World of Transportation* about the development of transportation is an excellent example from a trade book in which the author has developed a generalization which has broad utilization—man must move and needs mobility.

> Why does man move? He has many reasons: all the reasons of life itself—hunting, fighting, trading, mating, visiting, or just for adventure. As soon as a child can crawl, it tries to move away from its cradle. An instinct in all of us makes us want to search and discover the world.
>
> Originally, no doubt, the reason was hunger. Early man had to eat what he could: roots, berries, plants, fruits and animals when he could hunt them. Searching for these would force him to move. Easily caught animals would learn to shun men and move away to other pastures. To live, man would follow them. But only so many beasts could live off so much land. Only so many men off those beasts. Surplus people had to travel even farther.
>
> In time, early man colonized the earth, moving first in families and later in tribes, searching always for food and space. Little by little he fanned across Asia, seeking the new lands before him, and crossed into America from Siberia to Alaska by a land bridge or shallow sea. Down America, Africa and the Pacific islands, the strong drove the weaker before them, until the earliest wanderers were pushed to the edges of the world, to remote islands in the Southern Hemisphere like Tasmania and Tierra del Fuego.

Here and there people settled, grew food, raised cattle; but man still had reasons to move. Where tribes were small, young men would possibly leave home, as they do today, to seek wives and set up on their own. When a society prospered, and grew rich in goods, it would send merchants to exchange them with people living nearby. So trade began; still the most important reason for transport.

Another reason, even older than trade, was man's baser instinct for war. Poorer tribes, on hearing of wealthier neighbors, would often fall upon them and rob them. Nomads, whose cattle had died in drought, would raid the settled farmers for food. Expanding tribes, throughout history, sought new lands by invading others.

The first men to discover America were seeking food and somewhere to live. When Columbus later rediscovered it, he was looking for spices, gold and glory. It was also the spirit of adventure, the feeling of being first on the scene, which made him face the terrors of the Atlantic; the same spirit which drove our more recent explorers to the poles and to the top of Everest.

Today millions of people travel about the world in search of its many marvels—tourists who visit strange lands for no other reason than curiosity. Man is still, it seems, the most restless being on his ever-restless sphere. He possesses an instinct enjoyed by few other animals, which is simply to journey for pleasure.

(Laurie Lee and David Lambert,
The Wonderful World of Transportation, pp. 12–13)

In having the students develop the generalization (man must move and have mobility) from its supportative data, the student would list the facts and differentiate them from the generalization as in the following:

Facts
Early man moved to find food

Early man moved to trade
Early man moved to make war
Early man moved for adventure

Following a listing of these facts, the generalization that man must move and that he developed his interest in transportation in order to have mobility would be stated. Through this procedure, the student would perceive the relationship of facts and how they differ from the generalization, as well as utilizing the correct generalization from a series of facts.

Following the derivation of a generalization from a series of facts, the utilization of the generalization in other contexts would be made. In this instance contemporary man must also move in order to find employment and for reasons of health in some cases. In cases in which students are limited in experience and have difficulty utilizing the generalization, the cognitive map might be further organized by having students read pages from other trade books such as *The Winning of the West,* a story of westward expansion, or *Mario: A Mexican Boy's Adventure,* a story of migrant labor in California. Both of these books contain the basic generalization that man must move and needs mobility.

Another approach to the development of utilization abilities is the use of analogies as seen in this passage where a propeller is compared to a jet engine.

What is jet propulsion? In principle, it is really nothing new. Propeller-driven planes are, in fact, jet-propelled. A propeller not only thrusts air backwards, it moves forward itself with a reaction equal to the backward thrust of the air. Sir Isaac Newton worked out how this happens long before the propeller-driven plane had been invented. He proved that "action and reaction are equal in magnitude and opposite in direction."

You can prove this yourself by diving off the stern of a free-floating boat. You go one way, and thrust the boat in the opposite direction. In swimming, you move forward by pushing water backward. So it is in the air. One can move through it only by using this same principle of reaction.

Inventors found that a jet of gases could give a greater backward thrust than a propeller. So they made a jet engine which would drive a plane. How does it work? Scientists have invented several kinds.

The ram-jet is just a hollow tube, open at both ends. It can start working only when moving at more than 300 miles an hour. Then its speed rams air into the open funnel of the tube. Liquid fuel, injected into the tube, burns furiously in the oxygen of the compressed air. The burning mixture expands and pushes with great force against a forward component in the tube. By reaction, the plane built round the tube leaps forward with equal force.

Pulse-jets, on the other hand, are ram-jets with inlet valves that open and shut so that the air pulses through the tube instead of flowing in a steady stream. Both ram-jets and pulse-jets need special high speed launching methods.

The jets we most often see today are turbojets and turboprops. Unlike ram-jets, turbojet planes can take off unaided. A compressor fan inside the jet tube sucks in air at the speed that the ram-jet normally needs before it can start to work. Compressed air passes to combustion chambers where it mixes with injected fuel. A spark ignites the mixture, and it expands, as before, to thrust the aircraft forward. As it escapes from the combustion chambers, the expanding gas turns a set of turbine blades fixed to a shaft. The shaft itself spins the compression fan. The fan sucks in more air, and the cycle is repeated.

A turboprop works like a turbojet. But the shaft which links the turbine and compressor extends farther and ends in a propeller. Thus the gases in a turboprop are used to turn three "windmills" instead of two: turbine, compressor *and* propeller. Most of their thrust goes to turn the propeller.

Many people first learned of jet propulsion when they saw, and heard, British turbojet *Gloster* fighters chasing German pulse-jet flying bombs. But it is only since the war that we have really learned what ram-jets, pulse-jets, turbojets and turboprops can do: how they can help us to travel farther, higher, faster than man has ever moved.

(Laurie Lee and David Lambert,
The Wonderful World of Transportation, p. 74)

Other analogous examples of the use of action and reaction to transfer motion or energy may be explored: a boat propeller, a windmill, even such creatures as the ocean squid.

Being able to understand, apply, and construct analogies is a significant cognitive process which has many uses in advanced disciplines. Analogies drawn up as theoretical models have been widely used in the social sciences to explain some complex phenomena of human behavior. In one well-known model, the concept of political power—its acquisition, distribution, and use —was formulated to investigate and explain acts of government, the influence of pressure groups, and why people vote as they do.

Other types of utilizing abilities can be developed, using not only the generalizations derived from the actual content of the materials, but also the methods the author used in writing about the subject. One way to draw the student's attention to a utilization of a method of approaching written materials is through the table of contents. A table of contents of a popular biography, *America's First Spaceman,* is reproduced below.

CONTENTS

(Jewel Spangler Smaus and Charles B. Spangler,
America's First Spaceman)

Once having read the book, the student would be asked to work with the table of contents, which is divided into chapters roughly denoting important periods of the hero's life, and to itemize the steps used by the authors in collecting the information used in each chapter. After analyzing this, the student would be asked to outline the sources he would use if he were going to write a history of some famous personage such as Ralph Bunche, Dwight Eisenhower, Herbert Hoover, or Christopher Columbus.

Note that the last raises the abilities of utilization to a more complex level in that it produces more problems and does not provide as direct a model of utilization of the authors' methods as in the study of the three more contemporary figures. In the last example (Columbus) sources are more obscure and scattered, and the authors of appropriate sources are little known. Utilization of sources in the latter example requires more detailed investigation plus knowledge of a period of history in which the learner lacks firsthand experience.

Students who already have a relatively high level of cognitive development in utilization may be asked to make judgments of the sources of materials that were used and their relative value in writing an accurate account of the individual. However, regardless of the level of complexity in utilizing, the main process involves taking the generalization, fact, or method and being able to apply it appropriately in another context.

Discriminating

An area of cognitive abilities which is especially essential in mastering and manipulating written materials is discriminating. The ability to take a mass of materials and to begin to sort through the materials, developing a systematic way of viewing the material without being overwhelmed by the detail, is a functional scholarship skill useful in every subject area. Discriminating skills can be further subdivided into: *detecting* the facts used to develop a generalization, *differentiating* between different types of statements, *classifying* the different types of facts or statements, *relating* different types of facts and generalizations, and *seeing organization* in the way the material has been presented.

In discriminating, the act of classifying is central. After reading, the student may be asked to make an inventory of the facts the author has used in building his main ideas. Refinement in the discrimination of relationships within the written material can be practiced by having the learner select the main ideas from a given passage, and then make an inventory of the subordinate ideas the author uses to build the main ideas. By handling a longer passage, the learner can also look for relationships between main ideas and the way the author moves from one to the other.

As learners gain skill in their use of discrimination, the next logical step is to develop more elaborate classifications through categorizing facts according to some conceptual schemes regarding their function. The teacher can use a variety of categories, such as separating statements of fact from statements of interest, separating statements of motives for behavior from actual statements of description of behavior, separating the statements which give emotional feeling to the writing from those which specifically describe action.

Let us demonstrate how a teacher may develop in children various levels of discrimination skills, by using two short chapters from a trade book, *Up from the Sea*.

The Bell That
Saved Thirty-three Lives

[1] The science of marine salvage is constantly being called on to rescue not only ships but, as you have seen, their cargoes. And cargoes, not only of lambskins and ore but, as you will later see, gold, whiskey, spears, teeth, women's slippers, jewels, cannon, statues, and even the most precious of all cargoes, human lives.

[2] Generally, when a ship goes down, the human beings on board have a chance to save themselves in lifeboats or by swimming. But until recently, when a submarine has foundered, there has been no escape. The men were sealed up inside it at the bottom of the ocean.

[3] This catastrophe has occurred in the U.S. Navy a number of times, and on each occasion the impossibility of rescuing the men has shocked the whole nation. Surely, everyone said, there must be *some* way to save these men. Then came Commander Allan

McCann's invention and there *was* a way. But not until two of the worst submarine disasters of all time had given the country a terrible jolt.

[4] Both tragedies happened quite close together. In 1925 the *S 51* sank with her crew of thirty-seven after colliding with another vessel off the Massachusetts coast. Through a hole in her side the water poured in, drowning all but two of her men, and these suffocated in a watertight compartment before rescue could come. Two years later the *S 4* collided with the *Paulding*. This time forty men were lost by drowning or carbon dioxide poisoning while up above the rescue ship was tossing helplessly in one of the worst storms in memory and her divers were going mad with frustration.

[5] In 1939 came the *Squalus's* turn. Lieutenant Oliver Naquin and his fifty-eight men were putting this newest of U.S. submarines through a series of tests. Eighteen times the ship dived to the bottom and eighteen times every mechanical part worked perfectly. On the nineteenth dive the same routine was followed.

[6] When the engineer checked his indicator lights, those connected with the air-induction valves showed green: "All safely closed." The ship was airtight. He gave the signal to submerge.

[7] Down she went. Then suddenly from the control room came the terrifying, incredible message:

[8] "Water coming into the engine room."

[9] Somehow the lights had gone wrong; the air-induction valve was still open. The moment she had gone under, water had begun pouring in, and by the time the valve could be reached to turn it off, it was too late. The submarine was sinking rapidly.

[10] Within six minutes the *Squalus* hit bottom, 243 feet below. Almost at once her electric power went off, and now the fifty-nine men were isolated in total darkness and silence and bitter cold.

[11] Lieutenant Naquin, in the forward compartment, moved about cautiously, sizing up the situation.

The door to the stern end, he found, had been slammed shut. This meant that no water could enter the forward end—but it meant also that the twenty-six men in the rear had been immediately drowned. Sternly he forbade the survivors to speak of them; morale must be preserved—and so must the oxygen.

[12] "Don't let yourselves get excited," he ordered. "And don't talk. Don't even breathe deeply. Just wrap yourselves in blankets, to preserve your body heat, and lie perfectly still. Try not even to think."

[13] The *Squalus*'s equipment included a marker buoy bearing a sign: "Submarine sunk here. *S.S. Squalus*. Telephone inside." Lieutenant Naquin ordered it released and then, having done everything possible, he sat down to wait.

[14] When the *Squalus* had failed to report to Portsmouth Torpedo Base at the scheduled hour, an alarm had been sent out, and the *Sculpin*, a sister sub, began combing the area. As she passed overhead, Naquin, hearing the vibrations of her screws, sent up a bomb containing a smoke signal to attract attention to his buoy, and the *Sculpin* reported his position to all naval stations in the area. In a few hours the rescue ship *Falcon* was under way.

[15] On board the *Falcon* went a new and still-untested life-saving device.

[16] Impelled by the recent *S 51* and *S 4* disasters, Commander Allan McCann had invented a huge diving bell divided into two compartments, the lower of which had a bottom open as on an actual bell. It was designed to be let down by a cable onto the deck of the disabled submarine, where a diver would fit it into a circular groove. In the center of this groove was an escape hatch, and when the bell's rim, edged with a thick rubber gasket, had been fitted into the groove, operators inside would pump enough air out of the lower compartment to make it a kind of suction cup. When it was watertight, the hatch could be opened and the men could climb up through the lower compartment into the upper. The suction would then be

released by pumping the air back in, and the freed bell would rise to the surface.

[17] Such was the plan of the McCann Rescue Chamber now hurrying to the aid of the *Squalus,* and on its success depended the lives of thirty-three helpless men. Of course nothing had ever worked at such extreme depths before, but this was something new and until it failed everyone still stubbornly clung to hope. The entire U.S. Navy listened in to the operation by radio, knowing that this concerned not only the *Squalus*'s crew but every man jack in the service.

[18] The *Sculpin*'s captain, on finding the *Squalus*'s marker buoy containing the telephone, had immediately phoned down to Lieutenant Naquin. He was just trying to tell him that the *Falcon* was on its way when a huge wave hit his ship, knocking it sideways, and broke the phone line. After that there was nothing but silence below and the men could only sit still and hope.

[19] Racing against time, the *Falcon* arrived within twenty-four hours and dropped four moorings to fix her squarely over the submarine. Fortunately the weather was bright and calm, and diver Martin Sibitsky went down at once in a suit electrically heated to keep him from freezing to death. Landing on the *Squalus*'s deck, he looked for the cover of the escape hatch and hooked to it a line from the bell above. Now the bell, anchored to the hatch cover, slowly pulled itself down over it, the men inside pumped out air enough to make a suction, and the bell was locked into place. Down now dropped divers Badders and Mihailowski and entered the submarine.

[20] Many of the men were near death from carbon dioxide poisoning, and Lieutenant Naquin sent up six of the weakest, along with one officer to direct the rescue. At first everything went exactly as planned. As soon as one load of men was lifted out onto the *Falcon*'s deck, the bell went down for another and then another. Not until the final trip, late that night, did anything go wrong. Then it looked as if the coura-

geous Lieutenant Naquin, who had stayed until the last, might never see light of day again.

[21] The bell's guideline jammed halfway up. Inside, the mechanics strove frantically to free it; outside, divers did the same. Neither succeeded, and the bell was stuck. What to do?

[22] They could cut the line, of course, and leave the bell to rise of its own accord, lifted, like a balloon, by the buoyancy of the air inside. But any balloon cut loose from its string is completely out of control, and the bell might rise too fast, smashing itself against the *Falcon*'s bottom. If, on the other hand, they took on water to weigh it down to a balance, and accidentally took on too much, it might sink to the bottom forever. For three hours the mechanics balanced the heaviness of water against the lightness of air in an operation as delicate as a surgeon's. Sometimes the bell shot up a few feet in a frightening rush; then it plummeted down as breath-takingly. Sometimes it hung dead in midwater, neither up nor down, while they struggled to achieve that slight buoyancy that did finally lift it slowly but steadily to the surface.

[23] It was past midnight when Lieutenant Naquin and the last eight men dragged themselves out of the rescue chamber onto the *Falcon*'s deck. They were weak and shaking. But they were rejoicing, too. For not only had they escaped from a dreadful death, but they and everyone else knew now that rescue from a sunken submarine was possible and others need never fear that same dreadful death again.

(Nora B. Stirling, *Up from the Sea: The Story of of Salvage Operations*, pp. 51–62)

As an example of detecting and inventorying facts the author uses to describe a crucial episode in a story, the learner using paragraphs 11, 12, and 13 of the above selection could make a list of Lieutenant Naquin's actions in the sunken submarine. In this case the list would include: (1) he moved about cautiously, sizing up the situation; (2) he found the door to the stern end had slammed shut; (3) he found no water could enter the forward end, but that the twenty-six men in the rear had been immediately drowned; (4) he forbade the survivors to speak of them; (5) he ordered them not to get excited, talk, or breathe deeply, but to wrap themselves in blankets and lie still and try not to think; (6) he ordered the marker buoy released; (7) he sat down to wait. Paragraphs 16, 21, 22, and 23 also offer the learner possibilities for inventorying facts central to an episode.

In addition, this chapter offers opportunities for discriminating abilities to be brought to bear on differentiating between different types of statements. Students would be asked to discriminate between statements that give emotional feeling to the writing and those that specifically describe action. The phrases "Then suddenly from the control room came the terrifying, incredible message . . ."; ". . . her divers were going mad with frustration"; and "But they were rejoicing, too" are examples of phrases used by the author to give emotional feeling to the writing and need to be distinguished from phrases and statements which specifically describe action, as in the following: "Down she went"; "The submarine was sinking rapidly"; "They were weak and shaking."

Using the following chapter from the same book, students would be asked to use discrimination abilities in differentiating, classifying, and seeing relationships of different facts, statements, and generalizations.

The Meanest Freighter Afloat

The *Exminster* was an old rusty freighter with a long and honorable history. She was also probably the sulkiest, stubbornest, least co-operative ship in the U.S. service. During World War II, when all other vessels were doing their best to help win the war, the *Exmin-*

ster did everything she could to make things more difficult.

In 1942 she had been given an unusual responsibility. The United States was by now hard pressed for steel for war weapons, chiefly because of a shortage of chrome ore, and unless a lot more of this chrome were produced promptly from somewhere, serious trouble lay ahead. The *Exminster*, however, was expected to save the day, for the clumsy old tub was wallowing home from the Near East loaded with tons and tons of fine ore, and the men in charge of making munitions could hardly wait.

But they didn't know the *Exminster*. On the night of April 18 a storm blew up off Cape Cod. The *Exminster* was waiting with several other vessels to be convoyed down the coast to New York, and in that wild nor'-easter she and the *Algic* collided. Another ship might have tried to stay afloat to deliver its precious load. But not the *Exminster;* sulkily she gave up the ghost and went straight to the bottom, chrome ore and all.

The Washington munitions makers were appalled by her loss. "We'd rather lose a whole battleship," they told the Navy. "Go and get that ore up at once."

The Navy hurried to do as it was asked. But now it seemed that the injured freighter was determined to be as difficult as possible. The Navy had turned the job over to the nation's largest salvage firm, Merritt-Chapman & Scott, and on April 22 their Captain Frank Shepherd had gone down into her holds to size up the situation. He found that the two thousand tons of chrome in her bottom were keeping her upright in the mud, and that was good. But he also found that the other cargo—drums of oil, kegs of casein, bundles of Persian rugs and Persian lambskins—was tumbled about in an indescribable mess and was lying *on top* of the ore. And that was not so good.

A couple of oyster boats were fitted with cranes and pumps, and going alongside the *Exminster*, whose smokestack and masts just peeped out of water, Shepherd sent down two divers into the upper holds. Until the soggy mass there was cleared out they would not even see the ore underneath, and so, for days and weeks, they loaded rugs, lambskins, and oil drums into nets, from which they were dropped onto barges and carried to shore.

Three months went by thus, and all the time Washington kept demanding, "When?"

Shepherd finally sent word back, "October. Maybe."

And actually, on September 25, a dredge anchored alongside dropped its clamshell bucket into the hold and bit into the real thing. Ore came up, real win-the-war chrome ore, so everyone went ashore and celebrated.

But at that point the *Exminster* got really mean. Autumn brought bad weather, and in the October gales she rolled and pitched like a bad-tempered horse. When next Shepherd went down he found the ore shaken and packed together as solid as concrete.

"There's no way to get that stuff out of the ship now," he told the Navy. "We'll just have to raise the ship itself. With hatch cofferdams."

This sounded ridiculous; the authorities protested that no ship lying under thirty feet of water had ever been raised with hatch cofferdams before. But they mulled over the idea, and meanwhile the divers kept hacking the ore loose with pickaxes, a little bit at a time, and the weather got steadily worse. From twenty above it went to ten above; to zero; to six below. Snow lay five feet deep on the decks and the divers' air lines froze. During all November and December the men got barely ten hours' work done, and by December 20, when word came that the cofferdam idea was O.K., the storms were so furious that Shepherd had to call a halt anyway.

The next three months he spent in New York making the cofferdams—huge square boxes without tops or bottoms, the exact size of the three hatches over the freighter's holds and considerably more than thirty feet high, and in April he barged them to Cape Cod.

Washington's orders were, "By July 4—or else."

Shepherd first welded a huge metal patch over the gash in the side of the hull; next he sealed off every small opening, every drain and porthole and pipe, to make it watertight. Then came the cofferdams. A huge derrick was towed alongside, and, lifting them off the barge, it lowered them, one by one, over the open hatches. Fitted and bolted down, they protruded out of the water like three square funnels. And then all the men had to do was hang pumps over them and start sucking.

By May 30 everything was going so well Shepherd began to relax. But the cranky old freighter had not stopped fighting him yet.

With the water out of the upper holds, Shepherd and his assistant climbed down inside one of the cofferdams to make an inspection, for the *Exminster* should be floating soon and he wanted to be ready. And that was the moment, while he was inside her, helpless, that she chose to try to kill him. Suddenly breaking free of the mud, she started to rise, and in so doing lost her balance and tipped over. As the rim of the cofferdam touched the water a giant wave swept in, flooding the ship once more and plunging her back to the bottom. The men inside escaped drowning only by clambering up the side of the cofferdam like terrified monkeys.

But escape they did, miraculously. And the *Exminster,* having failed to do away with the captain, gave up and was no more trouble. A huge deep-sea derrick, the biggest in the world, was brought alongside to keep her from toppling over again, and this time, after a mighty pulling and pumping, up she came steadily and straight.

July 4 had been Washington's deadline. And on July 3, just under the wire, a dirty, sulky old ship with a patch on her side and a hold full of precious ore, slid meekly into a slip in New York Harbor. Captain Shepherd had licked the deadline—*and* the *Exminster.*

(Nora B. Stirling, *Up from the Sea: The Story of Salvage Operations,* pp. 31–40)

In this chapter students would be asked to find statements which can be proven as facts and those which are simply statements of interest and reflect the author's interest and judgment, as in the following examples. The statements "The *Exminster* was an old rusty freighter with a long and honorable history" and "A couple of oyster boats were fitted with cranes and pumps, and going alongside the *Exminster,* whose smokestack and masts just peeked out of water, Shepherd sent down two divers into the upper holds" are statements of fact. Whereas the statements ". . . she rolled and pitched like a bad-tempered horse" and "She was also probably the sulkiest, stubbornest, least co-operative ship in the U.S. service" are statements reflecting the *writer's* interest and judgment on the subject. These are statements of a very different order and purpose than a statement of fact.

Other types of classifications of statements are involved in the development of scholarship skills included in discrimination. The statements "On the night of April 18 a storm blew up off Cape Cod. The *Exminster* was waiting with several other vessels to be convoyed down the coast to New York, and in that wild nor'easter she and the *Algic* collided" contain descriptions of actual, verifiable behavior, whereas the statements "But the cranky old freighter had not stopped fighting him yet" and "Another ship might have tried to stay afloat to deliver its precious load. But not the *Exminster;* sulkily she gave up the ghost . . ." imply a motivation or behavioral reaction in the ship which is not open to verification. This classification is of a higher level of cognitive discrimination than discriminating single facts from broad generalizations.

A complex level of discrimination of a different order is obtained when the student can examine a piece of writing for the organizational outline which the

author used. A useful approach in helping students
discriminate organization is through surveying chapter headings. As an example, *The Quest of Captain
Cook* has the following chapter titles:

CONTENTS

(Millicent E. Selsam, *The Quest of Captain Cook*)

After surveying the chapter headings the student
would, before reading, try to detect the organizational
principles used in writing the book.

The organizational principle may have to do with
the author's purpose, point of view, attitude, or general approach to biography. In this illustration, the
organization is based on a chronological list of major
events in the person's life. After reading the book the
learner should check his hypothesis concerning the
organization the author used.

A further refinement and more advanced discrimination would have the student build a series of ways
the story might be reorganized using different basic
organizations such as the main aspects of a man's
career, the one highlight of his career, having the person tell his own story and comparing it with other
people's perception of the same events. Discrimination in the way material can be organized and dif-
ferentiated is a primary cognitive ability involved in
advanced levels of major disciplines.

In summary, discriminating abilities involve the
processes of sorting and differentiating among ideas

and methods. As with the other abilities there are many levels of complexity but the uniqueness of the process remains at any level.

Chaining

The cognitive abilities in chaining involve relating ideas to other ideas. However, chaining does not always involve relating ideas in a direct linear sequence. In some instances, chaining does require correct ordering and sequencing of ideas much as one might find in following a set of rules for a game, stirring up a recipe or similar set pattern where the fixed sequence is vital to the outcome. Nevertheless, chaining can require recombining of the ideas from written materials with other ideas from previous experience so that a new product may emerge which is greatly different from either of the two basic ideas.

Consequently, in the above instance, chaining differs from utilizing, inasmuch as it involves greater need for reconstruction and the likelihood that a new product will appear. A central feature of chaining is the cognitive search for directional properties beginning from a set of circumstances. Research on the cognitive processes indicates there are three variations of chaining.

One of the most direct forms of chaining is the direct leap from some given evidence to a solution, then the construction of the missing steps on the basis of the accepted solution. This form of chaining is called *extrapolation*. The following is an example of chaining by using a legend. The student would read only part of the story, the beginning and the ending, which are reproduced below.

Long years ago, the people of that land were sadly at the mercy of the wild, hairy folk who lived under the sea. To be sure, there were long periods when they were left in peace to do their fishing, though from their canoes they could look down into the waters and see the under-sea people walking on the sands at the bottom, very shadowy and vague though, in the greenish light. Still, it was clear enough, for those who watched, to see their hair-covered bodies, their long and serpent-like arms and their noseless faces.

But again, there were times when the under-sea men marched in great numbers out of the water and caught the land men, dragging them down to their deaths. In such numbers they came that there was no resisting them. Nor was there escape, for the under-sea people could walk on the water, going faster than the wind itself. With earsplitting booming they would form themselves into a wide circle about the canoes, then draw nearer in wild rushes or strange slidings and drag the frightened men into the green-gray water. Sometimes a few only were taken and those that were left, looking down, might see the under-sea folk dragging their fellows to great rocks to which they bound them with ropes of leathery kelp.

One day the under-sea people caught Na-Ha, a youth strong as a wild wind, whose muscles were knotted like oak branches, one who smiled when danger came. Five of the noseless people attacked him and of the five, Na-Ha sent three to the bottom of the sea with broken necks, for though he smote them with his clenched fist alone, they staggered back and swiftly sank, and the blood that gushed from their mouths made a spreading pink cloud in the water. But soon the sea was alive with wild, raging faces and the roaring of them was like the southeast wind in the forest trees, yet Na-Ha stood in his little canoe, cold and calm, and the smile did not leave his lips. Stealthily they crept toward him, none at first daring to attack, until with a fierce noise and clamour all rushed together, leaping upon him in his canoe and bearing it down by sheer press and weight, Na-Ha in the midst of the tangled mass of hair-covered creatures. Some who saw that fight said that the sudden silence when the water closed over them hurt the ears like a thunder clap, but the true hearted Na-Ha was the last to disappear, and while he smote the black-haired ones furiously, the smile of scorn was still on his face.

Like a picture in a dream some saw the fight among the rocks at the bottom of the sea, saw the noseless ones crowding about the lad, saw others leaping over the heads of those who did not dare to near him, saw others again creeping in the sea sand, trailing kelp ropes to bind him. Many fell in that battle under the sea and the low waves that lapped the shore were red with blood that day. How it ended none knew, for with the dying light and the sand clouds that hung in the water all became gray at last and then swiftly faded.

That night the land people wept for Na-Ha the untamed, Na-Ha whose spear was like lightning, Na-Ha whose canoe rode the waves like the brown storm-birds. Tales were whispered of how he never bent beneath a load, of how in the blackest night he drove his boat before the storm, of how once he swept out to sea after a great whale and slew it, so that his people were saved from the hunger-death.

But with the screaming of the morning sea-gulls Na-Ha came to them again, walking up out of the sea, and his face was set and stern. Nor did he say a word until he had eaten and thought awhile.

. . . .

Well and bravely stood Na-Ha while all this came to pass, scornful of the death that clawed at him. Nor did he lay down to die until the great cold had passed away and his people returned to find the under-water folk forevermore bound to their own place, powerless to harm, looking always with wide, wondering eyes, lest the mighty Na-Ha again steal upon them and bring the great white death.

(Charles J. Finger, *Tales from Silver Lands*, p. 33)

Following this the student would then construct the intervening steps and test his construction against the author's. In this particular case the student would not be expected to parallel the construction in specifics, but would be expected to maintain construction within the mood of the author, through attention to and sorting out of the cues given in the introduction and ending of the story.

A further variation of chaining through extrapolation using written materials, preferably short stories at first, is to read the conclusion of a story and then work backward in reconstructing the story before reading the author's construction. In arithmetic, one might start with the solution to the problem and work backward to develop the process. This latter approach in chaining is especially useful where there are problems with set solutions or quite tightly constructed written materials, as in this example taken from a story on pyramids.

> Perhaps the hardest problem was to make the base of the pyramid really square. The smallest error in fixing the angle at any corner would have thrown the whole building out of shape. Although the builders left no records, we may guess how they would do this.

For the benefit of the reader the solution is included:

> They might mark out a long straight line, by stretching a cord between two pegs stuck in the ground. Then to each peg they would tie an equal length of string, more than half as long as the line they had drawn. By keeping these strings stretched tight and moving the ends around, they could draw parts of two perfect circles. These part-circles we call arcs will cross each other at two points. When the builder draws a straight line between these two points, he will find it bisects the original line, that is it crosses it at a right-angle, cutting it into two equal parts.

> (Lancelot Hogben, *The Wonderful World of Mathematics*, p. 13)

In discussing the products of this form of chaining, the teacher assists students in examining their differences in construction of solutions or reconstructions of processes on the way to a solution if the working-backward approach is used.

There are some mistakes that students commonly make. Neglecting evidence through concentrating on a single rule is one of them. Failure to discriminate the significant cues is another, as is using highly selected evidence, missing out on important steps in application, and failing to see the significances of sequence.

In a variant of chaining called *interpolation,* which differs from extrapolation, some information is given, a gap is left, some more information is given, and the student fills in the information needed. Interpolation used with the famous myth "The Golden Touch" has the student reading separate paragraphs of the story and then supplying the intervening ideas, as in the following example.

As he dipped the pitcher into the water, it gladdened his very heart to see it change from gold into the same good, honest earthen vessel which it had been before he touched it. He was conscious, also, of a change within himself. A cold, hard, and heavy weight seemed to have gone out of his bosom. No doubt, his heart had been gradually losing its human substance, and transmuting itself into insensible metal, but had now softened back again into flesh. Perceiving a violet, that grew on the bank of the river, Midas touched it with his finger, and was overjoyed to find that the delicate flower retained its purple hue, instead of undergoing a yellow blight. The curse of the Golden Touch had, therefore, really been removed from him.

King Midas hastened back to the palace; and I suppose, the servants knew not what to make of it when they saw their royal master so carefully bringing home an earthen pitcher of water. But that water, which was more precious to Midas than an ocean of molten gold could have been, was to undo all the mischief that his folly had wrought. The first thing he did, as you need hardly be told, was to sprinkle it by handfuls over the golden figure of the little Marygold.

.   .   .   .

Her father did not think it necessary to tell his beloved child how very foolish he had been, but contented himself with showing how much wiser he had now grown. For this purpose, he led little Marygold into the garden, where he sprinkled all the remainder of the water over the rosebushes, and with such good effect that about five thousand roses recovered their beautiful bloom. There were two circumstances, however, which as long as he lived, used to put King Midas in mind of the Golden Touch. One was that the sands of the river sparkled like gold; the other, that little Marygold's hair had now a golden tinge, which he had never observed in it before she had been transmuted by the effect of the kiss. This change of hue was really an improvement, and made Marygold's hair richer than in her babyhood.

(Hamilton Wright Mabie, ed., *Myths Every Child Should Know*, p. 49)

After reading the first two paragraphs, the learner fashions the next sequence of events, keeping the story consistent and within the author's framework. As in this example, the learner needs to become aware of the relationship of the father and his child and the sequence of events between paragraphs two and three.

In this case, while exact reproduction of the author's ideas are not to be expected, the learner's ideas should conform to the main contextual outline of the story. In other instances, where a more formal logical structure is implicit in the written material, greater parallelism can be demanded and expected. Materials which rely heavily on a linear sequence for their meaning, as in following a list of rules in a game or in the construction of a toy, are good practice for interpolation.

Chaining involving interpolation is a useful approach in the students' development of the ability to order a sequence of processes and actions. A type of chaining which has had considerable use in creative writing is the construction of multiple endings starting from a given set of evidence. Encouraging students to develop highly original endings without doing injustice to the original evidence is one approach to developing the ability of exploring a broad range of solutions. An example of this type of chaining using an excerpt from the story "Royal Blood," illustrates how a student would read the beginning of a story, then construct several plausible endings before reading the author's.

They rode far that day, thirty miles over the steep mountains. The forest ranger drooped in the saddle, for the man, too, was weary almost beyond his strength.

Suddenly the ranger stiffened. A new forest fire was eating its way savagely through the trees. It was still small, but under the urge of the wind the flames were spreading rapidly. Like one in a dream the gray-green man unstrapped his tools and gave battle. In the path of the fire he began to dig a long trench down through the forest litter to the bare, uninflammable earth. When the flames reached this trench they stopped for lack of fuel. But again and again the wind blew sparks and bits of flaming wood across, so that the fire gained new foothold. The gray-green man was staggering. All that long afternoon Tuckee watched while the fire forced his master back and back, gaining headway with each victory. To the horse it seemed that his master had gone out of his mind. He was gasping, smoke-blackened, wet with perspiration. His efforts had ceased to be systematic. He ran back and forth, lashing at the flames with his ax. The struggle had long ago become hopeless, but he would not retreat.

The forest ranger was chopping frantically at a tree with its lower branches afire. In his haste he did not notice another tree, dead and with its roots rotted away, leaning against it. At the second jarring blow of the ax the dead tree shook itself loose and came crashing down upon him, knocking him headlong and coming to rest across his legs. The gray-green man gave a single cry, and then lay still.

> (Montgomery M. Atwater, "New Blood," in Pauline Rush Evans, ed., *The Best Book of Horse Stories,* p. 49)

The learner should be encouraged to explore the broadest range of probable endings, including ranking them from least to most probable with reasons for his rankings.

Extensive practice of this skill is a good way to help students avoid the dangers of circular thinking, in which stereotyped responses are provoked by the patterns of stimuli. The fairy tale, with its ending involving magical powers, stands as a prime example. As an added inducement to broaden chaining skills, students should be encouraged to explore the impact that various endings have upon the reader.

A third type of chaining, *systematization,* involves linking products and processes into a completed system. The system represents a cognitive map of products and processes all related, and structurally includes main generalizations, subordinate and supporting ideas, and facts ordered by specific rules governing their inclusion in the system and relationship.

One form of this procedure involves organizing a broad range of phenomena into generalizations or classifications showing their relationship. From quite diverse phenomena, students can develop idea anchors, discover relationships, and chain appropriate facts to these anchors as aids to retention. The following written material explains a basic scientific idea on classification of animals.

Any living thing on the earth that is not a plant is an animal. And so the animal kingdom includes far more than the four-legged creatures we are used to calling animals. It covers tiny little microscopic animals and giant-sized ones. It includes birds that fly, fish that swim, worms that crawl in the ground, and monkeys that swing in the trees.

There are over a million different kinds of animals known today. We tell them apart because they look different from each other. Anybody can tell the difference between an elephant and a dog or between a fish and a frog. But if we were to catalogue all the animals in the world and group together those we thought most alike, we might get into difficulties.

Scientists have done the job for us. They have classified all known animals into groups. Each year hundreds of new kinds are being discovered and added to the list. How do scientists name and classify a newly discovered animal?

They have to know a great deal about any particular animal before they can put it in its proper group. They have to know everything there is to be known about its *structure*—the way its parts are put together and the nature of each part. Scientists study the structures you can see on the outside—like the kind of skin, mouth, eyes, ears, the number and position of the limbs. They look to see what the inside organs are like. They describe the heart, the brain, the stomach. They cut up pieces of these organs to see what they look like under a microscope.

A study of the structure alone may show its proper place in the animal kingdom. But there are complications. Many animals look entirely different in their adult state from the way they look when they are growing up. Scientists therefore have to know the en-

tire life history of an animal in order to classify it.
A caterpillar has no meaning unless you know that it
is one life stage in the development of a moth or a
butterfly. The structure of an adult barnacle is very
different from the structure of young barnacles. Scientists could not classify barnacles correctly until they
studied the young forms.

Structure and developmental studies are most important. But every bit of available knowledge about an
animal helps scientists to put it in the group with the
ones it most closely resembles. Information about
where it lives, how it raises its young, how it gets its
food, what its blood chemistry is like, all help to give
valuable clues about its place in the animal kingdom.

On the basis of such studies, every animal in the
world has been given a scientific name which shows a
group to which it belongs. The name consists of two
parts. The first part is the *genus* name (plural—*genera*)
and the second part is its species name. For example,
all dogs are known as *Canis familiaris*. The genus
name *Canis* tells you that it belongs with other doglike
animals like wolves and coyotes. The species name,
familiaris, tells you that you are dealing with a dog
and no other kind of doglike animal. The name is
written in Latin—a language that is understandable
throughout the world. Whether in Africa, Europe, or
Asia, a scientist will know you are speaking of a dog
if you say *Canis familiaris*.

Using these basic units, the genus and species, animals are put into the same *family*. Families that have
something in common are put into a still larger group
called an *order*. Similar orders are put into classes.
Classes that resemble each other in some ways are
put into the same *phylum*—the largest group in the
animal kingdom. The whole animal kingdom has been
classified into groups that show more or less resem-
blances between the animals in them.

(Millicent E. Selsam, *Exploring the Animal Kingdom*, pp. 7–8)

In using the above passage, the teacher would want to have the students extract the idea anchor of the passage, which is the process by which scientists classify animals. Then, the learners would identify the separate detailed processes and link them to the total classification process. There is research evidence that memory is aided when the broad propositions or idea anchors are supported by relevant detail. In this particular case the student would be listing the specific procedures that a scientist uses in classifying an animal.

Most knowledge, particularly in the advanced disciplines, is arranged within supporting systems where related ideas support broad generalizations. In the social sciences, social systems of families, communities, cities, and nations are studied. In the sciences, atomic systems, ecosystems, and microsystems are prevalent ways of organizing related data. The ability to relate generalizations which make up the system and to honor the rules which order its organization is involved in chaining.

Judging

Judging as a category of cognitive abilities is more inclusive than those categories previously discussed. It involves decision-making and choice-taking. Judgments are involved in all of the other categories of cognitive abilities. Nevertheless, the ability of judging does have distinctive characteristics and identifiable components, which need to be given specific attention if the learner is to increase his cognitive capabilities.

Basic to judgment is the recognition and development of standards used in judging. Merely to say I like or do not like a particular passage and to let the judging remain at that is to use a standard which is not defined and open to appraisal. Judging is not simply unexamined tastes and preferences. It invokes discernible criteria.

As a category of cognitive abilities, judging and its exercise lie at the heart of human experience. For in the development of ability in judging we heighten our awareness of our values, attitudes, and other personality factors which bear directly upon our living and functioning as human beings. Such a quest is education at its best—self-knowledge.

In developing cognitive abilities in judging, there are two basic procedural steps to be observed: developing and using standards. Standards for judging can be developed *internally* to the written passage that is to be judged. Internal standards generally examine the author's statements for consistency. Is the author being logical, is the approach to solution of the problem or situation in keeping with the end desired or achieved, or both? Heightening student awareness of internal standards may be approached as in the following example.

> The destruction of wildlife continues today in nearly all parts of the world. Uncontrolled killing for profit has destroyed both the whales and the whaling industry of the North Atlantic. The "control" of natural predators, such as the leopard, has resulted in the emergence of almost uncontrollable numbers of baboons.
>
> It is common knowledge that the rhinoceros, the elephant, the zebra, and the lion are fast disappearing from Africa, and other species in Europe and North America are seriously threatened.
>
> Fortunately, there are international, national, and local agencies now at work to stop this senseless annihilation. The existence of our remaining wildlife will continue to be threatened, however, until a considerable percentage of the world's population becomes alarmed at the dangers involved in exterminating a species. Only then will real efforts be taken to put down illegal hunting and poaching. Only then will real

efforts be made to ensure that land is used in accordance with scientific principles.

(Roy Pinney, *Animals, Inc.*, p. 109)

In this passage the author's discussion can be checked for internal consistency with his conclusion stated in the last sentence. Is the relationship between the use of land according to scientific principles and the maintenance of wildlife made clear? The student needs to read further to see if the author is being logical in his arguments that there is a relationship.

The other procedural approach to developing standards for judging is the use of *external* standards. In external standards comparisons are made between the written material and other material. Are the author's facts consistent with other reliable sources? How does the written passage compare with other similar works? Is his approach in keeping with the approach of other authorities? External standards always involve using outside evidence to compare on some basis the written material under consideration. Given the following passage on wildlife and its extermination, students can be encouraged to develop external standards that are related to the cognitive abilities of judging.

The Arabian ostrich has suffered much the same fate. The cheetah, the leopard, and the lynx are also candidates for oblivion, and unless there is a drastic change in government policy nothing can be done to save them.

The story is the same in Iraq. Here the wild ass is extinct, and the gazelle, the leopard, and the bear are extremely rare.

A pleasant contrast to this state of affairs can be found in other parts of the world, such as the Netherlands Indies, where a magnificent system of wilderness areas and game reserves was established by the government in 1916. Within an area which includes Java, Sumatra, Borneo, the Celebes, Lesser Sunda

Islands, Moluccas, and New Guinea, some ninety-seven reserves and wilderness areas had been established by 1938, and by 1947 the number had grown to 120.

Few vanishing species have received more world-wide publicity than the large mammals of Africa, yet the slaughter of elephants, rhinoceroses, and lions continues. A recent estimate of the current situation in Africa charges that 75 percent of the total animal population in Africa is already extinct, and forecasts that all wildlife will be completely exterminated within the next ten to sixteen years.

In Kenya it is reported that seven important species are on the verge of extinction: the lion, rhinoceros, cheetah, roan antelope, serval, lynx, and wild dog. Despite this warning, the rhino, the male lion, the serval, and the wild dog are legal game.

The greatest danger to African wildlife is the poacher. Commercial hunters attracted by high profits account for a tremendous loss of animal life annually.

(Roy Pinney, *Animals, Inc.,* p. 116)

Implicit in using external standards is the raising of questions on accuracy of information, relevance, and authenticity of sources. After reading the passage, students would need to raise questions concerning the author's thesis, or facts used to support the thesis. In this particular case students would need to develop an awareness of the need to examine more current sources for later information on the problem such as the *New York Times Index.* Other sources on the same problem may be consulted such as *Serengeti Shall Not Die,* which is a scientific study of wild game animals in Africa. The significance of using current materials where the dynamics of problems are in a state of flux is an essential aspect of the skills involved in judging and has a bearing on the validity of the standards.

In working with students in building standards, one

of the common cognitive patterns that must be re-examined is the making of global judgments without identifying the standards on which they are based. Early in the use of written materials in developing cognitive abilities of judging, the teacher should give attention to helping the student develop specific standards. If the student gives broad general judgments, then he should explore his basis for these judgments. In the judgment process it is generally advisable to emphasize with students at the beginning the need for building of standards for judgment rather than have students pronounce judgment and then build supporting standards.

Other factors enter in the building of standards in addition to specificity. There should be an awareness of the necessity of recognizing the appropriateness of class in comparing. To attempt to judge the literary worth of a fairy tale by scientific standards of accuracy in explanation is an example of inappropriate use of external standards. Therefore the development of judging cognitive abilities involves both recognition of the content of standards and the process of application. Judging abilities are related to the broad areas of problem-solving and critical thinking. Every trade book offers a myriad of opportunities for practice in developing external and internal standards and application of the standards.

Maurice J. Eash

CHAPTER II

DEVELOPING COGNITIVE ABILITIES WITH SOCIAL STUDIES TRADE BOOKS

Preparation for citizenship in a democratic society necessarily involves the development of cognitive abilities. It is difficult to conceive of an effective citizen who has not developed the ability to understand and evaluate the issues underlying social problems, the ideas of governmental leaders, and the governmental processes in our society. If a goal of the social studies is to assist in this preparation of students for effective citizenship in a democratic society, students must be given ample opportunity to develop the needed cognitive abilities.

Specifically, in a society where the mass media are so widely used as primary sources of information, students must develop early standards for evaluating the messages presented by the mass media. And they must learn early the importance of basing their decisions upon the best available evidence. Collecting information, evaluating information, establishing cause-and-effect relationships are but a few of the general functional scholarship skills related to using the many disciplines embracing the social sciences, as well as essential to the citizenship education of all learners.

It is important, therefore, that the concerned teacher have some framework to assist him in developing the needed abilities in his students. The five areas of cognitive abilities provide such a framework.

Understanding

In working with very young children it is important to provide opportunities for the children to determine the major idea of a passage without being misled by personal experiences or opinions. The following verse might be used for such purpose. It could be read to the children, and they could then be asked to tell what the verse is about. This particular verse might be used in conjunction with a unit on communities, a unit on where people live, or a unit on the city.

Buildings
by
Myra Cohn Livingston

Buildings are a great surprise,
Every one's a different size.
Offices grow long and high,
Tall enough to touch the sky.
Houses seem more like a box,
Made of glue and building blocks.
Every time you look, you see
Buildings shaped quite differently.

(Sidonie Matsner Gruenberg,
ed., *Let's Hear a Story,* p. 38)

Once the children have identified the major idea here, i.e., that buildings are of different sizes and shapes, one might broaden the concept by attempting to get children to identify subordinate ideas by asking them to cite parts of the verse which suggest how different buildings are shaped. One could then also ask children to draw different buildings, suggesting what each building is. If the children understand the subordinate ideas in this verse we anticipate that they would not draw houses which look like skyscrapers. Even though their own "house" may very well be an apartment in a skyscraper—should they draw this as a "house" they would be coloring the author's ideas with their own personal experiences, and not really understanding the author's ideas.

As a final step, the children then might be asked to compare their drawings with the ones provided in the book, to see if theirs are at all similar to the illustrator's drawings of offices and houses.

Another example of simply written material that could be used to develop understanding of an author's idea is provided by the book *Wild and Tame Animals*. Young children could be asked to read this book in its entirety and then to tell in a short sentence what the book is about. Obviously the book is about wild and tame animals, but children should also comprehend the author's idea that man has learned to tame some of the wild animals. Once children have apprehended this idea, they could then be asked to cite examples from the book of animals that man has tamed, and tell how the author says man uses them. For example, one might have children read only the pages on horses, which state:

> Once all horses were wild. They ran free on the plains in big herds and grazed on the wild grass.
>
> Now most horses live on farms and do farm work, and the farmers take care of them.
>
> People ride horses in rough country where there are no roads, or just for the fun of it.

(Dahlov Ipcar, *Wild and Tame Animals,* unpaged)

If the children understand the author's ideas, they should be able to recognize that this passage supports the major idea of the book, telling about one type of animal that man has tamed, and how man uses it.

As one works with older children, additional skills associated with the understanding ability should be developed using more complex materials and assignments. The following discussion illustrates how one might use the preface and the table of contents from a trade book in developing understanding ability with students at the upper elementary level.

PREFACE

California's story really began many thousands of years ago. Before any other peoples lived here, Indians roamed the oak-studded valleys and foothills; built their huts upon the river banks; lived along the beautiful coast and on the barren deserts. It is believed that there were about one hundred fifty thousand of them, more than in any other part of North America. They took food from the places they lived, as well as materials for their homes and all other things needed to meet the demands of their simple way of life. Not all the Indian groups throughout the state had the same customs and the story told here will not be right for all tribes. . . .

The story of the Indians is an interesting but sad one. Once Indians owned everything they could see from their villages. You will want to read about the changes that came and what happened to these early-day Californians who began the first period in the history of California. Much of the period is only a dim memory. Place names, stone mortars and tools, painted rocks, stories told by early explorers and pioneers—these are all that remain as a record of that time. We wish that we knew more about these people. As time goes on and places are found where Indians once lived, this story will be somewhat more complete. Parts of it may never be known, only imagined. It is hoped that those who read this book will gain an appreciation for and an understanding of the California Indians who lived here and called it their home.

(Helen Bauer, *California Indian Days*, p. 9)

In this preface the author states her purpose for writing the book, and suggests what some of the

topics of the book will be. To develop understanding,
the teacher, using this material, might begin by having
the students identify the major topics the author suggests she is going to be writing about. Then they could
compose what they think would be a possible table of
contents on the basis of the topics suggested by the
author in the preface (e.g., Where the Indians Lived,
What Their Life Was Like, What Happened to Them,
etc.). The students could then check their understanding of the author's major ideas as presented in
the preface, by comparing their table of contents with
the one provided in the book.

In this particular instance the table of contents,
shown below, lists rather specific topics.

CONTENTS

(Helen Bauer, *California Indian Days,* p. 7)

Considering this table of contents, the students
could be asked to identify chapter headings which are
subordinate topics for the major topics presented in

the preface. They could further be asked to see if they have identified as major topics themes which do not appear to be supported by any of the chapter headings and which may be at variance with the major themes which the author indicated that she intended to write about. In other words, the students may be asked to identify points at which they have made their own interpretations which extend beyond the author's intent, and to differentiate between their own interpretations and the author's intended themes.

Finally, inasmuch as some students may not be able to tell from the chapter headings whether certain chapters deal with the author's main themes, they can be asked to read the book and to attempt to identify from the context which chapters deal with the major themes identified, thus checking their understanding of the author's major ideas.

If the material being used is close to an emotionally tinged area of the student's life, it may be more difficult to apprehend accurately. This, however, should not mean that one should avoid using such material. Quite the contrary. The need for developing an objectivity that will allow one to understand such material without emotional coloration becomes even more acute. The student needs to develop an awareness of his own biases as well as an awareness of any biases held by the author, particularly in using those social studies materials dealing with other countries and peoples.

The trade book *Partners: The United Nations and Youth,* for example, presents a very favorable view of the United Nations and its work. Regardless of what biases the student may already hold about the U.N., in using this book he must be willing to accept the authors' ideas on their own grounds if he is properly to understand. This does not necessarily mean that the student need agree with everything the authors state—only that he understand what the authors' ideas are and how they support these ideas.

Students at the junior high school level might be asked to read a chapter of this book, such as that entitled "Human Rights," and to list the major ideas stated regarding human rights. Without making any judgments regarding the main ideas (one must first understand in order to later judge), the students may then be asked to list subordinate or supporting points made by the authors under each of the major ideas. In essence, students could be asked to outline major ideas in the chapter as a means of checking their understanding of the authors' ideas.

As another approach for using this trade book, one might wish to take selected passages, such as the two opening paragraphs of the chapter "Human Rights" cited below, and have the students write a sentence or phrase telling the major idea of each paragraph, then list supporting points of the ideas from each paragraph.

> Many of you young people probably wonder why the United Nations should pay so much attention to human rights. The real reason, of course, is that this is a subject which has been discussed down through the ages. Men have been struggling since the earliest days not only for existence, but also for certain human rights and fundamental freedoms. If in the United Nations we can get joint agreement among the various nations to observe certain fundamental human rights and freedoms, and gradually come to a mutual understanding of what we mean when we talk about these rights and freedoms, we shall probably have laid a good cornerstone on which we may eventually be able to build a peaceful world.

> War is a violation of human rights and freedoms. Once two or more nations are at war none of the people in these nations have any freedoms any more be-

cause the nation requires of them, if necessary, one of the most precious of human rights, the right to life.

(Eleanor Roosevelt and Helen Ferris, *Partners: The United Nations and Youth*, p. 179)

In using this technique the students must be cautioned to use only the authors' ideas, not their own. For example, in the second paragraph the major idea is obviously that war violates human rights, and the supporting idea is that nations, in support of war, may demand the right to life. These should be the ideas listed by the students if they understand the authors' ideas. At this point, the students should not be listing their own ideas, either to support or to object to the authors' ideas.

When working with materials such as this it is also important that the students understand the meanings of key words and phrases. A later paragraph from this same chapter states:

So far as the USSR and other totalitarian states go, naturally their interest lies in what the few men at the top consider fundamental for all people; namely, the improvement of their economic and social conditions. But any of the other equally important fundamental human rights, which actually emphasize the dignity of man as a thinking human being, do not seem very important to totalitarian nations.

(Eleanor Roosevelt and Helen Ferris, *Partners: The United Nations and Youth*, p. 180)

If a student does not understand what is meant by totalitarian he may have difficulty understanding this paragraph. Therefore, having him search for meanings for this term may be a necessary assignment. One must also stress to the student when working in areas such as this that words such as totalitarian, democratic, etc., frequently take on emotional coloration that blocks understanding. The student must be cautioned not to let his own feelings about such terms prevent his understanding of the authors' meaning and intent. He must also be assisted in learning to recognize when an author is using such terms emotionally to make a point, and to be advised to be wary of such usage.

Utilizing

In the lower grades, short passages from simply written materials in which the learner can draw easily identified principles or generalizations provide a good start in utilization. In the following passage from a book entitled *Benjamin Franklin,* the principle that the learner needs to discover, i.e., that wind can be used as power to move things, may be more of a scientific principle than a social studies principle, yet it is a principle that has broad applicability, and which might be used in conjunction with a unit on transportation, or with a unit on man's uses of power from natural sources.

> Benjamin lived near the sea, and he early learned to swim and sail. He never grew tired of watching the wind carry the boats over the water, just as it carried his kite up into the sky. One day, while he was swimming, he fastened the kite to himself as if it were a sail and he were a boat. It carried him gently over the water while his friends, who were kicking and splashing, looked on in astonishment. . . .
>
> (Ingri and Edgar Parin d'Aulaire,
> *Benjamin Franklin,* unpaged)

The first step in using this passage would be to have the students identify the principle that is involved. One might do this simply by asking the children why the kite carried Ben gently over the water.

The students should be led to see that Ben was applying his knowledge about the power of wind to move sailboats to a different situation. Children could then be asked to list examples, other than sailboats and kites, where wind is used as a power to move things. Or they might be asked to search other sources for examples of the way man has used the power of wind for his own purposes. If one wishes to pursue this still further, making still broader generalizations regarding man's use of natural forces for his own benefit, children might be asked to give examples of the way man has harnessed and used water power, and power from the sun.

At the upper elementary level, somewhat more complex materials may be used. The generalization may be more difficult to discover or there may be more than one generalization involved.

After the Americans came San Diego did grow. But many years later it was decided that San Diego grew up in the wrong place. "San Diego is not even close to the bay!" some said. "No ships can land closer than three miles from the town!" "But," said others, "there is no water over by the bay. Yes—and we'll probably never get any there either. It has been tried before." But there were some who thought it could be done. "We'll try until we do get water there," they said.

So it was decided that the new part of San Diego would be by the bay. Now the town really began to grow. . . .

(Helen Bauer, *California Rancho Days*, p. 19)

In the above passage two principles involving necessary factors for San Diego to grow are implied. The first principle that students will need to identify is that for the city to grow it needed to be located near a means of transportation that would make it possible for the city to carry on commerce with other cities. In this particular instance it was a location near a bay which would make possible commercial shipping. A second principle is that for the city to grow it needed an adequate supply of drinking water.

Students might be assisted in identifying these principles simply by asking the question, "On the basis of this passage, what two resources were needed if San Diego was to grow as a city?" Students might also be asked to read the statements of the citizens which indicate what San Diego needed to grow.

Once the students have identified these principles, they may then be given assignments which would provide opportunity for them to see how these principles can be applied to other large cities. One might have students do research on other cities, using maps, encyclopedias, and other references, which would provide information regarding cities' locations. Students studying maps might be asked to note, for example, whether the city they are investigating is located near a natural means of transportation, such as a river, a lake, a harbor. If not, can they discover how the city meets this need? Is it near a railroad or near some similar man-made means of transportation? They might also be asked to note if the city is near an adequate supply of drinking water, and, if not, to discover how the city meets this need. The important thing for students to discover here is that for any city to grow, certain needs must be satisfied. If these needs cannot be met naturally by resources near at hand, then ways must be devised to provide for these needs or the city will not grow.

As an example of a longer passage from which students might draw generalizations that could be applied in different contexts, consider the following:

The Confederates had no navy on the ocean and the few ships belonging to the Union government were scattered all over the world when the war began. Nevertheless President Lincoln declared all the coasts of the Confederacy under blockade. This meant that any ship belonging to any nation could be captured if it tried to go in or out. The Confederates did not take this seriously. A blockade does not count unless there is a warship at the mouth of a harbor. They knew that the Union had nowhere near enough ships to close all their harbors, and they thought English ships would bring them the things they needed.

But the Union began buying up every kind of ship that would carry a gun and sending it to the Southern harbors. Even side-wheel ferryboats from New York and Boston were given small guns and sent to join the blockaders. They were not intended for such work and their decks were so weak that they sometimes broke when the guns were fired, but they did close the harbors.

At the same time all the shipyards in the North began building new warships. One group of them were called "ninety-day gunboats" because twenty-three of them were built in three months from the time work began. Before the end of the year the Union had added over a hundred and fifty ships to its navy. The English ships did not come.

The blockade was one of the most important things in the war. It did not make much noise and it was very hard work, because no matter how cold and wet it was or how fiercely the wind blew the blockaders had to stay where they were. But the blockade hurt the Confederacy badly because there were almost no factories in the South. The Confederates soon found it hard to get guns and ammunition. Things like needles, matches, paper, medicines, dishes for cooking, wagon wheels, and even blankets became very scarce.

(Fletcher Pratt, *The Civil War*, p. 14)

Students working with the above passage should be able to understand the general ideas presented and then apply these understandings to other situations

and in different contexts. Although the major portion
of this passage is descriptive of a wartime naval blockade, the important specific idea to be identified here
is implied in the last paragraph—that the blockade
shut off access to the Confederacy. This made it difficult for the South to acquire needed supplies for carrying on the war. The important principle, based on this
idea, to be identified, is that the purpose of a blockade
is to prevent passage or progress and is a strategic
tactic.

Students should readily identify this principle if
asked simply, "What is the purpose of a blockade?"
Once they have identified it, they could be asked to
find and list other historical examples of military or
naval blockades. However, in order for students to
demonstrate utilization abilities which indicate they
understand the generalization or principle, they must
be able to apply this principle in other than military
situations. To check this, the teacher might provide a
list of various items, asking students which they feel
are, or could be, examples or types of blockades and
why. By way of illustration, a teacher might provide a
work sheet as follows:

Item	Blockade (Yes or No)	If Yes—When and/or Why
Filibuster		
Ice		
Mountain		
House Rules Committee		
Dam		
Corral		

Using this particular list, if the students understand
that blockades prevent passage or progress, they
should see that in *certain* situations each of the items
listed can serve as a blockade. More than that, how-

ever, they should be able to suggest where the principle of the blockade is being applied as a strategic tactic, thus demonstrating utilization ability. Students might also be asked to compose their own lists of blockades, noting especially where the strategic principle is being applied. One assignment that might prove interesting along these lines would be to have students suggest when and how the principle of the blockade is applied in games they play.

If the trade book being used is not too complex, students may be asked to work with the entire book rather than with isolated passages, discovering and listing principles or generalizations that have broad utilization, and suggesting situations where the principles might be applied.

In order that the students may have a framework to guide them, the teacher may wish to provide beforehand a list of pages on which appear principles or generalizations having broad utilization. Students could then be asked to discover the principles, cite how they are applied in the text, and then give other examples of their utilization.

The trade book *North Pole: The Story of Robert E. Peary,* suitable for use at the junior high level, is one such source that might be used in this fashion. Throughout this book Peary is faced with many problems and difficulties which he eventually overcomes, frequently by utilizing some principle in an unusual context. To cite but one example, Peary demonstrates by analogy how he plans to use the principle that a rounded surface can be lifted by pressure in the following passage:

Meanwhile, in his spare time, he [Peary] designed a 600 ton polar ship. She was to be 184 feet long and 35 feet wide. One evening in the spring of 1903 he showed drawings of the ship to Josephine [his wife]. She would have 1,000 horsepower engines, ex-

plained Peary, enough to move three or four ships
her size. She'd have a sharp, chisel-like bow of iron
to split open ice. Her propeller would be easy to repair
if damaged by ice.

"We'll be able to pull up her rudder on deck in
ice-packed waters," Peary said. "And she'll have a
smooth, rounded bottom to lift her."

"Lift her?" asked Josephine.

"That's right. Ice won't be able to grip her curved
sides and crush them. As the ice closes in, she'll lift
right out of it—almost the way a pit squirts out of a
squeezed orange. . . ."

(Tony Simon, *North Pole: The Story of Robert E.
Peary,* pp. 98–99)

The job of the students, as stated previously, is to
discover this principle as well as others presented in
the text, seeing how the principle is utilized, and then
suggesting other ways of utilizing it.

This particular trade book also provides much information about discoveries made by Peary and knowledge gained by him on his many trips to the north,
which proved to be of much value to later Arctic explorers. Thus, another assignment using this book
could be to ask students to list some of the discoveries
made by Peary, and to suggest how the things Peary
discovered and learned were later applied by other
explorers.

One of the most important findings he made was
that the North Pole was not on a land mass, but located in the sea, over several thousand feet of water
(Tony Simon, *North Pole: The Story of Robert E.
Peary,* p. 134). Students who are familiar with the
Arctic journeys of the *Nautilus* certainly should be
able to suggest how this finding was applied.

In working with students at this level, other types
of utilization exercises of a more sophisticated nature
might also be used. One technique recommended for

using biographies is to ask students to study the methods employed by an author in collecting information for each chapter, and then to outline sources they would use if they were to write a biography of some famous personage. Obviously, this same technique might be used with other types of books. For example, *Worlds without End: Exploration from 2000 Years B.C. to Today,* while biographical in nature to the extent that it provides information about many explorers, is broader in scope than a single biography, providing a chronology of famous explorations.

In using this trade book, students could first be asked to check the table of contents, noting the general organization of the material. They should readily see that the main portion of the book is divided into four major areas of discussion, i.e., The Early Explorers, The Great Age of Discovery, Great Explorations of the Eighteenth and Nineteenth Century, and The Later Explorers (*Worlds without End,* pp. 7–10) —essentially a chronological organization. Students might then be asked to suggest why this particular type of organization would appear to be a good one, and to suggest other feasible organizational patterns that might be used for a book of this nature.

Students could then be asked to read the book, noting how each major section is organized, and how each chapter in each section is organized. Students should also be encouraged to note certain techniques used by the author for making the material more interesting and giving it more of a story flavor, such as her frequent use of conversations among the leaders and the men under their command. Students should also note her inclusion of maps to clarify the routes taken by the explorers.

In reading the book, students should be led to see how the author uses an introductory and a concluding chapter to "tie" the book together into a unified whole.

Still another assignment which might prove useful in assisting students to understand the organizational methods used in writing a book of this nature would be to have them note the index at the back of the book, and to check certain of the entries, finding what is stated about the entry on the referral page.

Once students have read the book and done the aforementioned assignments they could then be asked how they would organize a book about explorations, or some similar topic such as inventions, discoveries, or other types of pioneering. They should also be asked to suggest what sources they would use and how they would collect their information. In other words, students are now being required to understand and utilize methods of organization and of collecting information.

A similar technique for assisting students to utilize methods and techniques would be to ask each student to read only one chapter in the book, noting how the chapter has been organized. Each student could then be asked to suggest how he would organize such a chapter and how he would collect materials and information for writing the chapter. If one so desires, the student could then be asked to write a report of his own about the particular explorer or exploration his chapter discusses, or about some other trail blazer not mentioned in the trade book, utilizing various methods and techniques for organizing material and collecting information.

Discriminating

When working with young children, we may not expect them to make fine distinctions among various types of statements, or to classify statements into a large number of categories, but they can begin early to differentiate and to classify statements along broad general lines.

Many materials written for children at this level deal with heroes from the past. Using such materials, children should learn early to distinguish statements that are so grossly exaggerated as to be unbelievable from statements that can be believed. For example, one might read to children the following short passage describing a trip of Leif Ericson from Norway to Greenland:

> And Leif hoisted his sail and steered straight to the West, for now he wanted to do a feat that no other sailor had done before, and sail without stop from Norway to Greenland. But in a great storm the waves rose so high they nudged the moon, and his ship swayed like a rocking horse. For a long time it was thrown about on the sea.

> (Ingri and Edgar Parin d'Aulaire, *Leif the Lucky*, unpaged)

One might then ask them to suggest if there are parts of the passage that are hard to believe, and why. Or one could reread the passage a statement or a phrase at a time, asking after the reading of each statement, "Could you believe this?" "Why could (or couldn't) you?"

Children could, of course, be asked to draw upon their own knowledge and experience to explain why they could or could not believe in each statement, and through careful questioning they should be helped to see when a statement is too exaggerated to be believed. One could then continue this by asking children to classify other statements from this book along the lines stated.

Another technique for using material about a hero which would require children to distinguish among still other types of statements on broad general lines would be to ask the children to read passages much as the following from *Buffalo Bill:*

At night they made camp, sat around the fire, sang, and told stories. Then they all rolled up in their blankets and went to sleep. The stillness was broken only by loud snores and howling coyotes. Life on the plains was wonderful, thought Bill.

(Ingri and Edgar Parin d'Aulaire, *Buffalo Bill,* unpaged)

When asking the children to read this passage the teacher might suggest to them that three sentences are describing something, while the other sentence is not, and that when they have finished reading the passage they should write down the sentence that is not describing something. Once this is done, of course, one can pursue this further by discussing with the children what makes the one sentence different from the other three.

At the upper elementary level, the skill of differentiating among various types of statements would appear to be a particularly important skill to develop in the social studies if the students are not to take everything they read at face value and as bald fact. In order that students might be able to deal with materials critically, they need to be able to differentiate, particularly between statements of fact and other types of statements. Students reading about groups of people and their practices, for example, can easily be misled into accepting everything stated as fact, unless they have developed the ability to differentiate and classify statements along some categorical line.

For this purpose one may use short passages such as the following:

In the Northeast lived the powerful Iroquois Indians. They were enemies to many neighboring tribes and they waged fierce wars with bows and arrows and *tomahawks.* The goal of war was to prove courage and power. And the hope of every Indian boy was to prove himself courageous in battle, in the hunt, and in sport.

(Ernest Berke, *The North American Indians,* p. 9)

The teacher might employ a number of techniques which would assist the student in developing the skill to differentiate among various types of statements. One technique, particularly with a passage this short, would be simply to take each statement in order and ask students how one might "prove" or substantiate the statement if it is meant to be a statement of fact.

For example, the first statement, "In the Northeast lived the powerful Iroquois Indians," might be approached by asking first of all, "How could you prove they lived in the Northeast?" Students may suggest that this portion of the statement could be supported by written records which substantiate this or by first-hand evidence such as the discovery of Iroquois artifacts in this region of the country.

One could then ask, "How could you *prove* they were a powerful tribe?" Students may suggest that this portion of the statement could be supported by written records which indicate that the Iroquois were usually victorious in their wars with other tribes, thus were "powerful." But this is more difficult to prove as fact since "powerful" is a descriptive term which denotes comparison, and students should come to recognize that this portion of the statement is really not the same kind of "fact" as the first portion of the statement—that, indeed, there might be some who would hold the opinion that the Iroquois were not powerful. In other words, while the first portion of the statement quite likely could be verified as a fact, the second portion can only be supported as an opinion. Although one might find so much support for this opinion that it comes to be accepted as a fact, it is still nevertheless, a point of view, rather than a fact.

Students should be led to recognize that the last sentence in the paragraph, "And the hope of every Indian boy was to prove himself courageous in battle, in the hunt, and in sport," cannot be supported by any type of firsthand evidence. While it looks like a statement of fact, it is, in reality, a sentence stating what the author (quite probably along with many others) believes to be the motive underlying the Iroquois's behavior. It is a statement of motive, not necessarily a fact; and in attempting to find ways to prove this as a fact, students should come to recognize the differences between statements that can be proven as facts and statements which present a point of view and cannot be proven as facts.

In working on discriminating abilities with materials at this level, a somewhat simpler approach than the one just described would be to ask the students to read a passage, and then list only those statements dealing with a particular point. For example, one might ask students to read the following passage and then write down only those statements which describe facts about what the firemen did to fight the great Chicago fire.

On the evening of Sunday, October 8, 1871, the people of Chicago were aroused by the clanging of fire bells and loud cries of Fire! Fire!

They could see huge flames and great columns of smoke rising a few blocks west of the Chicago River. They knew this was a district of wooden houses, where every shingled roof was bone-dry because there had been no rain for three months. They could see that a strong southwest wind was sweeping the flames toward the heart of Chicago.

The firemen were dead tired. They had been out the night before, fighting a fire that burned up four square blocks of buildings. Now they had to battle a new fire. They responded with all the men and pumping engines they could command. But the fire spread so rapidly that they were baffled. They were facing what was to become known as the most destructive fire the country had experienced. It wiped out all but a small part of Chicago.

It is legendary that the fire was started by an unruly cow. It is said that Mrs. O'Leary, who lived in DeKoven Street went into her barn to milk her cow, while carrying a lighted lamp. She set the lamp down to attend to the milking, and the cow kicked over the lamp. The barn caught fire and soon the whole place was lost to the flames.

A stiff breeze fanned the flames and they spread to adjoining houses. They jumped across the narrow south branch of the Chicago River and ignited business houses in the main section of the city. The firemen were not strong enough to stop the fire. They sent frantic appeals to nearby towns to rush fire engines and men. They used dynamite to blow up buildings in the path of the fire, hoping to create barriers. But clouds of swirling, red-hot embers swept over the ruins and set on fire buildings blocks away.

(Harry Hansen, *The Story of Illinois*, p. 46)

Students who are discriminating among types of statements should recognize that at most there are only three statements in this passage which describe facts about what the firemen *did:* (1) "They responded with all the men and pumping engines they could command"; (2) "They sent frantic appeals to nearby towns to rush fire engines and men"; (3) "They used dynamite to blow up buildings in the path of the fire, hoping to create barriers." If students list statements other than these, they are not differentiating this particular type of statement from the others, and will need to be assisted in discovering the difference between the type of statement called for in the assignment and other statements. One method for doing this would be to have them compare the statements which they have written with those that are statements describing what the firemen *did,* and search for key words and phrases which describe *doing* something, rather than describing feelings, thoughts, etc.

Inasmuch as this entire report of the Chicago fire is relatively short (the remainder is reproduced below), one might ask students to read the entire report, then list statements from the report which best fit a number of categories, e.g., statements describing what the firemen *did,* statements describing what the people *saw* when the fire started, statements describing what the people *did* to get away from or protect themselves from the fire, etc. With this assignment, the teacher may wish to prepare beforehand a work sheet with categorical headings, and a number indicating how many statements belong in each category. Such a work sheet would provide a valuable guide to assist the students.

> By early morning of October 9 the courthouse was on fire. All the records of property owners were destroyed. Then the fire swept toward the main branch of the river, which divided the business section from the residences of the North Side.
>
> The river was filled with vessels—freight schooners, fishing boats, barges, steamships, and tugs. Some of the latter got away, but the sailboats were caught. Flames ran up their masts and the place seemed filled with blazing trees. Then the masts crashed and the decks burned to the water's edge. The old bridges also had much wood in their construction. They burned and fell into the river. Then the fire swept over the North Side, destroying its fine homes and churches. Here only two houses were saved by a change in the direction of the wind.
>
> The people of Chicago fled in a panic. The city had 335,000 inhabitants at this time. Those whose houses

were in danger packed a few possessions in bags and loaded up carts. The streets were so jammed with fleeing people that many carts had to be abandoned.

Cabmen and teamsters were in such demand that they could get preposterous pay for hauling goods. At first drivers charged $10, then raised the price to $50. A bank cashier paid $1,000 to a driver for the cartage of a heavy box to a railroad station some distance from the fire; the box was delivered safely. It was said to contain the bank's money—$600,000.

Because the heat of the fire was intense many persons rushed to the sandy beach of Lake Michigan and stood in the water for a long time. On the North Side people ran to Lincoln Park, where they found safety. The park was crowded, and all through the night men and women wandered around hunting members of their families. Although they had lost everything, they were thankful to be alive. People also huddled in two tunnels that ran under the Chicago River. Here they were safe, though the air was torrid.

A heavy rain fell that night. It had no effect on the fire, which had burned itself out, but it added to the discomfort of the people, who had no shelter. Several hundred persons had died in the fire. The main part of the city was a mass of ruins. On the North Side only the Chicago Water Tower and a few church spires stood out against the bleak landscape.

When the country learned how vast was Chicago's loss, it rallied help at once. Trains carrying food and clothing were despatched west. Money was raised in other cities to aid impoverished families. Businessmen constructed one-story stores and shacks for offices and started business anew. Within two years Chicago was filled with many fine new buildings and was booming.

Because the major fire took place on October 9, the whole nation now observes that date as Fire Prevention Day.

No Illinois city has suffered any disaster comparable with the Chicago fire. But Chicago was the scene of two tragedies that claimed a much greater loss of life.

On December 30, 1903, fire broke out in the Iroquois Theater. In the stampede for exits many persons were crushed to death and others died from gas fumes. In all 602 perished there. On July 24, 1915, occurred an even greater disaster. The pleasure steamer *Eastland* was loaded with employees of a large concern about to go on an excursion. Presumably the boat became unbalanced by the uneven distribution of the load as the vessel lay moored in the Chicago River. It turned on its side and 812 persons were drowned.

(Harry Hansen, *The Story of Illinois,* pp. 47–48)

At the junior high school level many students should be ready to do relatively complex assignments for developing discrimination abilities. Social studies materials such as biographies, especially if the materials are not too complex, may provide useful passages that can be used in a variety of ways, as illustrated in the following discussion.

At fifteen, Harriet was a woman. She was not beautiful. Her hair was short and crinkly, her mouth large, her heavy-lidded eyes blackest black. She was only five feet tall, and her broad, hard-muscled body was clothed in an ill-fitting castoff dress from the Big House, or in a coarse cotton shift. A red and yellow bandanna, wrapped tightly around her head to protect it from the glaring Maryland sun, was her only adornment.

Despite her plain appearance, there was a magnetic quality about Harriet. When she ran barefoot across the fields with her head erect and her firm muscles rippling under her dark, lustrous skin, men and women stopped to admire her grace and strength.

"She's strong as any man," her brothers boasted.

"She can beat the lot of you," Daddy Ben declared.

Tales of Harriet's strength spread across the plantation from the slave quarters to the Big House. When visitors arrived, Master brought them to the fields to see the sights. Leaning on their gold-headed canes and puffing their cigars of fine Maryland tobacco, the gentlemen marveled at the young girl who could lift huge hogsheads and pull a loaded wagon like an ox.

Conscious of their stares, Harriet's eyelids drooped over her shining eyes and her lower lip protruded, as it had done when she was a child. "They look at me as if I was an animal," she thought, and she deliberately turned her back on the gawking men.

Although she was a valuable field hand, performing the task of an able-bodied man, her sullen expression and rock-like chin made Master uncomfortable. There was a rebellious spirit here which had to be watched and curbed. . . .

(Dorothy Sterling, *Freedom Train: The Story of Harriet Tubman,* pp. 40–41)

Once the students have read the above passage they can be asked to develop their own categories for classification and to place each statement under the category where it best fits (numbering the statements in the passage and placing numbers rather than entire sentences under the categories could be done for ease and speed). The students might then compare their categories and classifications with each other and discuss the merits of each.

A second approach would be for the teacher to provide a list of categories such as statements descriptive of behavior, statements descriptive of appearance, or other useful categories, and to ask the students to list under each category those statements which best fit. Some statements may fit under more than one category, however, inasmuch as a part of the statement may fit one category while another part may better fit under another category. Students could, of course, be asked to write only the parts of the statements that best fit under each category.

A third approach might be to analyze certain paragraphs internally, attempting to see the relationships among the parts of the paragraph as a point is made, and to identify the assumptions that are involved in making that point. For example, one may ask students to consider only the last paragraph. They could be asked to identify the major point here (that the Master thought Harriet rebellious), then to identify the basis for his thinking (her sullen expression), and then to identify the assumption underlying the Master's reasoning (that a sullen expression implies rebelliousness). Of course, the students should be made aware that this whole passage is merely the author's interpretation or thought on this—that she could not really verify that this was what the Master thought—and that the author is, in essence, making some interpretations that cannot be verified as facts.

Once the students have analyzed this paragraph internally they could then be asked to analyze other paragraphs internally, and to compare the various paragraphs, differentiating among the ways the major point of each paragraph is supported: i.e., is it supported by an assumption regarding motives for behavior, or is it supported by descriptions of behavior rather than motives?

Using this technique, students should be led to see that the last paragraph of this passage is quite different from the first. While both paragraphs are judgmental to some extent, the first paragraph provides descriptions of Harriet's appearance to support the judgment that she was not beautiful, while the last paragraph makes judgments about her behavior based not only upon descriptions of her appearance, but also based upon the assumption that certain types of appearance imply certain types of behavior.

This particular trade book might also be used in other ways for developing discriminating abilities. At this level many students should be ready to make discriminations regarding the organization of material.

Using this trade book, which has a bibliography, students might be asked to check other books listed on Harriet Tubman in the bibliography, then to read these books and to compare the organizational patterns of these books with *Freedom Train*.

They might also be asked to seek out other materials on Harriet Tubman, and to compare these writings along organizational lines, keeping in mind the authors' purposes, points of view, approach to telling the story, and points emphasized. The students could then be asked to develop an organizational pattern of their own for writing a report on Harriet Tubman. In this fashion, students can be assisted in learning to discriminate among various organizational patterns. Along with this, students should also be beginning to develop some standards for judging the reliability of various sources to assist them in various levels of discrimination, a judgmental ability which will be discussed in a later portion of this chapter.

Chaining

The search for directional properties beginning from a given set of circumstances is cited as a central feature of chaining. In working with young children chaining abilities may be developed by using simple stories from which children can order a sequence of processes and actions, and then move on to a process of problem-solving. By reading to the children simple stories relating a series of events which lead to a problem that requires solving, they can be asked to identify the important events, and, on the basis of these events, suggest possible solutions to a problem.

By way of illustration, the story of a little Mexican boy, "Pancho," might be used. One would probably wish to use this story by reading the first part of it to the children, up to the point where Pancho is faced with a very serious problem.

Don Fernando, the richest man in the village, was angry!

A wild bull with a crooked tail coaxed the best cattle in his herd to run away.

So Don Fernando offered a purse filled with gold to anyone who caught the bull with the crooked tail.

Cowboys from nearby ranches came to win the prize. First Alfonso rode out on the range. He was sure he would win the purse filled with gold.

But the wild bull ran away with Alfonso's broken lasso trailing from his horns.

Alfonso went home.

"I'll win the prize," shouted Carlos as he galloped away in a cloud of dust.

Carlos lost his hat as well as his lasso, but he did *not* win the prize.

Then Jose, Juan, and Paco tried and failed. No one could catch the bull.

Don Fernando grew angrier and angrier. He offered a silver-trimmed saddle and the biggest hat in all Mexico as well as the purse to anyone who caught the wild bull.

He put the prizes in the window of his store for everyone to see.

All the best riders on the finest horses in the whole state came to try to win the prize.

Every day these cowboys rode past the adobe hut where Pedro, the potter, lived with his wife and young son Pancho. The little family made pots, plates, and bowls to sell in the village. Every morning Pancho led his little burro to the market place.

Pancho often stopped to look at the big hat and the saddle trimmed with silver in the window of Don Fernando's store. No one wanted to win the reward more than Pancho. But he was only a little boy and he had no swift horse nor fine lasso with which to capture the wild bull.

Early one morning Pancho loaded his burro with all the pots his father had made and all the gay colored plates his mother had painted and set out for the market place. As he walked along he thought how fine it would be to ride in a saddle trimmed with silver, wearing the biggest hat in all Mexico, and how happy he could make his father and mother with the purse filled with gold.

"Heee-Haw!" The burro stopped at the turn in the road and so did Pancho.

Right in the middle of the road stood the *wild bull* with the crooked tail!

The cowboys' broken lassos trailed from his horns and he was angry.

Pancho turned about and the burro turned, too. They ran as fast as they could.

Whipped by the lassos, the bull ran after Pancho and the burro.

He knocked the pack from the burro's back!! Pots, plates, and bowls rolled in all directions. The bull kept running and Pancho felt his hot breath just as he scrambled to safety in a big oak that grew beside the road. The bull stamped on Pancho's hat and tossed his head. He snorted and bellowed. He was a very mad bull.

"*Vamos*," shouted Pancho. But the bull would not go away. Pancho was a prisoner in the tree!

He wondered what to do. He looked at the lassos trailing from the bull's horns and thought hard.

Then he broke a hooked branch from the tree. . . .

(Sidonie Matsner Gruenberg, ed., *Let's Read More Stories*, pp. 76–78)

The teacher should then ask the children to identify Pancho's problem, which is not only to find some way to get out of the tree, but secondarily to find some way of capturing the wild bull.

The children can then be asked to list the various events that led up to Pancho's predicament, and to note events that created situations that will aid him in solving his problem, e.g., the bull had ropes on his horns, Pancho broke off a *hooked* stick, etc. Once this has been done students could then be asked to propose various solutions to the problem—keeping in mind what Pancho wanted, and keeping in mind the evidence they have listed. As they propose solutions, each solution could be checked against the list they have constructed to see if the proposed solutions are possible in light of their evidence.

Finally, one could have the children compare their solutions to the problem with Pancho's solution as told in the story:

> Quickly he fished up the nearest lasso and fastened it firmly around the trunk of the tree. The bull pawed the ground angrily and moved closer.
>
> Pancho fished up the other lasso and tied it firmly, too. Then he jumped to the ground and ran.
>
> The bull charged after Pancho, but the lassos soon stopped him.
>
> (Sidonie Matsner Gruenberg, ed., *Let's Read More Stories*, p. 78)

As they read this solution, they will want to note facts they have listed which make this a very plausible and probable solution.

In the upper elementary grades, social studies materials which can be used by students to construct multiple endings, starting from a given set of evidence, may provide opportunities for developing chaining abilities. The following introduction to an anecdote about Daniel Boone provides an example of how students may build endings on the basis of evidence provided in the material, and on the basis of their own knowledge and experience.

> The Indians had been watching the lone white man throughout most of the day. They had never seen any-

thing like him before and could not quite make up their minds what to do.

Some of the half-naked braves wanted to slip in close enough to shoot him with their arrows before he knew they were there.

Others insisted on capturing the strange intruder and taking him back to their big village, to be kept like a wild animal. Perhaps they would tie him to a stake and torture him with fire to give excitement to one of their wild dances.

But they finally made up their minds. They would wait until the white man was sound asleep in his crude shelter. Then they would completely circle the place and close in from every side.

The moonlight streamed down through the tree tops and lay like a soft gray blanket upon the quiet scene. The white man's little fire had died down until only a few sparks glowed in the ashes. His shelter was hardly more than a lean-to with a sloping back-wall of logs and a couple of deerskins tied over the top to keep out the rain.

Back underneath, the white man lay on the hide of a large black bear. He was dressed entirely in well-worn buckskins; and a long-barreled flintlock rifle lay close beside him. He was a young man, still in his twenties. His name was Daniel Boone.

The stillness of the night was broken by the soft call of a bird and from another direction, the chatter of a squirrel. The white man's eyes snapped open and his head jerked up. Instinctively his hand closed tightly on the gun that lay beside him. Wide awake now, he held his breath while he listened.

There was nothing very unusual about the call of a bird or the chatter of a squirrel in the night. But there had been something about these calls that immediately awakened Daniel Boone. Would they come again? He dared not go to sleep until he was absolutely sure what they meant.

This young white man was so thoroughly familiar with the wilderness and all the creatures in it that he

could instantly recognize the call of every bird and
animal. He knew exactly what the different calls
meant. He also knew that the Indians had a clever way
of imitating the calls of birds or the chatter of squirrels
as a means of signaling back and forth as they slipped
through the dense forest.

The calls came again. This time they were closer.
Daniel Boone was now fully awake, and he did not
hesitate. He knew exactly what to do and he acted
quickly. . . .

(Harold McCracken, *The Winning of the West*,
pp. 7–8)

Once the students have read the introduction to
this particular anecdote, the assignment would be to
have them write an ending to it suggesting what happened to Daniel or what it was that he did.

Of importance here, however, is the necessity of
having the students construct their endings upon the
basis of what they know about the situation from the
description provided, and what they may already know
about Daniel Boone that would be applicable. In other
words, the endings they write should be plausible endings that can be based upon knowledge and reality.

To assist them in this, one might first ask the students to list the items related in the introduction that
might have some bearing on the type of action that
Daniel might take: items such as it was night, he was
alone, he was armed. One might also have the students
list facts they might already know about Daniel that
would assist them in writing plausible endings, such as
the fact that, since he was in his eighties when he
died, to write an ending which suggested that Daniel
was killed at the time of this story would not be
plausible.

When the endings have been written, one could
pursue this further by having the children read each
other's endings and see if, in the light of what they

know, and of what is told in the introduction, the endings are plausible, and if things could have turned out the way they describe. One then might have the students read the ending to the story as it appears in the trade book, and compare it with their own.

The examples cited thus far for chaining have used only the introductory portions of stories which provide evidence to assist the students in solving particular problems or in writing multiple endings. Another chaining activity that might be used involves providing both the beginning and ending of a passage, but omitting the middle portion which suggests the steps used to solve a particular problem. The task of the students is to suggest what the steps to the solution are on the basis of evidence provided in the material, and on the basis of their own general knowledge. This type of chaining problem frequently occurs in the study of history, where gaps and unknowns exist in the available evidence.

The following material from *The Quest of Archimedes,* a trade book suitable for use at the junior high level, suggests a problem and indicates that the problem was solved; but the paragraphs suggesting the steps in the solution are omitted.

Alexandria's emergence as a capital of science was by no means an accident of history. It was due largely to the actions of two great rulers: Alexander the Great and Ptolemy I, king of Egypt.

It was Alexander the Great who chose the location of Alexandria in about 332 B.C. The city was then named and built in his honor.

During his short lifetime (356–23 B.C.) Alexander had conquered most of the known world. He pushed the frontiers of the Greek empire into North Africa, far into western Asia, and as far west as Spain. Greek culture began to spread out, away from the city-states such as Athens, and mingle with the other, older cultures around the Mediterranean. The two most important of these cultures were in Egypt and Mesopotamia. By absorbing the scientific insights of these older cultures, Greek science grew in wisdom and awareness.

Then, when Alexander died, the government of Egypt fell to one of his most gifted generals, Ptolemy. In 306 B.C., Ptolemy appointed himself king of Egypt —Ptolemy I, "The Savior"—and ruled for twenty years.

Ptolemy I was a shrewd and capable administrator, and he was determined to make Egypt the finest, richest and most respected kingdom on the Mediterranean.

Having chosen Alexandria as his capital, he called in the best architects and city planners to make it one of the most attractive and well-designed cities of the ancient world.

Fortunately for science, Ptolemy realized that wealth and prosperity alone would never gain Egypt, or himself, the sincere respect of the world. He set out to make Alexandria an intellectual center, too, as Athens was: a center of the arts, literature, and science.

Somehow, Ptolemy knew, he had to attract the attention of learned men in the cities and settlements all around the Mediterranean. He did this in a direct and brilliant manner. . . .

However questionable his motives and tactics, Ptolemy I eminently succeeded in making Alexandria one of the most active and influential intellectual communities in all history. For over a hundred years it was the spiritual home of Greek science. Like a great magnet, Alexandria drew to itself a host of bright intellects seeking knowledge and inspiration.

(Tad Harvey, *The Quest of Archimedes,* pp. 19–21)

Once the students have read these paragraphs, one technique that might be employed, which would require the students to reconstruct the data and then suggest steps in the solution of the problem, would be to prepare a worksheet for them to complete, as in the following example:

   I. Ptolemy's major concern.
      A. His subordinate concern.
         1. His basic problem.
   II. Data from the written material that one must know to suggest possible steps in the solution of the problem.
   III. General knowledge you may have, not provided in the material that may suggest possible steps in the problem solution.
   IV. Some assumptions you might make on the basis of information provided in the material and on your general knowledge that might assist you in identifying steps in the problem solution.
   V. The step-by-step solution you would propose.

In using this type of approach, on the first section of the worksheet the students are merely being asked to narrow the problem on the basis of the information provided; i.e., students should be able to identify that while Ptolemy's major concern was to make Egypt the most respected kingdom on the Mediterranean, to do this he had to fulfill the subordinate purpose of making Alexandria an intellectual center, and to do this he had to attract learned men to Alexandria. This last concern being the basic problem, Ptolemy had to deal with it if his other desires were to be satisfied. Once the students have thus identified the basic problem, they may then proceed to the other sections on the worksheet.

In the second section of the worksheet students are asked to list important information from the written material that will assist them, while the third section provides them with an opportunity to list points from their own knowledge that may contribute. Depending upon how far one wishes to go here, of course, for this section one could recommend that students read other

sources on Alexandria or Ptolemy I that may provide
them with information.

In the fourth section one is simply providing students
with an opportunity to make some assumptions that
may allow them to see relationships between their
information and possible solutions. The fifth section,
of course, is to be the students' actual proposals.

The important thing with this sort of technique is
that a *building* process is going on by which students
see relationships among various facts and assumptions leading to possible solutions.

If it is felt necessary, the teacher may assist the
students by providing clues through questions such as
"Would Ptolemy's position of leadership suggest to you
certain things he might do? What are some essentials
the learned man needs in order to gather knowledge?"
One may also wish to suggest to the students that
basically Ptolemy did two things or had two steps in his
solution to the problem of finding ways to attract
learned men to Alexandria. This might be done in order to provide for students still more of a framework
within which to operate.

Once the students have made their proposed step-
by-step solutions they may then check their solutions
against the steps in the book. In this fashion the students can also evaluate their work. If they have proposed rather wild solutions, they may be led through
discussion to see where they have made assumptions
or seen relationships which were not warranted by
the material.

If one wishes to use this material without employing quite as complex an assignment one might simply
have students read just the last sentence in the passage, "Like a great magnet, Alexandria drew to itself
a host of bright intellects seeking knowledge and inspiration." One could then work with the students,

asking them to list those things which might attract
intellectuals to the city, by posing a question such
as: "What must a city have that will cause a person to
go there who is seeking knowledge?"

They could then be asked to read the first portion
of the selection identifying Ptolemy's problem. Then,
on the basis of those things they listed as needs for
the city they can suggest what Ptolemy may have
done. Once this is completed they could check their
suggested solutions against what was done as stated
in the trade book.

Judging

Judgment is undoubtedly involved in all the previously discussed categories to some extent, since
each involves decision-making or choice-taking at
some point. Basic to the use of judgment, however, is
the recognition and development of standards being
used in judging. Even young children should begin to
develop standards for judging the worth of written materials. As suggested previously, it is advisable to
build standards, then judge, rather than to make a
judgment and build supporting standards.

In working with young children one may wish to
assist them in developing standards for judging materials internally. One simple approach, particularly
useful with materials wherein the author states what
a major theme will be, is to have the children identify
the theme, suggest what the author might do to support this theme, then judge the merits of the book by
determining how well the author follows the theme.
Books of pictures and verses, centered on one theme,
provide particularly useful sources that can be used
for developing judging standards.

For example, Katrina Thomas, the photographer for

My Skyscraper City, states in her dedication to the book:

> You see, I was a country child and until I met Apwick [the boy in the story] I had had the mistaken notion that the world of city children was paved only with asphalt, confined to the sidewalk and the playground. It was Apwick who proved me wrong and showed me how much fun city children really have.

(Penny Hammond, *My Skyscraper City: A Child's View of New York,* p. 7)

The teacher will want to read this portion of the dedication to the children, and to assist them in identifying what the major theme will be, or what the book is to be about. One may do this by asking the question, "What is the photographer going to try to show in her pictures?" Once the children know that the photographer is going to try to show how much fun children have in the city, one might then ask children to list things that are fun, and to tell why they are fun. In other words, the children begin to set up rather crude standards for judging whether the pictures really show Apwick having fun in the city. One could then read the book to the children, showing them the photographs and asking whether the picture really shows the boy having fun in light of what they have said about what things are fun and why things are fun.

Another approach for using this particular source would be to read each verse, then ask what sort of a picture they would take to accompany the verse if they were the photographer. The children can then be shown the photograph in the book and asked to judge whether the photographer's picture really shows what is said in the verse. For example, one might read the following verse:

> Whenever I don't feel like being alone
> I've so many friends to call on the phone

I'll race them, I'll chase them,
   play tug-of-war, too
In a city so big, there's so much to do!

(Penny Hammond, *My Skyscraper City:
A Child's View of New York*, p. 16)

The teacher could then suggest that two pictures
are used to illustrate the ideas in the verse. "If the
photographer is really doing her job, what should the
pictures show?" might be a question the teacher could
ask. On the basis of this verse they should be led to
see that one picture should show the boy talking on
the phone, another showing him playing tug-of-war.
The children can then be shown the photographs in
the book and asked to judge if this is what the photographer shows, or if she shows something else.

At the upper elementary level, in the social studies,
materials that are frequently used consist of stories
about folk heroes. It is important that children early
develop standards for judging the accuracy of the reports in such materials, and that they learn to determine the difference between what is accepted as
fact and what is accepted as legend. Among other
things, it is of utmost importance that children early
develop an attitude of suspended judgment, a willingness not to accept one account of a hero or incident as
fact without first comparing it with other accounts,
before making a decision about the hero or the incident.

For example, there have been written numerous
stories and accounts of such famous incidents as the
Battle of the Alamo, providing ample opportunity for
children to read about this battle, make comparisons
of the accounts, and make some judgments about
which accounts are the most accurate. Students at
this level could be asked to read two or more simple
accounts of the Battle of the Alamo and then attempt

to determine where these accounts appear to be in agreement and where they disagree. In cases where the accounts appear to disagree, children can be asked to develop ways of determining which is the more accurate, and thus develop standards for judging the material.

By way of illustration, one might ask children to read the account of the Alamo in *The Winning of the West* and the account of the Alamo in *The Story of Texas*. They could then be asked to make a list of facts such as who were the leaders of the forces and how many defenders were there at the Alamo, and compare these two accounts on the various facts.

For example, regarding the question of leadership of the defenders of the Alamo, *The Story of Texas* states:

> Though there was some dispute over who should take supreme command, Bowie or Travis, the fact that Bowie was in bad health to start with and was later injured by a fall from one of the gun galleries left Colonel Travis in solitary command.

(George Sessions Perry, *The Story of Texas*, p. 11)

The Winning of the West states:

> A small group of Americans had gathered together to defend the city and Texas liberty. There were only 187 of them, under the leadership of Colonel Jim Bowie—after whom the famous "bowie knife" was named.

(Harold McCracken, *The Winning of the West*, p. 52)

This latter account makes no reference to the role played by Travis, and seems to at least imply that Bowie was in supreme command. Children, having noted this discrepancy in the two accounts, can now be asked to determine which of the two accounts is the more accurate on this point.

First of all, the students might be asked to compare the two paragraphs internally. Does either account suggest *why* or do they merely *state* that one or the other individual was the leader? In this case, obviously the first account is the only one that suggests why Travis became the leader (Bowie was too ill), while the other account merely states that Bowie was the leader, without any particular support.

This, however, still does not necessarily make the first account more accurate than the second, and children may be asked to verify the accuracy by reading other material on the same subject.

One source that is usually readily available to the teacher is an encyclopedia, and students can be asked to check to see which man is credited with leadership in these accounts. The more sources students can check, the better their opportunity for building a case in support of one of the two reports cited. Students can then base their judgments about the accuracy of these reports on the evidence they gather. However, the students need to be advised that they may later discover other evidence which runs counter to this judgment; and that they need to keep an open mind, being willing to change their conclusion should later evidence tend to better support another contention.

At the junior high level, quite similar techniques for judging the accuracy and reliability of materials may be employed, although one may wish to assist students in developing more criteria or in devising other methods for judging materials. The following discussion suggests ways one might use a particular trade book to assist students in developing standards for judging at the junior high level.

Profile of Nigeria, a simply written account of that country, provides numerous short passages that can be used for internal judging of whether the author's conclusions logically follow his arguments, or his evi-

dence, or both. In the following passage, entitled
"Why We Have Never Heard of Nigeria," the author's
conclusion is stated in the title—i.e., we haven't heard
of Nigeria. After reading this passage, students can
be asked to list those points the author makes to
support this conclusion, then to judge whether they
really do.

Students should be led to see that, primarily, paragraph five lists particular points to support the general
conclusion. However, in judging this passage, students
also need to note supporting evidence or arguments
for the particular points made in the paragraph. For
example, when the author suggests in paragraph five
that we have not heard of Nigeria because it has not
had racial clashes, the assumption is that we would
have heard of it, had it had racial clashes. The question then becomes, "How does the author support
this assumption?" In this case, in paragraph three the
author notes countries we have heard of because they
had racial clashes. Students can thus be asked to take
each point the author lists to support his general conclusion, note the assumption underlying it, and check
to see if the author provides information to support
the assumption. Thus in reading this particular passage, the students should judge whether the author
provides support for his assumptions.

While students may disagree with the general conclusion or some of the author's assumptions, their
job here is only to judge the internal consistency of
this passage. If the author supports his assumptions
then he is being internally consistent, and this should
be the judgment on the passage. If students choose
to disagree with the conclusions or assumptions, then
they must be made aware that they too must be able
to support their point of view—not just disagree. If
the author does not support his assumptions, then
students should be ready to question the reliability of

this report—not just accept it without further investigation.

Lots of people have asked recently, "If Nigeria is so big and so important, why haven't we heard about it?" The answer is fairly simple, even though it has several parts.

Actually most of us have known very little about the entire continent of Africa, let alone its individual parts.

We have heard about the Union of South Africa and Kenya because of the clashes there between the white and colored people. We have known something about the Belgian Congo and the Union of South Africa because of their gold, diamonds, and uranium.

We have kept track of Liberia because of our interest in its rubber and because some of its citizens are descendants of former slaves in the United States who went to Liberia a long time ago. We have learned a little about Ghana, Morocco, Tunisia, and a few other spots because they have recently gained their independence.

Nigeria, however, has not had racial clashes. It has not had tremendous mineral resources in which we have been interested. It has been a British possession and we have had no special political ties with it. And it has not been independent until recently.

So it has been a blank spot in the maps of Africa which we all carry in our minds.

(Leonard S. Kenworthy, *Profile of Nigeria,* p. 11)

Obviously, this particular trade book can also be judged externally by comparing it with other sources on Nigeria, checking for consistency of reports. The author, in his acknowledgments, suggests how he collected information, names people who assisted him, and lists sources for information, other than photographs, which might be used for comparing with this particular trade book. In cases where there seems to be disagreement among the various sources, the students will need to be asked to suggest why such disagreement exists and how one might resolve the disagreement. One thing the students should be made aware of in this type of assignment would be the need to determine the purposes of the various authors' writings and the contexts within which they are writing.

For example, has the author's purpose been to present only a glowing picture of Nigeria which suggests none of its weaknesses? Has the author's purpose been to present only a negative picture of Nigeria? Has the author's purpose been to discuss only one aspect of the country? If the students can determine authors' purposes and intents (frequently the foreword or preface of a book can be used for this purpose), it may assist the students in seeing why various sources disagree—i.e., because they are written with different purposes in mind.

Students may also be assisted in determining which of several sources appear to be the more reliable by the development of criteria for determining the reliability of the author's sources for his research. For example, has the author writing on Nigeria visited the country and talked with the people, has he made wide use of a variety of sources (books, pamphlets, letters, maps, films, interviews, etc.), are his sources up-to-date, are his sources written only by Americans or are there some by Nigerians, etc.? Or, for that matter, does the author really give any indications of what his sources have been? In other words, the student who is asked to judge the reliability of a particular source by comparing it with other sources needs to be assisted in developing criteria by which the reliability of all the sources examined can be evaluated.

In asking students to judge the reliability and accuracy of this particular trade book, one might have them work with passages that are particularly concerned with facts about the country, then compare the facts listed with facts on the same topics in other sources. For such an assignment one might use the following passage:

On most maps of the world Nigeria looks like a speck. Even on most maps of Africa it seems very small. Though it is tiny, it can be found easily in at least four different ways.

One is by locating it at the southern tip of the big bulge on the western coast of Africa.

A second is by finding the Niger River, which flows through the heart of Nigeria and empties into the Gulf of Guinea.

A third method is to spot the equator and then to move your finger north a short distance on the map until you come to Nigeria.

A fourth and more accurate way to locate it is to find the area between meridians 3 and 14 east and parallels 4 and 14 north. That is the method a geographer would use to describe it in professional terms.

To the north of Nigeria is French West Africa. To the east is French Equatorial Africa. To the south is the Gulf of Guinea. And to the west are Dahomey and French West Africa.

We have said that this country seems small on most maps. It is small if you compare it with Russia, China, Canada, Brazil, and the United States. But it is very big if you compare it with many countries we know in Europe. For instance, Nigeria is three times the size of Norway. It is four times the size of Great Britain. It is ten times the size of Portugal. It is nearly 32 times the size of Belgium.

You could place all four of these countries in Nigeria, and they would still have room to bounce around.

It is also big in another sense. In it there are approximately 35 million people. That makes it the largest country in Africa in population. Its nearest rivals are Egypt and Ethiopia, and they are not even close competitors, for Egypt has about 25 million people and Ethiopia about 20 million.

(Leonard S. Kenworthy, *Profile of Nigeria,*
pp. 9–10)

Students might actually employ the methods suggested for locating Nigeria on the map, judging whether the methods described really work. They can be asked to check atlases, almanacs, encyclopedias, geographies, and other sources reporting on size and population of the country and the countries with which it is compared, to see if they report the same data, being especially aware of the date of publication on data regarding population figures. They can then note whether the author's facts are consistent with the reports on these facts in other sources, and judge the accuracy of this report accordingly.

The development of standards for judging written materials should be but a step toward the development of standards for judging in many other areas. Inasmuch as students will be asked to make many important decisions as citizens, it is of utmost importance that they develop and recognize standards for judging the worth of the available evidence, and that they base their decisions upon that available evidence which can best meet the judgmental criteria.

Richard J. Nichols

CHAPTER III

DEVELOPING COGNITIVE ABILITIES WITH LANGUAGE ARTS TRADE BOOKS

The study and use of language is the primary goal of language arts learning. It requires the systematic communication of thought processes by means of the spoken and the written word. It would be an anomaly indeed to conceive of language arts learning in the absence of the development of areas of cognitive abilities. Similarly, it would be inconceivable to think of developing areas of cognitive abilities without the use of trade books. Therefore, upon his ability to think—more specifically, to understand, utilize, discriminate, chain, and judge what he reads—depends the child's effective manipulation of the basic skills of listening, speaking, reading, and writing.

Another major goal of language arts learning is the child's ability to participate intelligently in civic and social events. It, too, requires preparation in areas of cognitive abilities, for whether the child is faced with a social or civic event or any other event, he needs to communicate effectively in highly divergent situations. There are situations not only when he needs to comprehend simple ideas but there are also situations when he needs to understand complex phenomena as well as the linguistic patterns that order such phenomena. Trade books are fertile matrices for practice exercises in understanding varying linguistic patterns in their specific functions and meanings. Trade books, particularly, cover a wide range of materials, from picture stories to highly sophisticated literary forms.

(This chapter presents a sampling of materials that might suggest ways of developing cognitive abilities with children in kindergarten through Grade 8 through the use of trade books. It is predicated upon the two-fold idea that *reading is thinking* and that the child's ability to read is therefore an index of his ability to think.)

This chapter also places emphasis upon the importance of trade books as indispensable tools of language arts learning. Such emphasis seems necessary because of the growing misapprehension among teachers about the usefulness of trade books, especially with the nonreader, for the teaching-learning act. Not infrequently faced with populations of nonreaders, teachers tend to revert to instructional media other than trade books, depriving the child of vital experience with books as records of language, namely, as records of thought processes. Why this should be so is, of course, unclear. Is it possible that teachers, in their enthusiasm for teaching facts, facts, and more facts, are losing touch with books as records of dialogue between author and reader—records whose focus is not fact but thinking? In the light of this observation, the impact of trade books upon learning to think cannot be overstated.

Understanding

The first area of cognitive abilities is *understanding*. It is defined as the ability to decode (to read) the author's meaning without confusing it with individual experience or application. Developing understanding ability through the use of language arts materials achieves important objectives intimately related to understanding meaning and understanding the structure of the language. First, language arts materials—poems, stories, novels, plays, essays, and the like—should be read at two levels: *statement* and *meaning*. Reading a passage as *statement* means understanding *what the author is saying;* reading a passage as *meaning* implies understanding *what the author is intending*. Second, language arts materials, because of their highly conscious word-ordering and other contextual structures, more than non-language arts materials, invite careful exploration of words and word systems (sentences, paragraphs, essays, and longer units of thought). The child reading a literary selection cannot presume to be another Humpty Dumpty of *Through the Looking Glass,* the self-styled critic whose words mean just what he chooses them to mean and who therefore, rather than discovering a word's meaning from its context, invents its meaning freely. The child reading a literary passage must learn to comprehend it in its contextual environment, for a word takes its meaning from context and not in isolation.

The teacher selecting practice materials for children in K through Grade 8 in understanding a passage at the levels of statement and meaning might begin with passages in which statement and meaning are quite obvious. The author's statement and meaning are clearly demonstrated in the following selection:

If you read the labels on food containers, there are two big words you probably see quite often—Pasteurized and Homogenized. This is what they mean:

Pasteurize. Once there was a scientist named Pasteur who wanted to find out how to get rid of germs. He knew germs were tiny little things that seem to be everywhere, even in our food. Some germs make the food spoil or turn sour. Others don't change the taste of food, but they make us sick, particularly the ones that get into milk. Pasteur worked and worked and at

last he found a way to make milk pure. You just warm
it a long time. The milk doesn't have to boil or even
get hot—just warm. This was such a wonderful discovery that it was named pasteurizing after Pasteur.
Food factories now pasteurize milk, butter, cheese,
and ice cream. Cider can be pasteurized, too, so that
it won't turn to vinegar.

Homogenize. Some foods are made up of different
substances that don't always stay mixed together. In
ordinary milk the cream separates out and rises to the
top. And if you let a glass of fresh tomato juice stand
on the table, the tiny bits of red will sink to the bottom, leaving an almost clear liquid on top. Food scientists have discovered a way of keeping the particles of
cream or tomato from separating. They put the food
into a container that is fixed so that the liquid can be
squeezed and squeezed through a tiny hole. This is
called homogenizing. The word means that all the
different substances in the food are mixed up evenly
and will stay that way. Ice cream can be homogenized,
too.

(Mary Elting, *The Lollypop Factory and Lots of
Others,* pp. 31–32)

The teacher should provide reading practice with this
and similar passages before attempting more sophisticated forms of statement and meaning.

Next, she might seek out selections which give children practice in reading amalgams of statement and
meaning. Amalgams of statement and meaning are
usually analogies, most frequently appearing as similes
and metaphors. Below is an example of an amalgam of
statement and meaning:

By chance, a ray of sunshine broke through the dull
round of Eleanor's social duties. One afternoon, on a
train trip to visit her grandmother, Eleanor looked up

and found her cousin Franklin standing next to her. She hadn't seen him since she was 14.

(Miriam Gilbert, *Shy Girl*, p. 111)

In the above passage, joy is expressed as "a ray of sunshine" and a segment of Eleanor's life as "the dull round of Eleanor's social duties." Further, the verb "broke" hovers between literal and figurative language and as such functions to amalgamate what the author is saying and what he is meaning. Such use of language is a frequent literary mode, especially in story writing.

Another understanding ability the teacher should develop with children in K through Grade 8 is the ability to comprehend what the author is saying when what he is saying is different from, or the opposite of, what he means. This kind of language is referred to as irony, and both young and older children frequently speak in ironies. For example, it is not uncommon to hear a child promised a picnic on a scheduled day that threatens rain to exclaim, "Oh, what a beautiful day for a picnic!" Or for a little girl who has soiled her white party dress with chocolate to whimper, "Just look what a lovely picture I make."

Trade books, especially poems and short stories, are replete with selections that can be used as practice exercises for helping the child to distinguish between what an author is saying and what he means under the figure of irony. Helen Ferris's *Favorite Poems Old and New* is one such trade book. Among the poems collected in this edition appears Lewis Carroll's "The Walrus and the Carpenter," a fine example of ironic language. The Walrus feasting on the young and unsuspecting oysters exclaims:

"I weep for you," . . .
"I deeply sympathize."

This, in turn, is followed by the author's ironic comment:

> With sobs and tears he sorted out
>> Those of the largest size,
> Holding his pocket handkerchief
>> Before his streaming eyes. (p. 330)

And, similarly, the Carpenter, after his banquet of the captive oysters, says:

> "O Oysters," . . .
>> "You've had a pleasant run!
> Shall we be trotting home again?"
>> But answer came there none—
> And this was scarcely odd, because
>> They'd eaten every one. (p. 331)

Still another understanding ability the teacher should develop with children in K through Grade 8 is the ability to understand word associations. Mary O'Neill's *Hailstones and Halibut Bones,* adventures in color, is highly promising as practice material for learning to make word associations. The teacher might have him read a passage on the color gold:

> Gold is a metal
> Gold is a ring
> Gold is a very
> Beautiful thing.
> Gold is the sunshine
> Light and thin . . . (p. 15)

[At this point the child suggests other associations.]

Similarly, with young children the teacher might develop understanding by using picture stories requiring the correlation of "viewing" and "saying" to comprehend the author's statement and meaning. A fine picture story that might be used in this way is Charlotte Steiner's *Birthdays Are for Everyone*. Each page illustrates some kind of birthday. A verbal description accompanies each illustration. These, in turn, lead into the author's generalization: "The best thing about birthdays is that they happen every year to everyone" (p. 30). At the end of the story, the author explains what she intended the story to mean, namely, "the more you enjoy other people's birthdays the more they will enjoy yours with you" (p. 30). Early experience with picture stories at the levels of the author's statement and meaning should result in better comprehension later of unillustrated stories.

Older children might be given stories in which a key word signals both the author's statement and meaning. Thus Jay Heavilin's *Fast Ball Pitcher* might be read at the levels of statement and meaning as they are made known through a key word chain. Passages such as the following might be cited from the beginning, the middle, and the end of the novel:

He [Scotty] reached for the resin bag at his feet, knowing the resin powder would help him change to the grip he needed to throw the curve. "Boy, I hope my curve is on today," said Scotty. Scotty was as uncertain about his curve ball as he was sure of his fast ball. . . . (p. 34)

Scotty looked at the ball in his fingers and wondered what would happen if he threw the ball with a forward spin. He changed his grip and fired at Felix. The spots on the ball spun backward.

"Keep trying," Felix shouted. "Flagg has me curious, too."

Scotty changed his grip half a dozen times. . . . (p. 73)

Scotty grinned. Thanks to Coach Flagg and Coach Hudson he felt that now he had as firm a grip on his future as he did on the hard, white baseball in his hand. (p. 143)

[Underscorings are my own.]

Even the few passages above indicate quite clearly the function of the key word *grip*. As statement, the word "grip" signals simply that Scotty, after much practice, learned to have a firm grip on the ball. As *meaning,* it signals not only that Scotty learned to have a firm grip on the ball but also on life. The meaning of the story is the theme, and both young and older children need practice in extracting the theme of an author's statement.

The teacher in K through Grade 8 might also find it helpful to prepare work sheets of titles and lead questions asking children to present what the author is saying in one sentence and what he means in another sentence. This understanding ability is closely related to the discriminating ability in that it does develop the child's ability to differentiate ideas of statement from ideas of meaning. Again, the meaning should be identified as the *theme*. On the following page is an example prepared from some language arts stories for young children which appear in Sidonie M. Gruenberg's *Let's Read More Stories.*

As noted earlier in this chapter, language arts materials are also useful for developing understanding ability because they are marked by highly conscious word-orderings and structural systems wherein form and content usually inform one another, and the ability to perceive how form and content coalesce for meaning becomes an understanding ability. Poems, for example, frequently must be perceived through the organic fusion of content and form. Further, denotative (direct and basic) and connotative (suggested or implied) meanings must be grasped, for words in language arts materials function dramatically to evoke feelings, attitudes, and ideas. They direct the reader to see, touch, feel, smell, hear, and experience what an author did. They are a "way" in which the author shares an experience with the reader.

TITLE	QUESTION	STATEMENT	QUESTION	THEME
The Penny Puppy (pp. 13–20)	Who is the Penny Puppy?	He is a lonesome dog.	What is the author actually trying to tell the reader about Penny Puppy?	To the balloon man, he means luck.
That Rapscallion Cat, Sneakers (pp. 28–32)	Who is the rapscallion cat?	The rapscallion cat is Sneakers, a mischievous cat.	What is the author actually trying to tell the reader about Sneakers?	Sneakers' mischief is so very funny that it makes others laugh.
Meow! (a poem) (p. 53)	Who is Meow?	Meow is a beautiful Siamese cat.	What is the author actually trying to tell the reader about Meow?	Beauty is not always useful. (Meow seemed not to like to catch rats!)

However, in K through Grade 8 the teacher should not require any formal analyses of word structures and their functions. Instead, she should provide ample practice with words and word systems in aural-oral readings. Aural-oral experience with words is the comprehension of the auditory-vocal system of language through the basic skills of listening and speaking. It can be, and should be, enjoyed through choric reading of selections especially responsive to aural-oral interpretation. Yet seldom has choric reading been used for developing the understanding ability in K through Grade 8. Is it perhaps because its potential as practice material for this learning still needs to be explored?

In promoting understanding abilities through aural-oral interpretation Helen Ferris's *Favorite Poems Old and New* lends itself well to choric recitations. The poems in this volume are arranged by topical interest, but they can be easily regrouped into the five major categories of choric reading, namely, into refrain, antiphonal, solo, solo-narrator-solo, and unison poems, providing a range of experience from the simplest to the most complex. In order to assure the best possible use of these materials, the teacher needs, first, to become familiar with the sound patterns of the various selections and also with the voice range of her class, and second, to divide the class into voice groups appropriate for interpreting the varying sound patterns. A class of boys and girls might be, for example, divided into high and low voices, or among the girls into soprano and alto and among the boys into tenor and bass and assigned parts accordingly.

It might be best to begin choric reading with *refrain* poems, since in such poems repetition, the simplest of sound patterns, is usually used to carry the theme, or at least to underscore it, and a little observation on the teacher's part should convince her that repetition, though elementary, does help the understanding ability. In the Ferris collection appears the following poem, which is especially striking in its refrain for reinforcing meaning:

Laughing Time
(William Jay Smith)

Girls: It was laughing time, and the tall Giraffe
        Lifted his head, and began to laugh:
 All: Ha! Ha! Ha! Ha!
Boys: And the Chimpanzee on the gingko tree
        Swung noisily down with a *Tee Hee Hee:*
 All: Hee! Hee! Hee! Hee!
Boys: "It's certainly not against the law!"
Girls: Croaked Justice Crow with a loud guffaw:
 All: Haw! Haw! Haw! Haw!
Boys: The dancing bear who could never say "No"
        Waltzed up and down on the tip of his toe:
 All: Ho! Ho! Ho! Ho!
Girls: The donkey daintily took his paw,
        And around they went: Hee-Haw! Hee-Haw!
Boys: The Moon had to smile as it started to climb;
        All over the world it was laughing time!
 All: Ho! Ho! Ho! Ho! Hee-Haw! Hee-Haw!
        Hee! Hee! Hee! Hee! Ha! Ha! Ha! Ha!

(p. 327)

"Laughing Time" is a sensitive choric tapestry, its phonetic features in words such as those of the refrain appearing in contrastive rather than similar spellings. Basic to the child's understanding of language is, of course, the ability to make high-speed response to the contrastive features of words and word systems.

Next, the teacher might give children practice with *antiphonal* poems, poems which lend themselves to group recitation for interpretation. Young children might be asked to recite group poems such as the following:

Tugs
(James Tippett)

Group I: Chug! Puff! Chug!
          Push, little tug.
          Push the great ship here
          Close to its pier.

Group II: Chug! Puff! Chug!
          Pull, strong tug.
          Drawing all alone
          Three boat-loads of stone. (p. 195)

From the above poem it can be observed that antiphonals might be especially used for developing an understanding of comparisons and contrasts. In this poem, for example, the power of the "little tug" is contrasted with that of the "strong tug." Tone and mood poems also are amenable to group readings. Older children might enjoy reciting the psalms, such as Psalm 23, "The Lord Is My Shepherd," antiphonally.

The third grouping in choric poems is the solo poem. The solo poem is the "line-a-child" sequential poem. Poems in which diction is especially colorful in imagery, rhyme schemes, rhythms, reiteration, alliteration, personification, and the like are very responsive to choric reading. The following poem could be rendered very well chorically as a solo poem:

When Icicles Hang by the Wall
(William Shakespeare)

Voice 1: When icicles hang by the wall,
      2: And Dick the shepherd blows his nail,
      3: And Tom bears logs into the hall,
      4: And milk comes frozen home in pail,
      5: And blood is nipped and ways be foul
    All: Then nightly sings the staring owl,
         "To-whit! To-whoo!" A merry note!
         While greasy Joan doth keel the pot.

Voice 6: When all aloud the wind doth blow,
    7: And coughing drowns the parson's saw,
    8: And birds sit brooding in the snow,
    9: And Marian's nose looks red and raw,
   10: And roasted crabs hiss in the bowl,
  All: Then nightly sings the staring owl,
       "To-whit! To-whoo!" A merry note!
       While greasy Joan doth keel the pot. (p. 65)

The solo-narrator-solo recitation is best suited for narrative poems, for, as the name implies, the poem can be divided for individual parts and for a sustaining narrator's part. Solo-narrator-solo recitations are quite difficult to master because they require a wide range of voice coloring for chaining ideas; but, once mastered, they interpret very effectively plot, character, theme, and style through sound-sense patterns of words. Again, the Ferris poems might be used here.

The fifth grouping in choric poems is the unison poem. It is perhaps the most difficult, for performance in unison demands bringing into as close proximity as possible all voices so as to create a unified impression. In unison recitations poems especially rich in stress words (particularly monosyllabic words) should be used, because "stress," or accent, can serve as an important directional property in performing in unison. The teacher should avoid using poems marked by sophisticated phonemic colorings, deviations from normal punctuation, spelling, or capitalization, word inversions, and the like. Premature use of such poems for aural-oral performance might well result in dislike for choric reading. She should instead select poems that are relatively simple in both structure and texture. An example of a poem which might be effectively recited in unison is Edgar Allan Poe's "The Bells." On the other hand, poems by writers such as Ogden Nash and E. E. Cummings, which are usually written in uncommon word orderings and word creations, should

not be used. Children in K through Grade 8 should
enjoy what they perform orally. Therefore language
patterns which deviate from natural speech patterns
should not be introduced in choric performance.

Thus far, two ways of developing cognitive abilities
through language arts materials have been presented:
(1) reading a selection both as statement, i.e., what
the author is saying, and as meaning, i.e., what the
author is intending; and (2) reading selections in
choric performance in order to capture the *sense* of
language through its *sound* patterns. How the utilizing ability can be developed with children in K through
Grade 8 through the use of language arts materials is
discussed next.

Utilizing

If language arts learning is to be a thinking process,
then utilization assumes a major role in building cognitive abilities through trade books. We have defined
utilization as "the ability to take an understanding
from one context and to use it in another context."
Observing how an author utilizes materials for ad-
vancing his own thinking and also for making reading
a contributing force to learning is truly a scholarship
ability. What trade books, then, might the teacher of
K through Grade 8 use to help children to do more
than merely understand what they read? In other
words, what "practices" might she give them to
strengthen their abilities to make what they read truly
their own?

The answers to these questions lie perhaps in a
careful inventory of the skills integral to the utilizing
ability. The following list is offered as a teacher's
guide, therefore, in selecting language arts materials
for developing the utilizing ability:

(1) Restating the author's theme or informing idea and applying it to an understanding of other materials, problems, or situations

(2) Recognizing organizational patterns, styles, and informing ideas as they appear in literary forms and knowing how to imitate them for expressing one's own ideas

(3) Recognizing how tables of contents, indexes, glossaries, titles, and other orientation features serve as directional properties for the author's statement and meaning

(4) Recognizing an author's "like . . . as" systems to clarify ideas

(5) Outlining an author's idea with an awareness of his developmental techniques and using those techniques in new contexts

Restatement as a utilizing ability is the ability to abstract an author's intent or theme and to put it into other words without altering its original validity. In practice it is an individual and imaginative act, especially when what has been restated is utilized for other learning. An example of how restatement and its application to other learning is a utilizing ability can be illustrated from the following story, "My Mother Is the Most Beautiful Woman in the World," by Becky Reyher, one of the stories in Gruenberg's *Let's Read More Stories* (pp. 98–106).

This is a story of a little Ukrainian girl, Varya, who, following her mother in the fields at harvest time, gets lost. Varya wanders alone in the wheat fields for some time before the villagers stumble upon her. The villagers try in vain to learn her name so that they might take her back home to her mother, but sobbing Varya can only stutter, "My mother is the most beautiful woman in the world." Finally, the village leader, Kolya, announces to the village that a child who has

the most beautiful mother in the world is lost, and
women, hopeful of meriting the accolade, rush from
all parts of the village to Varya's side. Suddenly, a
big, broad, toothless woman appears, and Varya
rushes into her arms, crying, "My mother is the most
beautiful woman in the world." Kolya, seeing Varya
safely cuddled in her mother's arms, comments pro-
verbially: "We do not love people because they are
beautiful, but they seem beautiful to us because we
love them."

First, the teacher might require the child to restate
the above story at the level of statement. She might
ask: What is the story? And the expected answer
might be, of course, that the story is one about Varya,
a little Ukrainian girl, who was lost but finally found
by her mother. Next, the teacher might require the
child to restate the story at the level of meaning. She
might ask: What is the author trying to tell us? What
is he trying to make us understand? And the expected
answer is Kolya's proverbial comment: "We do not
love people because they are beautiful, but they seem
beautiful to us because we love them."

Practice in applying the proverbial meaning to his
own learning is a utilizing ability which might be for
the child more complex but also more interesting.
The teacher might have him develop his own story,
using the proverb as the core of meaning. The purpose here is to give the child practice not only in
understanding what he read but in using the understanding in a new context as well.

Young children should be permitted to restate and
to apply what they have learned in oral language
rather than written. When required to write too early,
they often refrain from saying all they wish to simply
because they do not have a sufficient writing vocabulary. Finally, the teacher need not adhere strictly to
the method outlined above but may create other meth-

ods suggested by the style and content of the materials
which she is at that time using.

Second, practice in recognizing organizational pat-
erns, style, and informing ideas as they appear in
literary forms might be best provided through "prac-
ice pattern" writing. Practice pattern writing is the
systematic study of language through close imitation
of already established patterns among recognized
writers. It is a derivative of the principle of linguistics
that language is patterned human behavior. As such,
it emphasizes *models of writing*. Trade books contain
numerous models that can be studied, understood,
and easily emulated by children in K through Grade
. Used frequently enough as a practice exercise,
model writing can result in a meaningful and integrated
construct of language principles upon which the child
can draw and which he can utilize to give expression
to his own thinking. Without such practice, he re-
orts of necessity to rules of writing divorced from
actual practice.

The first step in practice pattern writing is wide
reading for the purpose of developing sensitivity to
natural speech patterns as they are translated into
writing patterns. Speech, it is well to remember, is
primary; writing is secondary, and a derivative of
speech. The teacher might offer very young children
icture stories in which pictures and words inform
ach other to denote or to suggest the author's mean-
g. A fine picture story which might be used with
ry young children is Marjorie Flack's *Tim Tadpole
d the Great Bullfrog*. This is a picture story in
hich the struggles of Tim Tadpole are not only well
escribed verbally, but are illustrated—first, in the
ctures themselves, and even in the typography. The
llowing passage illustrates how typography lends to
e tiny tadpoles quivering movements as he learns

to swim and to develop into a frog like the great bullfrog:

                    So
              all day long
              Tim swam
          and he swam,

                    and all night long
              Tim swam
          and he swam

                              and
                            he never
                    had time to feel
                    sorry for himself
                              at all. (unpaged)

The use of typography for meaning might seem in-
significant to the adult, but the young child can find
it particularly illuminating.

Older children as well as the young should also be
given assorted reading materials that are written strikingly at the audio-visual level, namely, materials
marked by stress-texture words. Stress-texture words
are words which become meaningful through their
rhythmic and pictorial functions, as in the following
poem:

A Birthday

My heart is like a singing bird
    Whose nest is in a watered shoot;
My heart is like an apple tree
    Whose boughs are bent with thickest fruit;
My heart is like a rainbow shell
    That paddles in a halcyon sea;
My heart is gladder than all these
    Because my love is come to me.
Raise me a dais of silk and down;
    Hang it with vair and purple dyes;
Carve it in doves and pomegranates,
    And peacocks with a hundred eyes;

Work it in gold and silver grapes,
In leaves, and silver fleurs-de-lys;
Because the birthday of my life
Is come, my love is come to me.

(Christina Rossetti, "A Birthday," in John Hollander and Harold Bloom, eds., *The Wind and the Rain,* p. 21)

Every line of the above poem moves in flawless iambs and is rich in concrete images which suggest color, motion, and other appeals to the senses. The poem is also a good example of the author's "like . . . as" system in which the "heart" becomes so many things. Another source of practice materials at the level of audio-visual appeal is Mary O'Neill's *People I'd Like to Keep,* in which portraits of familiar people are drawn through rhythmic word patterns and concrete imagery.

Before moving into the next step in practice pattern writing, the writing itself, the teacher should be sure that the child has had plenty of practice in reading stress-texture words so that he has a wide experience vocabulary. One approach to practice pattern writing itself with children in K through Grade 8 is the "punch-card" technique. The punch-card technique is the process of simultaneous extraction and substitution of words at choice junctures of a language structure. The language structure may be as simple as a single sentence or as complex as a short story. While the child carries out this process, he should be encouraged to introduce, if at all feasible, a fresh concept into his model writing. Below is an example of how a teacher might prepare a passage for punch-card practice:

There are *hundreds* of *these markets* in *Nigeria. Some* are *small* and *serve only* the *people* within *walking distance. Others* are *huge, extend*ing for a *mile* or *two* in *all directions* from the *center. People come to them* from *distances* of *hundreds* of miles, *traveling* by *donkey* or *camel, canoe,* or *boat, auto* or *jeep,* or *truck.*

(Leonard S. Kenworthy, *Profile of Nigeria,* p. 43)

The teacher may anticipate that what the child writes according to the above model may be contextually quite different from the model itself, but structurally it will resemble it. In its resemblance of the model it is a way of learning the grammar of a language as a built-in-language system, and is indeed functional learning. The child transforms a series of sentences of identical grammatical structures into another series of identical structures, using this series to transmit his own ideas. He learns thus not only what principles govern language structures but also what principles he himself might utilize to express his own thinking. The punch-card technique is only one of the many ways in which the teacher can teach practice patterns.

Third, recognizing how tables of contents, indexes, glossaries, titles, and other orientation or extrareferential materials give direction to the author's statement and meaning is a utilizing ability which can be developed also through trade books. Most children in K through Grade 8 know very little about the functional application of those materials which give meaning to an author's writing purpose, approach, or emphasis. The teacher therefore needs to pause and to examine with the child matters such as introductions, contents, biographical notes, and the like before beginning the reading of a book having these materials. For example, in beginning a reading of Jonathan Swift's *Gulliver's Travels* in the Doubleday Edition illustrated by Leonard Weisgard for young readers, the teacher should guide the child in studying the frontispiece as an illustration of one of Gulliver's adventures. She should also read with him the introductory biographical note explaining Swift's credentials as politician, churchman, writer, and man of public affairs, which qualify him to write a book of such scope. Finally, she should ask the child to explore the contents and to relate the contents outline to the author's narrative. Such a preliminary survey of extra-referential materials should help the child to comprehend better how the author himself has utilized materials and what his writing craft is. Further, while the child would not attempt to write anything of Swiftian scope, he might be inspired to utilize some Swiftian manner in his own writing.

Fourth, practice in recognizing an author's "like . . . as" systems, namely his use of metaphors and similes and other figures of speech, to clarify an idea is also an important utilizing ability which the teacher of K through Grade 8 should promote. A child sensitive to an author's effective use of metaphors and similes is likely to use these figures of speech in his own language. As a beginning exercise, the teacher might require the child to read selections in which the meaning of the metaphor, though unexpected, is clear. For example, she might require the child to take inventory of the "like . . . as" systems in Janet Lewis's *Keiko's Bubble,* the story of a Japanese girl. The child may draw up a list such as the following:

The rice cakes would be diamond-shaped. (p. 11)
They [wooden floats] looked like a curtain of huge wooden beads. (p. 15)
It was an enormous radish, as big as a turnip. (p. 17)
Keiko nodded, and again her hair swung like tassels. (p. 18)
The beach was curved like a half-moon. (p. 36)
Then he held up a fish that was short and plump and pink as cherry blossoms. (p. 45)

Frequent experience in sighting an author's use of "like . . . as" systems can enhance the child's own perception of diction.

The teacher might next introduce the child to "like . . . as" systems in which more subtle meanings are presented. Again, the Ferris volume is an excellent source of practice materials of this kind. For example, Emily Dickinson's "The Locomotive," appearing in the Ferris volume, might be studied to see how a common object like a locomotive can take on new meaning when compared to another object. First, the child might observe the metaphorical meanings behind the verbs in their order, namely, the verbs *lap, lick, feed, step, crawl, complaining, chase, neigh,* and *stop*. The child may be asked what these verbs suggest. He may say, "A horse," and the teacher might then inform him that the first locomotive had been called "an iron horse." Next, the child might be asked to explain the meaning of the noun *stable* as it completes the horse metaphor. If the poet's comparison is effective, it should finally lead the child to a new understanding of both the locomotive and the horse. In the extended metaphor of the train and the horse the child should be able to perceive similar attributes: both the locomotive and the horse are dependent, both must be fed, both are powerful, and both complain.

Finally, practice in outlining an author's idea in order to comprehend better his technique in developing the idea is a highly important utilization ability for children in K through Grade 8. Not only might the common literary forms be briefly explored with children in K through Grade 8, but, more important perhaps, the contents outlines should also be explored, if they are included in the trade books. The child's awareness of the function of a contents outline as used by a writer should lead him to an awareness of the function of idea ordering in his own writing. This need not be at any sophisticated level, but it should enter the child's perception of writing as thinking as early as possible. Further, the child might be encouraged to keep a file of sample outlines gleaned from book contents which he has studied in class and which might well serve as models of developmental techniques for structuring ideas in written form. Trade books offer numerous samples of contents outlines from simple running notes to sophisticated typographical forms.

Chaining

Chaining is the ability to relate ideas to other ideas not only in a linear sequence but also in the ordering of ideas as one might find in following a set of rules for a game or for stirring up a recipe, or in recombining ideas to bring about a new idea. The central feature of chaining is the search for directional properties of selections, namely, the search for a given set of linguistic circumstances or ideational details which advance the established meaning in a reasonably recognizable line with respect to both content and structure.

With children in K through Grade 8 the teacher should confine herself to the use of relatively brief selections. This is not to suggest that longer selections, even entire plays and novels, might not be used for analysis and breakdown insofar as detecting relationships between plot sequences and idea chaining is concerned. On the contrary, plot sequences and idea chains are more perceptible in long works than in short ones, and therefore the over-all structure is also better understood in long works than in short ones. However, children in K through Grade 8 generally respond more efficiently to analysis of short selections rather than long works.

One chaining process children in K through Grade 8 should explore and develop through the use of language arts trade books is *extrapolation,* whereby the beginning and the end of a selection are given and the child is then given rein to speculate on the middle. The following Grimm's tale is an example of the kinds of materials which might be offered as practice in extrapolation:

The Rabbit's Bride

There was once a woman who lived with her daughter in a beautiful cabbage-garden; and there came a rabbit and ate up all the cabbage. At last said the woman to her daughter,

"Go into the garden, and drive out the rabbit."

"Shoo! Shoo!" said the maiden. "Don't eat up all our cabbages, little rabbit!"

"Come, maiden," said the rabbit, "sit on my tail and go with me to my rabbit-hutch." But the maiden would not.

Another day, back came the rabbit, and ate away at the cabbages, until the woman said to her daughter,

"Go into the garden, and drive away the rabbit."

"Shoo! Shoo!" said the maiden. "Don't eat up all our cabbages, little rabbit!"

"Come, maiden," said the rabbit, "sit on my tail and go with me to my rabbit-hutch." But the maiden would not.

Again, a third time back came the rabbit, and ate away at the cabbages, until the woman said to her daughter,

"Go into the garden, and drive away the rabbit."

"Shoo! Shoo!" said the maiden. "Don't eat up all our cabbages, little rabbit!"

"Come, maiden," said the rabbit, "sit on my tail and go with me to my rabbit-hutch."

And then the girl . . .

On the basis of this beginning the child is instructed to supply a middle to the story, keeping in mind the following ending:

And the rabbit thought that he had killed his bride, and he went away and was very sad.

(Jakob and Wilhelm Grimm, "The Rabbit's Bride," *Grimm's Fairy Tales*, pp. 7–8)

The child may be told that the key word in the story is "bride" so that he can determine an idea focus for the middle he has been asked to supply. He will perhaps emerge with a story quite different from the original, but it is also likely that the structure and style of his version may come quite close to the structure and style of the original tale. In this discovery, the child will observe that there is a certain ordering of an idea that must be sustained from the beginning into the middle and finally into the end of a narrative.

Another practice exercise suitable especially for very young children in learning chaining is observing echo words which function to chain related ideas or to give frame to a piece of writing. An example of a trade book in which echo words for chaining an idea are highly functional is *All Aboard the Train,* by Ethel and Leonard Kessler. The following passage has been taken from this book:

> Waiting—
> Waiting—
> Waiting for the train,
>
> looking down the long, gray tracks.
>
> I think I hear the train.
> I see the train!
> Here it comes,
> zooming down the tracks.
>
> Is this our train?
>
> There is no huff,
>   no puff,
>   no chug,
>   no choo.

The diesel train is zooming through.

Fast.

Whizzzzzzzzzzzz.

Hold on to your hat.
Cover your ears.
Feel the platform shake.

Whizzzzzzzzzzzz.

It is gone! (unpaged)

The teacher can observe that echo words cement the idea of the speed of the train and in this function actually give the passage a highly poetic texture. Trade books, particularly stories for young children, make ample use of this device.

Perhaps one of the most attractive ways of developing older children's chaining ability is through practice in seeing relationships of clues in mystery stories. The Happy Hollisters Series provides excellent materials for such study. In the mystery story a lattice of events leading to a plausible solution of a mystery is established through plot development and clue chains. While the mystery might at first thought seem to be most appropriate for interpolation practice, the chaining ability which will be next discussed, a variation of extrapolation might be stimulating to attempt also: namely, a working backward from the solution to a presentation of the problem to be solved by skipping the beginning and giving the child the middle and the conclusion.

There are, fortunately, a number of short-story mysteries which boast a logical, sequential development of plot together with a progressive layering of evidence in the form of clues. Such mystery stories fit in ideally with the interpretation of chaining as the ability to anchor on to something when reading. *Best Book of*

Mystery Stories, edited by M. A. Donnelly, offers excellent practice exercises.

Another chaining ability, the ability to complete information, is *interpolation.* Practice in interpolation entails providing the child with the beginning and the middle of a passage, and requiring him to supply the end on the basis of the body of materials he has before him. Again, with children in K through Grade 8, brief selections should be preferred. The teacher might go so far as to supply all but the last line of a selection, asking the child to complete only that line. Or she might ask him to "fill in" certain chaining words omitted from the original version, as in the following poem:

The Cupboard
(Walter de la Mare)

I know a little cupboard,
With a teeny tiny key,
And there's a jar of Lollipops
    For me, me, me.

It has a little shelf, my dear,
As dark as dark can be,
And there's a dish of Banbury Cakes,
    For —, —, —.

I have a small fat grandmama,
With a very slippery knee,
And she's Keeper of the Cupboard,
    With the —, —, —.

And when I'm very good, my dear,
As good as good can be,
There's Banbury Cakes, and Lollipops
    For —, —, —.

(Helen Ferris, ed., *Favorite Poems
Old and New,* p. 42)

In the above poem clues for the omitted words are signaled in the first stanza. The omitted word in line 8 is anticipated in the refrain line 4, and, similarly, the omitted word in line 12 is anticipated in line 2. The omitted words in the final line are further anticipated by the already established refrain: "For me, me, me." Even a poem as structurally simple as this can be rewarding practice in recognizing echo words as a way of chaining a major idea.

Other exercises in interpolation through the reading of poems might include: (1) having children write the final line to each stanza of a poem, observing both the original rhyme and rhythm, while making sure of maintaining a focus on the poet's meaning; and (2) having children write the concluding stanza, thus giving them an opportunity to create other plausible endings. An exercise in summarization would be: after showing them what the author had written for a concluding stanza, having children prepare a single sentence of theme.

Virtually made for interpolating are humorous stories with surprise endings, for example the stories written by Twain and O'Henry. The same can be said of many mystery or suspense stories having a "twist" or bizarre ending. Trade books for Grades 5–8 are rich with such materials.

A variation of interpolation is the ability to supply or to anticipate an answer to a question raised by a picture illustration. A case in point is Robb White's *Candy,* a delightful adventure story for girls in which pictures serve as clues to the story ending. In one picture, for example, the question is raised, "What's That Horrible Object?" The child might be asked to anticipate what that object is before he actually reads the author's statement. Another picture shows Candy trying to sell her much-prized boat, the *Faraway.* She is seen talking with her two friends, Chuck and Ryan, and exclaiming, "Oh, no! I want the money. I've got something special to do with it." The child might be again asked to speculate what that something is that Candy wants to do.

Of all the chaining skills perhaps *systematization,* the ability to perceive the logic of writing, is the most valuable to children in K through Grade 8. One type of systematization the child might practice is recognizing a definite *time order* in a sequence of events. The teacher might, in varying degrees of complexity, ask children to put into their proper arrangement a random sampling of sentences. The sampling below might be used this way (the numbers in parentheses show the correct time order):

(2) I was aboard my ship again by noon.

(6) She might warn Nate Hurley, who in turn might inform his brother.

(1) At ten o'clock I went to the Marine Tower to see Mr. Blakemore.

(5) What did we know about Mrs. Stauffer anyway?

(3) At one o'clock Inspector Cameron phoned to say he wanted me to call off my own inquiries.

(4) One of his men had interviewed Mrs. Stauffer and she had told him that a Mrs. Moran had been there the day before asking questions.

> (Howard Pease, *Mystery on Telegraph Hill,*
> pp. 179–80)

A similar exercise can be done with the following sentences from an example-order paragraph:

(2) One bouncer separates the oysterettes from each other when they come out of the oven.

(4) And the biggest bouncer shakes the flour and salt and baking powder together to make them smooth before they are stirred into dough.

(1) A lot of gadgets in the cracker factory bounce up and down.

(3) Another knocks all of the crumbs off the band
    before it goes back to get a new batch of
    crackers.

(Mary Elting, *The Lollypop Factory and Lots of
Others*, p. 66)

The paragraph which follows could be used the
same way, or it could be used in another type of practice exercise in systematization. The children could be
required *to find the anchor idea* (Now he understood
the trampling) *and to underline it twice*. They could
then explain the relationship of the surrounding ideas
to the anchor idea.

> Little Toomai stared again and again. The clearing,
> as he remembered it, had grown in the night. More
> trees stood in the middle of it, but the undergrowth
> and the jungle-grass at the sides had been rolled back.
> Little Toomai stared once more. Now he understood
> the trampling. The elephants had stamped out more
> room—had stamped the thick grass and juicy cane to
> trash, the trash into slivers, the slivers into tiny fibers,
> and the fibers into hard earth.

(Rudyard Kipling, "Toomai of the Elephants," *The
Jungle Book*, 1931 ed., p. 255)

The paragraph below from "Rip Van Winkle" could
be used in a practice exercise in systematization because of its *orderly arrangement in description*. It
could also be used as an exercise in extrapolation by
giving the child the first two sentences and the last one
and having him fill in the middle. Although only very
bright children could fill in a description in historical
context, average children should realize that some type
of character description belongs in the middle and
should be able to provide it:

> On entering the amphitheatre, new objects of won-

der presented themselves. On a level spot in the centre was a company of odd-looking personages playing at ninepins. They were dressed in a quaint outlandish fashion; some wore short doublets, others jerkins, with long knives in their belts, and most of them had enormous breeches, of similar style with that of the guide's. Their visages, too, were peculiar; one had a large beard, broad face, and small piggish eyes; the face of the other seemed to consist entirely of nose, and was surmounted by a white sugar-loaf hat set off with a little feather. They all had beards, of various shapes and colors. There was one who seemed the commander. He was a stout old gentleman, with a weather-beaten countenance; he wore a laced doublet, broad belt and hangar, high-crowned hat and feather, red stockings, and high-heeled shoes, with roses in them. The whole group reminded Rip of the figures in an old Flemish painting in the parlor of Dominie Van Sharch, the village parson, which had been brought over from Holland at the time of the settlement.

(Washington Irving, *Rip Van Winkle and Other Stories*, pp. 17, 20)

The above selections are but a mere sampling of trade books which might be utilized for developing chaining ability in K through Grade 8. Before concluding this section, one should observe that while chaining has been demonstrated here as a cognitive ability fundamental to reading as thinking, it is also particularly useful for teaching writing as thinking. Chaining brings to light models of good, sound writing. The challenges to the child are obvious: if he observes how an author performs in structuring his thinking through chaining devices, he can perform similarly in structuring his own thinking. Having learned first by close imitation, the child should be able eventually to strike out on his own and to create fresh writing patterns in which chaining devices are evident.

Discriminating

Discriminating is the ability to take a mass of materials and to begin to sort through them, developing a systematic way of viewing them without being overwhelmed by details. Children in K through Grade 8 may be taught discriminating through the use of trade books by reading them for (1) detecting a generalization and its supporting details in a mass of materials; (2) differentiating among major literary modes such as narration, description, and exposition; and (3) recognizing the over-all organization of well-written materials.

First, the ability to detect a generalization and its supporting details in a mass of materials might be developed by providing children with practice in reading single paragraphs in which the generalization (topic sentence) is quite obvious, as in the following paragraph:

It was weary work for Kotick. The herd never went more than forty or fifty miles a day, and stopped to feed at night, and kept close to the shore all the time; while Kotick swam around them, and over them, and under them, but he could not hurry them up one half-mile. As they went further north they held a bowing council every few hours, and Kotick nearly bit off his mustache with impatience till he saw that they were following up a warm current of water, and then he respected them more.

(Rudyard Kipling, "The White Seal," *The Jungle Book*, 1931 ed., p. 164)

Children may be required to underscore, as illustrated above, the topic sentence and to restate the supporting details. In the paragraph above, the supporting details explaining why Kotick was weary are clearly stated in the remaining two sentences: "The herd never went more than forty or fifty miles a day, and stopped to feed at night, and kept close to the shore all the time," and "As they went further north they held a bowing council every few hours." No matter what Kotick did he could not hurry them up.

In addition to reading single paragraphs for detecting a generalization and its supporting details, children may be required to read sequences of more than one paragraph, such as the one below:

There were some excellent swimmers in the Advance Class. Young Barrett Shane was one. There was no stroke he could not do well. And only Dink, Peg, and one twelve-year-old girl who did the back-stroke could beat him in a race.

Tina, the twelve-year-old, was Peg's find. The girl was not very good at the free-style-swimming with various strokes in class. But Peg had spotted Tina off by herself, doing the back-stroke with speed and grace. She had brought Dink to watch, and together they invited Tina to enter the coming meet.

There were several boys who showed promise and had been signed up. And Ellie was doing so very well that Peg had pulled her right into Advance Class, to train her for the Baby Race at the meet. But few other girls swam really well. Peg had selected the best of the lot and drilled them, but still she saw little chance for their team.

(Ann Finlayson, *A Summer to Remember*, pp. 54–55)

In this selection, the generalization is stated in the opening sentence of the first paragraph: "There were some excellent swimmers in the Advance Class." One example of an excellent swimmer is also given, namely, young Barrett Shane. But other examples are also offered, and these appear in the succeeding paragraphs: Tina, several boys, and, finally, Ellie. From this cluster of examples, serving to clarify the generalization that there were excellent swimmers in the Advance Class, children can observe that often the writer needs more than one paragraph to clarify a single major idea.

Young children as well as older ones can profit from practice in detecting a generalization supported by details that extend over more than one paragraph. An example of the kinds of practice materials that might be used with very young children is:

> Once upon a time there was a little engine. Her name was CHOO CHOO. She was a beautiful little engine. All black and shiny.
>
> CHOO CHOO had a whistle which went who-WHOOOooooo-oo! when she came to a crossing.
>
> CHOO CHOO had a BELL which went DING! DONG! DING! DONG! when she came to the station.
>
> And a BRAKE which went s-ss-ss-ssSSSSSWISH! And just made an awful noise.
>
> (Virginia Lee Burton, "Choo Choo," in Sidonie Matsner Gruenberg, ed., *Let's Hear a Story*, p. 88)

The teacher should elicit from the children the major idea by merely asking: What was Choo Choo? The children are expected to respond: Choo Choo was a beautiful little engine. To help them detect the details which the author gives to show that Choo Choo was a beautiful little engine, the teacher should further ask: How does the author tell that Choo Choo was a beautiful little engine? And the children are again expected to answer: Choo Choo was a beautiful little engine because (1) she was all black and shiny, (2) she had a whistle, (3) she had a bell, and (4) she had a brake. Thus the details which expand the author's major idea are brought into focus, and the children observe that rather than being written in a single paragraph they are written in a chain of three paragraphs in addition to the paragraph containing the major idea, namely, that

Choo Choo was a beautiful little engine, all black and shiny.

Another major discriminating ability is the ability to differentiate among literary modes such as narration, description, and exposition. Children in K through Grade 8 need not be given practice in recognizing literary modes in which these modes often appear together to provide for an author's varying purposes. For example, an author frequently uses both narration and description in exposition to provide vividness for what he is attempting to explain. Rather, children in K through Grade 8 should be given practice in recognizing literary modes in passages where a specific mode is strikingly evident, as, for example, in the passages below extracted from "Mowgli's Brothers," *The Jungle Book*:

(1) All day Mowgli sat in the cave tending his fire-pot and dipping dry branches into it to see how they looked. He found a branch that satisfied him, and in the evening when Tabaqui came to the cave and told him, rudely enough, that he was wanted at the Council Rock, he laughed till Tabaqui ran away. Then Mowgli went to the Council, still laughing. (p. 35)

[To lead the children into a recognition of this passage as narration (the telling of a story), the teacher might ask them questions such as: What happened? To whom? When? Where? Narration is basic to story-telling and practice in recognizing it as the method for revealing plot, characters, and setting is therefore invaluable.]

(2) A black shadow dropped down into the circle. It was Bagheera, the Black Panther, inky all over, but with the panther markings showing up in certain lights like the pattern of watered silk. Everybody knew Bagheera, and nobody cared to cross his path; for he was as cunning as Tabaqui, as

bold as the wild buffalo, and as reckless as the
wounded elephant. But he had a voice as soft as
wild honey dripping from a tree, and a skin softer
than down. (pp. 19–20)

[To help the children recognize this passage as
description (a picture of the Panther through language
appealing to the senses), the teacher might ask them
questions such as: What words help us to see the
Panther? to hear him? to feel him? What are some
of the "like . . . as" words the author uses to help
us see, hear, and feel the Panther vividly?]

(3) The Law of the Jungle, which never orders
    anything without a reason, forbids every beast to
    eat Man except when he is killing to show his chil-
    dren how to kill, and then he must hunt outside
    the hunting-grounds of his pack or tribe. The real
    reason for this is that man-killing means, sooner
    or later, the arrival of white men on elephants,
    with guns, and hundreds of brown men with
    gongs and rockets and torches. Then everybody
    in the jungle suffers. The reason the beasts give
    among themselves is that Man is the weakest and
    the most senseless of all living things, and it is
    unsportsmanlike to touch him. They say too—and
    it is true—that man-eaters become mangy, and
    lose their teeth. (p. 7)

    [To guide the children in seeing this passage as ex-
    position (the kind of writing that seeks to explain and
    inform), the teacher might ask them questions such
    as: What is the author explaining? What is the *real*
    reason for this law? What is the reason the beasts give
    among themselves? Questions such as these will lead
    the children to see that in exposition the author is
    explaining and informing.]

It cannot be overemphasized that whatever practice
children in K through Grade 8 are given in differentiating literary modes the teacher should be sure that such

practice does not distract from *experience* with trade books for sheer enjoyment. Cognitive abilities with children in K through Grade 8 are best developed if children are permitted direct confrontation with trade books at the level of reading experience rather than at the levels of analysis and synthesis.

Finally, both young and older children might be given practice in discrimination through the use of language arts materials by attempting to recognize an author's over-all organization of materials. For example, very young children might be given selections such as the following and asked very simple questions related to the author's orderly arrangement of parts:

CHOO CHOO had an engineer. His name was JIM. Jim loved the little engine and took care of her. He would shine and polish her till she looked like new and oil all the parts so they would run smoothly.

CHOO CHOO had a fireman. His name was OLEY. Oley fed the little engine with coal and water. The tender carried the coal and water.

(Virginia Lee Burton, "Choo Choo," in Sidonie Matsner Gruenberg, ed., *Let's Hear a Story*, p. 89)

After reading the first paragraph, the child might be asked: What did Choo Choo have? What was his name? What did he do? Then the child may proceed to read the next paragraph and might be asked the same questions. This may be followed by an assignment to conclude some pattern practice writing beginning with some such statement as: Choo Choo also had a ____. His name was ____. ____ ____ and so on, modeling this writing on the pattern of the two preceding paragraphs.

Older children might be given practice in recognizing the over-all organization of larger units, and perhaps even of units in which the ordering is less explicit and therefore ruled by some such pattern as from simple to complex, basic to less basic, ordinary to unusual, less important to more important ideas, or even from less persuasive to more persuasive ideas as illustrated in the selection below. For material of essay length, such as the selection below, the child might be provided with its basic framework, which can guide him through the main points and subpoints in their orderly arrangement. In this case the framework might be (1) thesis sentence, (a) writer's position, (b) others' position (as interpreted by the author); (2) purpose in writing; (3) conclusion.

I suppose the average fifteen-year-old girl would consider it a disgrace to be imprisoned in her room. Not I—I don't mind it at all. In fact, my room is a haven for me. Here I am safe from friends who want to know what *really* happened, from my two brothers, and especially from my parents. At least they have stopped grilling me, a useless proceeding anyhow because they refuse to believe a word I say and I can't change my story. How could I, when I am telling the plain truth? Now they are simply feeding me though in a grudging manner, and locking the door the minute I finish my tray.

Like other prisoners before me, I have decided to begin writing down the true story of what happened, partly to fill the empty hours but also because I want them to know that I am innocent in case I die here or something.

First, I think I ought to make it known that I never had any real idea of eloping with Richard Starr for two reasons: he did not ask me to and I still have to finish high school and maybe college. And as for the story about deliberately running over the man from Hollywood and the reporter, nothing could be more ridiculous. It was not intentional at all. It just happened, the way things always do happen to me. But it's time I got to my story which will explain, I hope, my innocence of intention, if not of deed. I have always meant well toward everyone, no matter what they may believe.

(Jane Hinchman, *A Talent for Trouble*, pp. 7–8)

The provision of some skeletal outline to guide the child in recognizing the over-all organization of material of essay length is desirable to help him see better the necessary connection of ideas, both major and minor, for expressing an author's point coherently and with due emphasis. Further, practice in studying how an author organizes materials into a coherent pattern should be useful to the child in helping him to organize his own materials similarly. Children from Grade 6 and up, who have had frequent practice in studying the over-all organization of writing as seen in trade books, should be able to emulate varying useful patterns in their own writing.

But ability to organize, whether a single paragraph unit or an essay of many paragraphs, requires wide experience with samples from well-written materials. Trade books are replete with such materials. It might be very useful for the teacher himself to outline a number of essays in trade books, noting their parts, the order in which the writer chooses to present them, and the particular interest of each before deciding what materials might be effective exercises for his class.

Judging

Developing judging ability as an area of cognition in K through Grade 8 through the use of objective materials such as those in the examples in the chapters on science, mathematics, and social studies, can be attempted in all three phases, namely, experience, reflection, and reaction. However, developing judging ability as an area of cognition in K through Grade 8 through the use of language arts materials, materials usually volatile in statement and meaning, should not be attempted in all three phases. Reflecting upon and reacting to an author's statement and meaning implies invariably the ability to analyze and to synthesize what one reads. While the very bright child in K through Grade 8 may be capable of analysis and synthesis, research findings report that the average child and below-average child do not have these abilities, and premature effort to teach them these abilities could result in over-simplification of the judging process. Basic, then, to developing judging ability with children in K through Grade 8 through the use of language arts materials is *experience*. Experience means *enjoyment* of what one reads through direct confrontation with the author's work rather than through the breakdown processes of analysis and synthesis.

This does not imply, however, the random selection of trade books. On the contrary, it requires careful selection according to vividly discernible criteria. For example, the teacher should find useful the following list of suggested criteria as a guideline for making selections:

Criteria of Judgment

1. Communicability
   a. Clarity
   b. Intelligibility
   c. Economy
2. Extra-referential content
   a. Connotative values
   b. Directness of approach
3. Personalization
   a. Identifiability
   b. Relatability
   c. General and specific import of the situation
4. Feasibility
   a. Possibility of occurrence
   b. Authenticity
   c. Timeliness

5. Aesthetic appeal
   a. Originality in structure and concept
   b. Style
   c. Over-all art form

The criteria outlined above do not attempt to set the judging ability into any set mode, and the importance of each criterion in the spectrum of judgment can be determined only when the criterion is applied more or less independently to the materials being judged. It is possible, for example, that a specific work may be desirable material at the level of communicability but not so in its extra-referential content. A word of clarification of each criterion may be in order.

When the teacher of K through Grade 8 presents language arts materials to the child she must be sure that the passage communicates to the student. Only then will the child become conscious of its precise structure of sentence ordering and also of its economy of expression through the proper use of vocabulary, without meaningless verbosity. He might also examine the passage for its precise and appropriate use of words in their denotative values. An example of a passage that communicates well to the student is the following:

> After another reflective silence, Tom said: "Hucky, you sure you can keep mum?"
>
> "Tom, we *got* to keep mum. *You* know that. That Injun devil wouldn't make any more of drownding us than a couple of cats, if we was to squeak 'bout this and they didn't hang him. Now, look-a-here, Tom, less take and swear to one another—that's what we got to do—swear to keep mum."
>
> "I'm agreed. It's the best thing. Would you just hold hands and swear that we—"

(Mark Twain, *The Adventures of Tom Sawyer*, Junior Deluxe Edition, p. 84)

The passage communicates well because the sentence structure and also the word denotations are precise and appropriate for informing the reader about two young boys enjoying an adventure of secrecy.

(The teacher should realize also that children in K through Grade 8 are frequently troubled with words and sentences that do not have direct references but instead indirectly connote meanings. Therefore the child needs wide experience in reading passages which incite the imagination through so-called extra-referential content, namely, through diction in all its connotations. The passage below illustrates the kinds of language arts materials the teacher might use with very young children to give them experience with the extra-referential content of writing:)

> One, two, three steps up,
> There's a seat . . .
> the big red bus starts down the street.
>
> Clink!
> the coins
> go Clink!
>
> Beep Beep!
> the horn
> goes Beep!
>
> Whir-RRRRRR-
> Whir-RRRRR-RR
> the motor roars!
>
> round and round and
> round and round . . .
> the wheels go round
> as the big red bus goes down the
> street.

(Ethel and Leonard Kessler, *Big Red Bus,* unpaged)

The teacher might, especially with young children, refer to these words and sentences as "talking" words: they "say" and "mean" at one and the same time, and therefore can be judged to be a desirable communication system between author and reader. Similarly, passages rich in connotative meanings might be offered to older children.

The third criterion, personalization, means the ability of the child to identify with a character, or, if identification is impossible, at least to relate the character to someone from his own experience. This ability also refers to relating what one reads to what one does, thus personalizing the material. The question "Have you learned anything from what you read?" might be a valid one in terms of judging ability because it does exact from the author a statement of import and application. *Tom Sawyer,* cited above, is a good example of a trade book which passes the criterion of personalization. What has happened in the story must, of course, be understood by the child before the implications of the experience can be sensed or valued.

The fourth criterion, feasibility of material, might serve best in judging the merit of science fiction where authenticity and timeliness are most easily verifiable. The author's bias might also be checked here. In checking the possibility, authenticity, and timeliness of materials as well as the author's bias, the teacher is actually judging them for their reliability. Trade books of science fiction such as Ray Bradbury's *S Is for Space,* designed especially for young children, and his *R Is for Rocket,* for older children, might be useful here. The teacher might also have the children look into the author's background to determine how qualified he is to write science fiction.

The last criterion, aesthetic appeal, cannot be defined universally because it can occur under any circumstances within any of a variable set of parameters. There are, however, certain aspects of aesthetic experience which the teacher might seek out in the materials he is selecting. For example, he might examine the passage for its ability to create sense impressions which in turn bring about emotional response and perhaps even intellectualization on the part of the reader. In other words, the teacher might judge the materials for their responsiveness to communication at the levels of sensation, emotion, and intellect.

Of course, the teacher should be aware that judging a work for its aesthetic appeal means examining its over-all art form, a form that has perhaps been given shape in a cultural or temporal context, in multiple layers of subject matter (extending from the purely informative to the purely experiential), and also in some function or use. Above all, he must be aware that language arts materials represent on the part of the author a selection and rearrangement of details, usually from life itself, for the purpose of recording some human experience in an objective and concrete form. Thus the author's product is actually synthetic, whereas the reader's process of judging that product is analytic. The teacher should, then, realize that in applying the criterion of aesthetic appeal to a passage he will not, and should not, try to judge every detail of the passage. Sufficient for selection purposes might be simply judging the unified structure of the selection as it achieves the author's purpose. For example, the teacher might approach an examination of the story "Pancho" by Bertha and Elmer Hader for its aesthetic appeal by noting stylistic devices such as its dramatic, stagelike opening sentence; its emotional tensions; its precise and descriptive vocabulary; its echoic strands for informing at the level of statement and meaning; its dramatic center, narrating Pancho's confrontation with the wild bull; and finally its appeal of identifying with Pancho directly or with Pancho's brilliant stroke of strategy in capturing the bull.

First, "Pancho," the story of a little Mexican boy

who caught a wild bull that no one else, not even the smartest cowboys, could catch, begins on a very forceful dramatic note: "Don Fernando, the richest man in the village, was angry!" The growing tensions of Don Fernando's anger are reported throughout the story. The reader learns that Don Fernando was not only angry but as he fails to catch the bull he "grew angrier and angrier." The emotional tensions are sustained by Don Fernando's offer of, first, a "purse filled with gold," and then "a silver-trimmed saddle and the biggest hat in all Mexico as well as the purse to anyone who caught the wild bull." Poised against the mounting difficulties of the cowboys and the ranchers in their efforts to lasso the bull stands little Pancho, when right in the middle of the road "stood the *wild bull* with the crooked tail!"

The story of Pancho's direct confrontation with the bull is told in precise and emotive language:

Pancho turned about and the burro turned, too. They ran as fast as they could.

Whipped by the lassos, the bull ran after Pancho and the burro.

He knocked the pack from the burro's back!! Pots, plates, and bowls rolled in all directions. The bull kept running and Pancho felt his hot breath just as he scrambled to safety in a big oak that grew beside the road. The bull stamped on Pancho's hat and tossed his head. He snorted and bellowed. He was a very mad bull.

"*Vamos*," shouted Pancho. But the bull would not go away. Pancho was a prisoner in the tree!

He wondered what to do. He looked at the lassos trailing from the bull's horns and thought hard.

Then he broke a hooked branch from the tree. Quickly he fished up the nearest lasso and fastened it firmly around the trunk of the tree. The bull pawed the ground angrily and moved closer.

Pancho fished up the other lasso and tied it firmly too. Then he jumped to the ground and ran.

The bull charged after Pancho, but the lassos soon stopped him.

He bellowed and stamped his hoofs in a rage, but he could not get away. He was tied fast to the tree. The wild bull with the crooked tail was now a prisoner.

(Sidonie Matsner Gruenberg, ed., *Let's Read More Stories*, p. 78)

Further, the echoic phrases, namely, "the wild bull with the crooked tail," "a silver-trimmed saddle and the biggest hat in all Mexico," throughout illuminate the theme of the story, namely, that success in an encounter deserves reward, as Pancho's encounter with the wild bull merited for him the much prized saddle and hat. Stylistically, the author's purpose is clear: to point up the brilliant stroke of strategy exhibited by Pancho. Stylistically the purpose is achieved with the sentence: "Everyone was happy except the wild bull with the crooked tail." Young children reading the story, the teacher might validly anticipate, could easily identify themselves personally with Pancho, or at least identify someone they knew with him. The story, "Pancho," then might be said to pass the test of aesthetic appeal, and might be well utilized for developing young children's judging ability at the level of experience.

Particularly significant in the child's *experience* of reading as a *judging ability* is his ability to raise questions about what he reads. The teacher should therefore encourage a questioning mind, and if answers to his own questions are not forthcoming from the child, he should provide the answers. There is no better way to prepare him for discerning what is and is not "good" reading. It is likely that his questions will be inroads into the structure and the content of what he is reading, and as such prepare him for the analysis and synthesis of what he reads as he matures in his cognitive processes. Wide and frequent exposure to carefully selected language arts materials should result in the child's better understanding, utilizing, discriminating, chaining, and, ultimately, judging ability. But the importance of *experience*—direct confrontation—with reading for enjoyment cannot be overstated, for unless the child experiences worthwhile language patterns as expressed in trade books, he cannot possibly recognize and develop standards which govern such patterns.

What has been offered in this chapter is merely a sampling of what the teacher attempting to develop areas of cognitive abilities through language arts materials might use. It is hoped that the suggested materials might ricochet into an exploration by the teacher of similar or significantly different materials. But even this limited sampling should make the teacher aware of cognition as the superstructure not only of language arts learning but of all learnings as well. To fail to provide practice exercises in thinking is to fail to teach, for learning is thinking and endures only where thinking situations exist.

Marilyn Carrol

CHAPTER IV

DEVELOPING COGNITIVE ABILITIES WITH SCIENCE TRADE BOOKS

Recently, I was asked to evaluate an elementary school science program. I visited about six schools and spoke to all the principals and most of the teachers. Without exception, their chief complaint about the science program was the lack of experimental apparatus. Unwittingly, they told me more. Their comments revealed how little they know about elementary school science, or science in general for that matter. Science is not shiny equipment, or cookbook exercises, or writing up "experiments" in a stereotyped format. Science is understanding concepts and utilizing them in new situations, discriminating, relating, or sequencing ideas, and making judgments based on explicit standards.

These cognitive abilities are enhanced by providing opportunities for children to engage in classroom activities involving observation, working with simple materials, and collecting and graphing data. Often these activities require manipulation of the environment. But there are limitations to what can be manipulated in the classroom—limitations of space, of time, of materials, and of the nature of things. For example, how can one teach the effects of society on science, as in Galileo's case, or the effects of science on society, as in automation, by manipulating the environment?

Although there are no substitutes for classroom "messing around," there are ways of supplementing and complementing classroom activities. It may be that the potential usefulness of trade books to teach cognitive skills in science is grossly neglected. There are many excellent sources of material to enhance scientific inquiry. Although many references are not on a reading level suitable for children, they could certainly be read aloud by the teacher and then discussed.

Piaget's work with children indicates that they do not attain the ability to think abstractly until early adolescence, or until they are out of elementary school. However, in one of his own studies he reports that city children attain advanced levels of thinking at a slightly more accelerated rate than country children. Investigations in Israel for the last ten years show consistently that educationally disadvantaged children enrolled in special programs providing varied experiences make enormous strides in improved mental ability. Here in the United States, directors of Headstart programs are getting feedback that appears to establish the effectiveness of early experiences for children.

What is the implication of these studies for teaching cognitive skills? Simply this—if we want children to think scientifically and to use the methods of science and scientists, we must provide opportunities for them to practice the cognitive skills that are involved. The earlier and the more often they use these skills, the more likely they are to learn them and make them part of their repertoire.

Moreover, children must learn that these skills are not compartmentalized. How many scientists make every effort to be objective in the laboratory while conducting research, but are authoritarian, dogmatic, and unreasoning outside of the laboratory! The only way to develop critical thinking in adults is to teach children that cognitive skills are just as applicable in history or science as on a camping trip, and then give them the chance to transfer these skills to all areas of their experience.

The following quotations have been selected to illustrate how trade books read by the children or by the teacher to the children may be used to promote the cognitive skills. In most cases questions are suggested to guide the children's thinking. Wherever possible, the discussion includes suggested experiments or audio-visual aids which will help to give the ideas a concrete foundation. Abstract thinking, the highest type of thinking, is more likely to develop in those children who have many and varied sensory perceptions to draw on. In other instances, children are encouraged to draw on their own past experiences for comparison or illustration.

Because we know that children's learning, indeed adults' as well, is affected by the individual's self-concept, questions relating to family and social relationships are also suggested. So many teachers become so deeply involved in teaching concepts that often they forget that they are teaching these concepts to people with needs. There are many instances in which this can quite appropriately be done within the framework of the science curriculum.

Understanding

In the book *A Chipmunk Lives Here* several opportunities for understanding of basic concepts of human needs are provided. The following passage would be suitable for use with very young children, either to read themselves or have read to them.

> The weeks passed. Late in April there came a day when the chipmunk felt that she would soon have her babies. This was tremendously important. She dug a little side room off from the main one. Then she went out and got fresh dry leaves and grass, and made a bed in the new place.
>
> There, the next day, her baby chipmunks were

born. There were only three of them. As each was born she picked it up, turned it over in her forefeet the way she did acorns and nuts. She looked each one over carefully, licked it thoroughly, then put it down and covered it with the grass and leaves.

The young ones were very small, no longer than a rather small person's thumb. They were pink all over and had no hair yet. Their eyes were closed, and so were their little rounded ears. And they had no teeth at all. The mother, having looked them over, was very content.

After a while she scratched the dry grass aside, lay down, and let the young ones suckle. Later she and the little ones fell asleep together.

Now that she had her babies the mother chipmunk did not go out so often. She watched over her young ones, and she fed them her milk many times a day. When she did go out for food and water, she hurried back to make sure they were all right. Many times she heard them squeaking for her as she came near.

(Irmengarde Eberle, *A Chipmunk Lives Here*,
p. 31)

Some questions the teacher may ask to clarify the learners' understanding of the author's ideas are: Where did the baby chipmunks come from? Can a mother chipmunk have a kitten or a puppy? Is a baby chipmunk like a baby sister or a baby brother? What do all babies need?

This kind of lesson could do more than teach children the understanding that "like reproduce like," that babies (mammal) are born helpless, that mammary glands provide milk for babies. It points up the understanding of the universality of reproduction, need for food, and reaction to mothers of animals. It's an opportunity for youngsters supplanted by new babies at home to verbalize hostilities and gain understanding of family relationships. Comparing chipmunks to other animals they have known indicates understanding of the basic concepts. Pictures of cats and kittens and of dogs and puppies would help to make the understandings more concrete.

The understandings which were developed in the passage from *A Chipmunk Lives Here* can be extended and elaborated with passages from other trade books, for example *The Wonderful Story of How You Were Born*:

I once knew a little girl whose mother was going to have a baby. The family already had three children, but no pets. So this little girl thought it would be more fun if her mother had a kitten instead of a baby.

Of course, her mother *couldn't* have had a kitten. People can have only human children like yourself and your friends. Dogs can have only puppies, and cats only kittens. Pine trees can make only the seeds that grow into other pine trees, and robins only the eggs that grow into robins. (p. 8)

At the beginning of you, you were no bigger than a dot—a tiny dot, much smaller even than the dot on this page. Smaller than the point of a pin, or the dot a pencil makes on paper, or a single grain of sand. So small that the dot could not be seen at all, except through a strong magnifying glass. The dot that was going to be you was like a tiny little round egg. And that is what you really were—a tiny, tiny little egg.

Everybody you know started to be and started to grow from just an egg. Your mother did and your father did, and your sisters and your brothers, and your cousins and your teachers and your friends. No matter how big anyone is now or how small, he began in exactly the same way. No matter whether a person has white skin, or brown skin, or yellow skin, whether he lives in America, or India, or Africa, or China, he began as a tiny little egg.

Everything else on earth that's alive started out as a tiny dot of an egg, too. All the furry animals you know—from the biggest bears to the smallest mice.

Yes, and the crickets and the flies, the frogs and the fish, and every kind of plant and vegetable and tree— all of these started from a tiny dot-sized egg. In most plants, these eggs grow into seeds.

But even though every living thing began from a little dot, each one is different. Each new plant and each new animal grows to be the same kind of living thing as its parents.

(Sidonie Matsner Gruenberg, *The Wonderful Story of How You Were Born,* pp. 4–7)

In the second passage there are two basic ideas introduced: (1) All plants and animals grow from eggs. (Not always true of one-celled plants and animals or vegetative reproduction, but suitable on this level.) Children can plant radish seeds, look at soaked lima beans that have been split to show the embryo, hatch fertile chicken eggs, and watch shrimp eggs hatch on a microprojector to make understandings concrete. (2) All human beings start life the same way regardless of race.

Many trade books contain science material which can be used to promote understanding among middle grade and junior high students. Below are listed several examples of such passages and their use.

Nearly all of the major oil areas of the world are associated with present or prehistoric seas. The rich Oklahoma oil fields once lay at the bottom of a Paleozoic sea that covered regions in the western United States. In past ages the Gulf of Mexico, the Persian Gulf and other shallow seas have at times been land masses and at other times seas. Over the ages billions upon billions of sea creatures have died, sunk to the slimy ocean floor and enriched the sediments of such areas, all of which are today's treasure lands of petroleum. Saudi Arabia, Iran, and Iraq represent such oil rich areas in the Near East, and the Gulf of Mexico in North America.

Only within the past few years have oil companies begun prospecting for undersea oil in the Gulf of Mexico. Today off the coasts of Texas and Louisiana oil geologists are tapping rich supplies of oil. One of their guides are salt domes, mile-wide underwater mountains of salt crust which have been forced up through five thousand to fifteen thousand feet of sediments. Oil companies are discovering that these salt domes often rest on top of oil rich areas and so serve as natural markers to guide drilling.

Each year chemists who study the sea are discovering a greater and greater storehouse of chemicals waiting to be taken for use by man. Today we are just taking our first steps in learning how to extract some of them economically. Most of them still lie beyond our technological grasp. In years to come as man uses up the ores and petroleum beneath the ground he may be forced to rely on the sea as his major provider.

(Roy A. Gallant, *Exploring Chemistry*, p. 110)

Questions the teacher may ask in guiding the learners are: Why are oil areas of the world associated with the seas? Can you name some continents that are oil rich? Why is the sea called a "storehouse of chemicals"?

These questions will direct students to the key ideas that oil represents the fossil remains of animals, that much oil remains to be tapped under the seas, that the seas contain many chemicals to be harvested. Use of commercial maps and student-drawn maps will tie these key ideas in with geography and history. Evaporation of sea water, or salt water in class with heat, in sunlight, and in the shade, with children tasting the residue would make the concepts concrete as well as teach some of the techniques of science.

The two examples below use passages from different fields of science but require the same fundamental approach to building understanding abilities—comprehending the author's main ideas.

The praying mantis, ten times as big as the froghopper, is also a bubble maker. This fierce-looking creature doesn't need a shelter when it is young. From the day it is born it is able to take care of itself. It feeds on mosquitoes and flies and beetles and big butterflies. Its bubble shelter is built in the fall, when the mother mantis is ready to lay her eggs.

She works upside down, holding onto a twig with her human-looking "hands." A sticky liquid oozes from the rear end of her slender body, and she whips it into a froth with her double-tipped abdomen. The fresh foam looks like well-beaten white of egg. It dries quickly, becoming hard and pinkish brown.

As soon as the foundations of her nest are firmly wrapped around the twig, egg laying begins. A layer of tiny eggs is deposited in the bubbly stuff and covered with a blanket of foam. Then another layer and more bubbles. Often it takes the mother three hours to complete the nest of froth. The finished product is a shiny ball, bigger than an acorn, which may hold as many as two hundred eggs. It shelters the eggs until they are ready to hatch next spring.

Birthday for the praying mantises is an exciting occasion. The babies squeeze out through openings on the front of the nest. These newborn mantises are tiny, pale copies of their parents, except that their bodies are soft and wingless. Hundreds of them wriggle out, hanging from their home by silken threads until they are dry. Then they crawl away, hunting for something to eat.

The hungry mantises devour enormous quantities of insect pests. People sometimes collect their bubble homes in the wintertime and fasten them to branches near their vegetable gardens. When the babies hatch, they go to work for the gardener. All summer long, they dine on beetles and caterpillars which would otherwise have eaten the lettuce or the tender young beans.

A praying mantis is one of the few insects which can be kept as a pet. Although it looks ferocious, it can't hurt you. If you pick one up, it will cling to your hand with its thorny forelegs and try to bite with its pointed mouth. You may be able to teach it to eat bits of raw hamburger and sip water from a spoon.

If you decide to collect mantis bubble balls for your garden, it's wise to keep them in a cool place until spring. Otherwise they will hatch early, before the beetles and flies and caterpillars do. If this happens, you'll see a strange sight. The hungry babies will turn cannibal and eat each other up. Instead of hundreds of mantises, you're likely to end up with just one!

(Dorothy Sterling, *Insects and the Homes They Build*, pp. 43–46)

The teacher may ask: What type of shelter does a mother mantis build for her eggs? What does a baby mantis live on? If you should collect mantis bubble balls for your garden, why should you keep them in a cool place?

To enhance these understandings the learners should examine closely the illustrations that accompany the text, or look at the insect and its bubble nest, if available.

The other major activity that goes on almost every day in any Pygmy camp is the repairing and alteration of the huts. New leaves have to be added, or the old ones changed to avoid leaks. If relatives come to visit, either the house has to be enlarged or a new one built. Whenever this happens there are repercussions throughout the camp, since people will have to change the entrances to their huts to avoid looking directly into the stranger's hut. The entrances also get changed if there are arguments between two families. The two disputants, though they may be next door to each other, will build little "spite fences" between them, so that their huts are turned almost back to back, the walls in effect turning the doorways to face in opposite directions. Then the doorway may face into someone else's hut, and if that family is not in sympathy, their doorway in turn will be changed, and so on.

These changes are usually made by the women, since the hut is considered the woman's property. This is one of the strongest points a woman has in arguments with her husband. I have seen a woman who has failed to get anywhere in a matrimonial disagreement simply turn around and start methodically pulling all the leaves off the hut. Usually the husband stops her halfway. In this case, however, the husband was particularly stubborn. He waited until she had taken all the leaves off, then remarked to the camp at large that his wife was going to be dreadfully cold that night. There was nothing for her to do, without losing face, but to continue; so reluctantly, and very slowly, she started to pull out the sticks that formed the framework of her home.

By this time the camp was agog, because it had been a long time since anyone had seen a domestic argument carried quite this far. The poor woman was in tears, for she was very much in love with her husband, and the final step, if he did not stop her, was for her to pack her few belongings and walk off, having completely demolished their home first. Then she would return to the home of her parents. It is the nature of a Pygmy never to admit he is wrong, and the husband was beginning to feel equally anxious. Things had gone too far for either of them to patch up the quarrel without being shamed in the eyes of all those who were watching to see what would happen next. He sat silent, hugging his knees, looking as miserable as his wife. Then he brightened up suddenly and turned around to see how far the demolition had gone. Only a few sticks had been pulled out. He called to his wife not to bother with the sticks, it was only the leaves that were dirty. She looked at him with a puzzled "Ayiiiiii?"—and then, understanding, asked him to help her carry the leaves down to the stream. This they did, and together they gravely washed every single leaf and brought them back. While she joyfully put the leaves back on the hut he stoked up the fire and then went off with his bow and arrows to see if he could find some game to bring back for a special dinner.

The pretense was that she had been taking the leaves off not because she was angry, but because they were dirty and attracted ants and spiders. Nobody believed this, but everyone was glad the quarrel was over.

(Colin Turnbull, *The Forest People,* pp. 133–34)

Some appropriate questions are: Why do Pygmies change the entrances to their huts? Whose property is the hut? Are Pygmies the only people who never admit they are wrong? How did this husband and wife make up?

The understanding conveyed by this charming selection is not strictly anthropological, to be relegated to discussions of African tribes. It has implications for behavior among all people. In a discussion, children should be encouraged to tell of times that they refused to admit they were wrong in encounters with other children, teacher, parents, and also tell how the problems were resolved.

Utilization

Utilization abilities entail being able to take an idea, principle, or piece of learning from one context and use it in another. The examples which follow have been drawn from the fields of biology, physics, and archaeology to illustrate the versatility of the content that trade books offer. An important principle that has broad application in many areas of human experience is developed in this selection on plants.

Plants, which add so much beauty to the pond, are as important to the pond community as the animals that live or visit there. Many pond animals depend solely upon plants for their food; all use the nutritious elements that plants produce.

Some animals that live in the pond or come to it for food eat only the leaves, stems, or roots of the plants that grow there. Through photosynthesis and through essential nutrients absorbed from the pond, these plants make food and store energy. This food and energy builds the bodies of the plant-eating animals. The animals that eat only meat get their nutrients from the plants of the pond indirectly by eating the plant-eating animals. So we can see that all animal life in the pond depends upon the plants, because only plants can make food.

(Melita Hofmann, *A Trip to the Pond,* p. 43)

Can children transfer the concept that plants are producers and animals are consumers to other communities? To ours? Children can be asked to trace food chains as one step in utilization of the concept.

A similar example of taking a principle which has many applications is seen in this passage from the same trade book:

In order to live, all pond animals use oxygen. It is produced by the green plants of the land and water through a process called photosynthesis. This takes place when light energy from the sun, shining on the green leaves of plants, combines with water in the plant and carbon dioxide which the plant takes in from the air. Photosynthesis is a chemical process that produces food and stores energy for the plants and gives off oxygen.

The oxygen is released into the air and water and some is breathed in by animals which in turn give off carbon dioxide. Some of the oxygen is used by the plants themselves. Animals take in oxygen and release

carbon dioxide, plants take in carbon dioxide and
release oxygen.

(*Ibid.*, p. 15)

Can children transfer the principle of the cyclic use
of oxygen and carbon dioxide by the pond community
to other communities? To ours? To increase the
utilization of the principle children might be asked to
make diagrams of the cycle using plants, animals, and
humans.

A description of utilization of the principle of gravity
suitable for upper grade children is contained in this
passage from the book *Space Flight and How It
Works*. An excellent diagram of the change in speed
needed to keep an object in orbit as gravity weakens
accompanies the passage in the book.

> Gravity weakens as the distance from earth in-
> creases (4000 miles up, an object falls only 4 feet the
> first second, instead of 16 feet). Therefore, a satellite
> must go slower at higher altitudes to balance the
> earth's weaker pull. That is why the moon stays in or-
> bit at a comparatively "slow" speed.
>
> To get the "feel" of balancing speed with the
> gravity at *your* altitude, "launch" a marble in a bowl.
> By swirling the bowl in a small circle at the right speed,
> you can—with practice—get the marble to orbit along
> the walls. If you swirl too slowly, the marble won't
> go fast enough to balance gravity, and the marble will
> fall to the bottom of the bowl. If you swirl too fast,
> the marble will go faster than needed to balance
> gravity and the marble will be hurled out of the bowl.

(William P. Gottlieb, *Space Flight and How It
Works*, p. 25)

Children should be allowed to do the experiment and
find out for themselves what happens when the marble
goes too slowly or too fast. Then get the children to
apply the principle to gravitational force on earth. Be

ing able to apply the principle indicates the mastery of the concept.

With the great interest in space exhibited by middle and upper grade students, materials concerning space flight provide opportunities to develop utilization abilities with basic science principles, as in the following selection:

Did you ever realize that our planet is a kind of natural spaceship, carrying us in orbit around the sun? Because of the special conditions that exist on earth, we are kept alive as we speed through space.

To carry humans successfully, a *man-made* spaceship must have a life-support system that can duplicate the one provided by our *natural* spaceship. Let's see what is required. . . .

How much atmosphere is needed?

The part of earth most important to life is the atmosphere, a layer of air, moisture, and dust held to our planet by gravity.

The atmosphere has density. At sea level it pushes on us from all sides with a pressure of nearly 15 pounds per square inch (usually referred to as "15 psi"). We don't notice it because our bodies contain air and fluids which push outward equally. But what would those inner pressures do to us if we suddenly went unprotected into high altitudes where the atmosphere has less density and pressure? (Ten miles up, the pressure is only about 1.5 psi.)

High up, an unprotected body would similarly swell if suddenly exposed to the thin outside atmosphere. In outer space, where there is *no* air and therefore *no* air pressure, an unprotected body would explode.

To prevent deadly swelling (and other disorders created by low air density), a spaceship must carry its own atmosphere. The ship must be perfectly sealed so that its atmosphere won't escape.

To help in emergencies, astronauts can wear suits that squeeze the body and thereby replace the outside pressure normally provided by the atmosphere. These suits also contain the proper atmosphere for survival.

How will oxygen, food, and water be supplied?

An astronaut needs about 10 pounds of oxygen, food, and water a day. On long trips, a complete supply would be too heavy for a rocket to lift. To save weight, scientists are developing ways to use air, food, and water over and over again, in imitation of the cycles on earth.

On earth, for example, our oxygen supply is kept fresh by green plants. These plants absorb carbon dioxide, which other living things *exhale,* and they release oxygen, which other living things *inhale.* In a spaceship, this cycle may be carried on by tanks of algae, a tiny, green water plant which can efficiently exchange undesirable carbon dioxide for life-giving oxygen.

The same algae, after proper preparation, may also be used for food. Algae can grow rapidly with the help of light, water, and human wastes such as carbon dioxide.

Water must be reused on long space flights. To see one method of purifying water, pour some salt (to represent impurities) into a kettle of water. Boil the water. The water will turn to steam and rise; but the impurities will stay behind. If the steam strikes a cool surface, such as a piece of metal, it will condense back into water droplets, which can be gathered in a plate. The new water supply will be pure.

(*Ibid.,* pp. 46–52)

The teacher might ask questions similar to these in prompting the learners to utilize the basic science principles: (1) What conditions does man require to stay alive on earth? (2) If he left the earth, how could he be sure that necessary conditions for life will be available? (3) Cap two test tubes with a balloon. Place one in a cold place, the other in a warm place. Which of these illustrates what would happen if man went into space unprotected by space suits? Explain.

Can the children transfer the needs for life on earth to all environments? This ability to utilize concepts in other situations is the real test of learning, and the only reason for schools. The information learned may not be useful in its present form. Therefore, children should be able to apply what they know to other situations.

Three more examples, from a trade book on jets and rockets, exemplify how basic science principles are used in space flight, and provide students suggestions for experiments on their own to promote utilization of the principle at their level of comprehension.

If it is difficult for you to imagine a gas in some different form, think of the fact that steam (a gas) comes from water (a liquid), which in turn can become ice (a solid). All three are the same substance, at different temperatures.

Like steam, oxygen can be turned into either liquid or solid form.

In a liquid-fuel rocket, tanks of liquid fuel and liquid oxygen are pumped into the combustion chamber, where they are ignited.

To get an idea of what can happen when fuel and an "oxidizer" combine, try this experiment outdoors:

First, get a bottle, a cork, some vinegar, baking soda (bicarbonate of soda), tissue paper, vaseline, a spoon, and several round pencils.

Put some vaseline where the bottle and cork will touch.

Then, half fill the bottle with a mixture of 50 per cent water and 50 per cent vinegar. (This is the "fuel.")

Put two teaspoonfuls of baking soda (the "oxidizer") in a piece of tissue paper and twist the ends.

Slip the baking soda into the bottle; and, before the paper can come loose and release the baking soda, cork the bottle and place it across several of the pencils.

When the paper comes apart and the baking soda combines with the vinegar, a strong chemical reaction takes place which releases a large quantity of fast-moving, expanding gases.

In a moment . . .

the cork and part of the contents are shot from the bottle, perhaps as far as 20 feet. As a reaction, the bottle has been pushed in the opposite direction.

Incidentally, toy flying rockets usually use chemicals similar to vinegar and baking soda.

In an actual rocket, fuel and liquid oxygen burn fiercely when they combine. The combustion heats and greatly expands these liquids so that, like water turning to steam, they become gas. The expansion takes place very rapidly and builds fantastic pressure.

Since there is a nozzle at the rear, the rocket shoots ahead.

(William P. Gottlieb, *Jets and Rockets and How They Work*, pp. 49–51)

After experimenting with steam, water, and ice, can children utilize these concepts to explain how solid and liquid oxygen are formed? After experimenting with vinegar and baking soda, can children apply these understandings to what they know of the way a rocket behaves?

Why are rockets the only engines that can be used for space flight?

The atmosphere which surrounds the earth gets thinner as altitude increases. At one hundred miles, it is almost too thin to measure. At two hundred miles, it scarcely exists. Still higher, there is practically nothing but space—empty, outer space.

About a fifth of the atmosphere is oxygen, a gas necessary for combustion (burning). If you light several candles and cover them at the same time with glasses of different sizes, you will find that the candle covered by the smallest glass will go out first. Why? Because the smallest glass contains the least oxygen and can maintain combustion for the shortest time.

Without oxygen, candles cannot burn and release

the energy which provides light and heat. And without oxygen, fuel cannot burn and release the energy which provides an engine's power. (That is why jet engines need huge intakes to scoop up air.)

Since there is no air in outer space, *ordinary engines* cannot operate above the atmosphere. *Rockets,* however, do not need oxygen from the air. They carry their own supply, either in the form of a liquid "oxidizer" or in solid oxygen particles mixed with solid fuel. Rockets can work anywhere, even in airless outer space.

(Ibid., pp. 12–13)

After doing the experiment, the teacher may check the principle through these or similar questions: Why does the candle under the smallest glass go out first? What relation does this have to the fact that rockets must carry their own fuel?

In this situation, the understanding of the experiment may be utilized to create a better, more concrete understanding of why rockets carry fuel. The common elements, of course, are fuel and oxygen, which provide heat and energy in both cases.

A different form of utilization of abilities which are part of the functional scholarship skills of advanced science is the using of data to formulate a theory, as in the use of fossils to date the earth's aging.

Once learners understand what fossils are, then they could be asked to probe the relationships which brought forth the theory. What was the relationship of fossils and layers? Here the aim would be to see that scientists have utilized discoveries of fossils in various layers of rock to develop the theory that the type of fossil identified the layer of rock. This is utilization of a very high order. From observing analogous situations, scientists developed a generalization. This high-level utilization is called induction.

Since scientific data are derived from experience,

utilization of principles demands that the learner apply and use the principles as nearly as possible within his experience. The demonstrations that are so prevalent in a good science program and that have been suggested with some of the passages in this section are in keeping with this widely accepted learning principle.

Discriminating

The area of cognitive abilities of discrimination, which involves, as a central ability, classification, is of particular significance in science. Every science is concerned with the classification of the data which fall within its specific field. To make sense of a mass of data, to organize it into a theory, and to apply data to a problem, classification at one or more stages is necessary. The following examples illustrate how children using trade books containing science information can practice discriminating abilities in many contexts. The first examples relate to basic principles of classification in biology.

> At the end of a path through the encircling woods or meadow a pond sparkles, dappled by bright spring sunlight and shadow . . . still and quiet. Tall spears of cattails and the leaves of other green and flowering plants sway gently to and fro along the edges of the pond.
>
> A soft splash breaks the watchful quiet. Near a water lily leaf the flippered feet of a frog are just disappearing into the mat of mossy green on the surface of the water. Through the opening among the pond weeds you can see where it went—below the surface of the pond—into a lively world of countless insects, snails, turtles, fish, and many other creatures, that crawl or swim about among the stems and leaves of water plants. Across the bottom of the pond move shadows made by insects walking, running, skipping, leaping, and whirling on the surface.

On the surface of the pond, near the cattails, where a turtle or possibly some furry little animal swims, the water's quiet film is cut in a V-shaped wake. Beside the pond animal tracks lead in and out of the nearby thickets. A salamander slithers among the wet leaves and over mossy clumps bordering the pond. A long-legged heron stalks out of the reeds to catch a tad-pole or fish. A duck leads her downy brood out across the pond, while songbirds sing in nearby trees and shrubs. A metallic-blue-green dragonfly, a brilliant creature on transparent wings, flies by in pursuit of an insect. It catches one in midair, and eats it without landing.

A trip to a pond is a visit to a busy community of plant and animal families. All the families in the pond community depend in some way upon one another, and on the water of the pond to live.

(Melita Hofmann, *A Trip to the Pond,* p. 11)

This example seems particularly suitable for primary and middle grade children as an introduction into the basic classification system of biology. The teacher might ask the learners questions such as: How many different kinds of living organisms live in the pond? Can you divide the organisms into two groups? How could the two groups be subdivided?

This quotation lends itself well to classification of plants and animals. Animals may be subdivided into those with backbones and those without. Similarities and differences of each group may be listed. Examples of some of each should be brought in for observation.

Two other basic biological science principles which require discrimination abilities, metamorphosis and pollination, are discussed in the following selections taken from the same book.

Insects that were born in the pond lay their eggs in the pond. Most of these eggs are laid on leaves, in the stems, or in crevices of water plants. Some are deposited there by insects living down in the pond. Others are dropped by insects flying over the surface of the pond. Millions of eggs are laid, each coated with a transparent, jelly-like substance which makes them hard to find and slippery to catch. Even so, not all have a chance to hatch, since so many are eaten by residents of the pond that depend on them for food.

However, many of these eggs do hatch and develop into adult insects. In the process of development some of these insects go through what is called complete metamorphosis. This means that there are four stages in an insect's development. The first stage is the egg. The insect hatches from the egg as a wormlike form known as larva. In the larval stage it eats continuously until it has reached its full growth. Then it changes into a pupa, when it needs no food. During this period it gradually develops adult organs and finally emerges as an adult insect.

Other insects go through a three-stage transformation called incomplete metamorphosis. From the egg a larva known as a nymph emerges. This nymph looks very much like an adult without wings. It eats in ways similar to those of its parents, until it is transformed into the adult stage. In complete metamorphosis and in incomplete metamorphosis the transformation from egg to adult may take a period of weeks or months, even a year or more. The time needed for metamorphosis depends upon the kind of insect, and on climate and other conditions.

(*Ibid.*, pp. 26–27)

As guides to learners' discrimination of characteristics of metamorphosis, the teacher can direct the learners' attention to the differentiation of complete and incomplete metamorphosis, and to the way organisms variously grow and develop. Children can compare growth and development of animals that go through metamorphosis and those that do not, noting similarities and differences. Pictures of various insects showing life cycles would clarify the comparisons. Children can bring in examples of insect eggs or pupa or both and watch metamorphosis in class.

When a flower appears on a plant, it contains tiny, tender eggs. These eggs will not grow into new plants until they have been fertilized with pollen from the flower centers. The fragrant odors, a bright color spot or gay, fluttering petals of most flowers attract insects and birds, which take a little pollen with them as they fly. Animals carry some pollen on their furry coats. And the wind often scatters pollen so that it may reach unripe seeds.

Pond lilies open their petals when the sun shines and close them late in the afternoon when the sun sets. During these hours all summer long many insects and birds, attracted by their fragrance, hover over them, sipping the nectar. Their bodies brush against the pollen, and they fertilize the seeds in other lilies with the pollen they carry. Seeds develop and are carried to the bottom of the pond as the pond lily's stem bends downward, or they may float along in the water to be carried to another spot by the wind, then drop to the bottom to take root.

Two underwater plants have unusual ways of scattering their pollen and their seeds. In early summer, one of the feathery pondweeds, the bladderwort, floats up from the bottom of the pond to the top, its countless bladders buoying it up like a lush green raft. From June to August its tiny flowers appear at the surface. The parts of the male flower which carry the pollen break off and float on the surface, where they settle on the other bladderwort blossoms. During the summer the seeds form. In the fall the plant sinks to the bottom and drops its seeds. By the next spring, new plants of the bladderwort which have grown from these seeds float up to the surface.

Pollinating its flowers in a unique way, too, is the ribbon-weed. Though native of Italy it is often planted here in ponds and aquariums. It grows a long-stemmed flower which during the summer reaches up to the surface from its roots and ribbon-like leaves at the bottom of the pond. Soon a shorter-stemmed male flower of the ribbon-weed releases its tiny sphere-shaped flowers. One by one each rises to the surface. Each opens its three tiny canoe-shaped petals and floats its clump of sticky pollen grains to the flower on the surface. The female flower encloses them and, inside, the seeds form and ripen. In the fall, the long-stemmed flower collapses its head and spirals down to the bottom of the pond to scatter its seeds.

Beside the pond, the golden catkins of the willows and the brilliant red flowers of the swamp (red) maples whirl and toss in the wind in the springtime, scattering their pollen. Between spring and fall, when the seeds of the willow in their flasklike pods are ready, the pods open to set them free in cottony masses. These are carried by the wind to a moist spot near the pond where they will take root and grow. The seeds of the swamp maple are also carried by the wind. On tiny red wings they are wafted to the moist ground below, to root and grow. These seeds cannot survive even a few days unless the soil upon which they fall remains wet.

By late summer the dangling seed pods of the jewel-weeds (touch-me-not) burst, scattering seeds far and wide as though flung from a slingshot. By autumn thousands of seeds develop in the velvety brown cattails. Sometimes the cattails stand throughout the winter before their seeds, each attached to a plumy fluff, are carried off by the wind, perhaps to be dropped down where they can take root and grow at the edge of the pond.

(*Ibid.*, pp. 48–49)

The learners may be asked to classify flowers according to the similarities in pollination. Children can compare the appearances of flowers which depend on insects, birds, wind, or water to scatter pollen. This might be a good place to introduce the concepts of teleology and adaptation. *Teleology* implies the existence of a reason for certain organisms to develop as they do. For example, we often hear it said that some flowers have fragrant odors *so that* they can attract insects. *Adaptation,* on the other hand, results from a chance variation which makes an organism successful so that it survives long enough to produce offspring to carry on the variation. Using the same example, we might hypothesize that originally roses had no odor. Through a chance mutation, one rose developed an odor. Insects were attracted to this rose in preference to unscented roses. As a result, pollen from the scented rose was scattered and more scented rose plants were produced. Because the unscented roses did not reproduce, they died out. Darwin called this natural selection. This discrimination between purpose and adaptation is a very difficult one for youngsters to understand. Plants brought into the classroom could provide examples of adaptation to aid in discrimination.

The next selection suitable for use with middle and upper grade learners emphasizes that a valid way of discriminating between opinion and fact is to do a controlled experiment. It also shows the distinction between a hypothesis and a conclusion. The students can replicate this experiment in order to learn the methods and techniques of science by inquiry.

For hundreds of years, scientists had believed in the spontaneous generation of small creatures. That is, they believed that small creatures had no parents or ancestors. Instead, these simply sprang into being in the substance in which they lived. Such a springing-into-being was called spontaneous generation. The Romans believed that bees came into being in the blood of a slaughtered ox or steer. An English scientist of the 1600s said beetles and wasps were generated in cow dung. A chemist of the same period told how to create mice at will. His formula: place in a container a dirty shirt and a few grains of wheat or a piece of cheese. In a few weeks, he said, fully formed mice would be found in the container. Even more remarkable, mice so created were always full grown.

By Pasteur's time, scientists no longer believed in the spontaneous generation of mice. But many still believed that other small creatures—among them microbes—simply sprang into being. A few scientists had made attacks on the theory. For example, they had taken up the question of spontaneous generation of worms in meat. They showed that if flies were kept away from the meat, no worms appeared in it. Such experiments, though, did not shake the faith of those who believed in the theory. They simply said that for some reason conditions had not been right for spontaneous generation; the experiments proved nothing.

Pasteur believed that the matter had to be settled for once and for all. It was important to science, and it was also important to his work on fermentation. He was culturing microbes. He could start with a few and the few would become billions. Did microbes breed microbes? Or did the billions of new microbes spring into being spontaneously? He believed that microbes bred microbes. But belief was not enough. He needed an answer drawn from experiments that could not be challenged.

He began by repeating some old experiments that had been performed by earlier scientists.

He put cotton in one end of a glass tube and attached a suction pump to the other end. Then he pumped air from his garden through the cotton. Dust caught in the cotton. When the cotton was placed in a yeast broth, microbes appeared and multiplied. This seemed to show that microbes, or germs, were carried on dust in the air.

Then he went at the same matter the opposite way. He put yeast extract, sugar, and pure water into a glass flask. He held the neck of the flask in a flame, melting the glass and drawing the neck out into a fine point. He held the flask over a flame and boiled the liquid in it for a few minutes; this killed the microbes and forced out the air. Finally, he sealed the flask.

No microbes grew in the liquid. This seemed to show that only microbes can produce more microbes; where there are none, none grow.

Pasteur repeated the experiment a number of times. Then he took several flasks and broke their necks. When air had rushed into them, he resealed the flasks. This time microbes grew and multiplied in the flasks. This indicated that they had been carried in on dust in the air. And it seemed also to prove that microbes breed microbes.

(Patricia Lauber, *The Quest of Louis Pasteur*, pp. 29–30)

What is spontaneous generation? What was Pasteur's hypothesis? Did Pasteur's conclusion support his hypothesis? List the facts which he used in supporting his hypothesis.

These questions can help learners discriminate facts from opinion, an important element in the scientific method.

Some people believe that all animals and plants were formed exactly as we know them by "special creation." Fossil evidence indicates that long ago, all the plants and animals on earth were very simple. Fossils found in successively earlier strata show that plants and animals became more complex as time passed. This idea of change is known as evolution. This selection may be used to discriminate between theory and fact.

A fact is defined as a piece of information that has been well-established by demonstrable, observable evidence. It is a fact that chalk deposits exist. It is also a fact that sea animals now existing produce chalk deposits. A theory is an explanation for observable, demonstrable facts that new information seems to fit, which in turn is a basis for seeking new information. Knowing that chalk deposits are made by sea animals, we might theorize that these rocks were formed in the sea. From the rate of deposition today, the age of the rocks can be calculated.

But since the formation of the rocks is not demonstrable (although it may be well-documented), we must say that evolution is a theory. We are using evolution to explain the facts we have; in addition it has explained much new information, and is the basis for seeking new information. Pictures of fossils found in various strata on a time line could clarify the concept of evolution and help to discriminate between a theory and a fact.

Chaining

The examples of materials for use in the cognitive areas of chaining, which involves relating ideas to other ideas, are drawn from selections on biology, astronomy, and archaeology. These examples are directed to the middle and upper grades. The relating of ideas to each other is of great value in the study of science—for this is the procedure of building theories and testing of relationships. The first example gives the learner an opportunity to chain the ideas of Pasteur as he formulates the evidence of fermentation being caused by living organisms.

But such findings were greeted with scorn by other scientists. Most of them agreed with the famous German chemist, Baron Justus von Liebig. He said that fermentation was a chemical change that required no living organism.

Pasteur, of course, had heard of other men's work on yeasts, but he had never studied them himself. It's doubtful if he was even thinking about them when he started to explore Bigo's problem.

His first step was to turn his microscope on samples from the vats of good alcohol. He placed a drop of liquid on a slide and began to study it. Somewhat to

his surprise, the drop was full of tiny yellowish globules. And their insides were full of curious dancing
specks. What could these be? Then Pasteur remembered—yeasts, of course. He went on taking drops out
of the good samples, studying them for hours on end.
Sometimes the little globules were alone; sometimes
they occurred in bunches or chains. He saw some with
buds sprouting from their sides. So Cagniard de la
Tour was right. Yeasts *were* alive.

Burning with curiosity, Pasteur turned to the samples from the vats of spoiled liquid. What could have
happened here?

In these samples he found no yeasts at all. Instead,
as he pored over drop after drop, he kept finding a
queer mass of specks that he couldn't make out. Finally, he managed to separate one of these specks and
put it in a drop of clear water so that he could see it.
Then he blinked in astonishment.

The speck was actually a great tangle of rod-shaped
things. Some were alone. Some were linked together
like a string of barges. All were far tinier than the
yeasts. And all were moving with what appeared as
constant vibration.

For days Pasteur could think of nothing but these
strange little rods. He forgot about meals, forgot about
going to bed. Every spare minute was spent at his microscope. He made another discovery. The liquid from
the bad vats contained no alcohol. But it did contain
lactic acid—the same acid that is found in sour milk.

Stranger and stranger, Pasteur thought. Why . . .
with a sudden flash of imagination, Pasteur guessed.
The little rods were alive. *They* made the sour-milk
acid.

(Patricia Lauber, *The Quest of Louis Pasteur*,
p. 18)

The teacher may want to raise questions similar to
these in directing the learner in using this passage:
What organism causes fermentation by producing alcohol? Describe what Pasteur found in the spoiled al-

cohol vats. What substance did the spoiled vats contain?
What sequence of facts led Pasteur to his conclusion?

Pasteur was able to relate what he saw to previous
discoveries. He then went one step further in discovering
rods, coming to a brand new conclusion that lactic
acid, too, is produced by living organisms.

As a further experience in using this selection, children can make wine in class by placing yeast and sugar
in a covered jar of fruit juice, just as wine makers do.
The alcohol produced is easily detected by odor. A
sample exposed to the air will turn sour just as in the
wine factory Pasteur was working with.

Another fine example of a passage involving chaining skills is seen in this passage on Pasteur's work with
vaccine as an immunization process:

> In 1796 Edward Jenner, an English country doctor,
> made an odd discovery. A number of his patients had
> caught cowpox, a mild disease, from the animals they
> handled. They believed that this illness somehow made
> it impossible for them to catch the very dangerous disease of smallpox. Other doctors said this was an old
> wives' tale, but Jenner was sufficiently curious to test
> it. He discovered that it was true. So he began to protect people against smallpox by inoculating them with
> cowpox. Jenner called this process vaccination.

> Vaccination against smallpox proved a great success. But there the matter rested for more than eighty
> years. No one knew whether cowpox and smallpox
> were the same disease or different diseases. There was
> no way of making the vaccine; it had to be drawn
> from a cow or a person suffering from cowpox. And
> no means of vaccinating against other diseases was
> discovered.

> Pasteur often thought about these matters, turning
> over in his mind ways to protect people against other
> disease germs. He had noticed something rather interesting, too. When sheep, for example, got anthrax,

some died but some recovered. The sheep that recovered were immune: they never got anthrax again. To test this observation, Pasteur had even injected such sheep with anthrax germs. They remained perfectly well.

This suggested an intriguing idea to him. Could people or animals be made immune by giving them just a small attack of a disease? Before he could answer that question, Pasteur had to find the answer to another one: how could he cause just a small attack of a disease? He didn't know, but the matter was seldom far from his thoughts.

In 1880 he found part of the answer when a piece of research went wrong. It was luck; but, as Pasteur liked to point out, luck is really the ability to recognize and seize an opportunity.

Pasteur had been working on a disease called chicken cholera, which swept farmyards, killing almost all the hens. The germ was a very tiny microbe that had been discovered by another scientist. He had tried to grow the microbe for study, but had failed. Pasteur succeeded in growing the microbe by using a special broth made from chicken gristle. He grew generation after generation of chicken cholera microbes for experiments.

Here chance intervened. Pasteur went away on his summer vacation. He left the germ cultures in the care of his assistants, Roux and Chamberland. However, they also went away for several weeks, leaving the cultures. On their return, they continued the experiments. They injected a hen with one of the cultures they had left. To their astonishment, nothing happened; the hen remained perfectly well. Several days later, they inoculated the same hen with a new culture. Again the hen remained well, though the same culture killed other hens.

By this time, Chamberland and Roux were both puzzled and worried. What were they going to say to Pasteur when he returned? And what would he say to them? As they well knew, Pasteur would not tolerate carelessness. Still, there was only one thing to do. They told him the truth.

Pasteur listened. Then, to their surprise, he simply said, "Keep quiet!" After a minute of thought, he said, "Well, everything explains itself—this hen has been immunized by being injected with an old culture." It was an accident, but Pasteur had seen meaning in it. He had found the answer to an important question.

(*Ibid.*, pp. 47–48)

A teacher could direct the learner in the chaining process with this passage through such questions as: What is vaccination? What were the steps in Pasteur's thinking about why the hen didn't die of cholera?

Here again Pasteur's work has given us an ideal example of chaining. Jenner established that vaccination with cowpox made a person immune to smallpox. Pasteur carried the idea further to consider making people immune to other diseases by giving them a small attack. He then went on to recognize that infection with an old culture could accomplish the same thing—immunity. As a further activity children might be asked to do some library research to locate methods of immunization for other diseases, such as polio or measles.

In the next selections, drawn from the field of astronomy, learners have a fine opportunity to chain together a sequence of ideas. In the first selection it is possible to follow the chain of ideas from the discovery of Uranus and its peculiar behavior to the hypothesis and subsequent proof that another planet lay beyond Uranus. What makes this selection particularly fascinating and unusual is that two people in different countries came to the same conclusions at the same time—Adams and Leverrier. Pictures of the solar system, an orrery, or student-made models may be used to demonstrate this discovery.

In some respects Galle's discovery of Neptune is more dramatic than what we know about the planet itself. The Neptune story began very soon after the Uranus story ended. One of the first tasks astronomers set themselves was drawing up mathematical tables that would show the exact path Uranus traced as it traveled in its orbit. By relying on such tables today astronomers know just where Uranus, or any other planet, will be at any given time. Uranus, however, turned out to be a planet that refused to be plotted. The tables showed that Uranus was scheduled to appear at a certain point at a certain hour. But sometimes astronomers found the planet ahead of its predicted position. Other times it was behind its predicted position. Why, they wondered? The French astronomer Alexis Bouvard was convinced that there was a planet beyond Uranus. This planet's gravitational attraction, he thought, must be influencing Uranus, making it speed up and slow down.

It wasn't until 1841 that someone tackled the job of solving the Uranus mystery. The someone was John C. Adams, a young college student attending St. John's College, Cambridge. In his notebook Adams wrote: "Formed a design, in the beginning of this week, of investigating as soon as possible after taking my degree, the irregularities in the motion of Uranus, which are not yet accounted for, in order to find whether they may be attributed to the action of an undiscovered planet beyond it and, if possible, thence to determine approximately the elements of its orbit, which would probably lead to its discovery."

Two years after graduation, Adams worked out an amazingly accurate mathematical scheme showing that there must be a planet beyond Uranus. He realized that the proof of his idea would have to come from an experienced observer, so he wrote a letter to Sir George Biddel Airy, the British Astronomer Royal, and asked him to look for the new "planet." For some reason, possibly because young Adams was unknown, Airy did nothing for seven long months.

Then in the summer of 1846 he asked James Challis, another British astronomer, if he would look for the planet. A month later Challis saw it in his telescope, but unhappily he did not recognize it as a planet.

As so often happens in science, other men were attempting to solve the same problem, unaware of Adams and Challis. In France, Urbain Leverrier had worked out the new planet's orbit just as Adams had. And the same month that Adams wrote Airy, Leverrier wrote the French Academy asking that its members search the skies for the new planet. He also wrote Johann G. Galle at the Berlin Observatory. Galle received Leverrier's letter September 23, 1846. That very night Galle pointed his telescope where Leverrier had instructed. And there it was, in clear view! The new planet! It was named Neptune.

This discovery shows the importance of mathematics in astronomy. Whenever the faster Uranus began overtaking Neptune, as the two planets circled the Sun, Neptune's gravitational attraction pulled Uranus along faster. This is the reason that Uranus was sometimes ahead of its position predicted by the star charts. After Uranus passed Neptune, Neptune tended to hold Uranus back and so slowed it down. For this reason Uranus lagged behind its position shown by the star tables.

(Roy A. Gallant, *Exploring the Planets*,
pp. 108, 110)

Once the learner has chained the sequence of ideas in the above example with assistance from teacher-aided questions such as "What was the difficulty in plotting the orbit of Uranus? How did Galle happen to discover Neptune?" the next illustration will be a good test of the learner's ability to use chaining in a similar context.

Pluto's story began forty-nine years after Galle observed Neptune. At first Neptune seemed to account nicely for the speeding up and slowing down of Uranus as it circled the Sun. But still, Uranus' actual position did not always fit exactly its position predicted by the star tables. Could there be still *another* planet lying far out in the dim reaches of the solar system, astronomers wondered? And could this planet also be disturbing Uranus' motion?

Lowell, the American astronomer, decided that there must be a ninth planet. Like Adams and Leverrier, he approached the problem with mathematics. By 1905 he had worked out some figures which accounted for "Planet X", as he called it. But he did not publish his findings until 1915.

Lowell said that Planet X lies about four billion miles out from the Sun, that it moves in a long elliptical orbit and that it takes about 282 years to make one trip around the Sun. He also said that the planet must be a small one because its influence on Uranus' motion is slight. For several years Lowell searched the skies for his Planet X, but he never found it. And his untimely death, in 1916, forever ruined his chances of seeing his planet. But other men carried on Lowell's work at other observatories and at the Flagstaff Observatory, which was named after Lowell. W. H. Pickering also worked out a mathematical Planet X, but Pickering based his figures on the planet's effect on Neptune, not Uranus.

In 1919, Milton Humanson of the Mount Wilson Observatory took up the search for Pluto with a telescope camera. He knew that if he took two or more pictures of the sky, three or so nights apart, he might be able to spot the planet. His first picture would show him a certain number of stars in "fixed" positions. His second and third pictures would again show the same stars in the same positions. But if a planet were moving among them, the planet would reveal itself by showing up in different positions on each photograph. Unhappily Humanson ran into some bad luck with his photographs and abandoned the search. But in 1930 Clyde W. Tombaugh, an astronomer at the Lowell Observatory, found Planet X. His photographs showed clearly that a point of light was moving among the stars. There could be no mistake. So fourteen years after Lowell's death his mystery Planet X was officially made a member of the solar system. It was given the name Pluto, the Greek god of the underworld.

(*Ibid.*, pp. 114–16)

Using material from archaeology, the following two selections demonstrate how materials can be used in having learners chain ideas.

In 1831, Darwin sailed as naturalist on board a British surveying ship, H.M.S. *Beagle*, on a voyage round the world. When he was in South America, he found fossils of many animals which were like, but not the same as, the animals living in that continent now. For instance, he found fossils of an armored animal called *Glyptodon* . . . , that was like an armadillo. It occurred to Darwin that perhaps they were alike because they were actually related. Perhaps each type of animal was not fixed, but could change slowly into a new type.

This idea was not new. What was new was Darwin's ideas of how this change, or evolution, took place. He started from two facts: 1. that each species (the scientific name of an animal type) produces many more young than can possibly survive—think of the amount of frog spawn you can find in a small pond; and 2. that no two members of a species are exactly alike. And if animals vary, some must be better fitted to living their way of life than others. Darwin realized that these better-fitted animals had a better chance of breeding; and that their offspring would be likely to inherit the characteristics that gave their parents the advantages over the others. In this way a species gradually changes and improves. We call the process by which it does so, in its natural surroundings, natural selection.

Darwin's book, *The Origin Of Species,* made people much more interested in fossils because it showed that fossils are the remains of the ancestors of the animals alive today. We can find series of fossils showing the changes that have made the animals we know. One of the best known series is that of the horse.

(William E. Swinton, *The Wonderful World of Pre-historic Animals,* p. 19)

This selection relates how Darwin took two observable, demonstrable facts, added further observations from South America, and came to a new conclusion —natural selection, the foundation of the theory of evolution. Pictures of the *Beagle* and of the animals on the Galápagos Islands would enhance this selection. In reading the selection teachers may wish to guide learners' reading with these questions: From what two facts did Darwin devise his theory of evolution? What is natural selection?

The following passage gives the learner an example of how *interpolation* works in chaining together the sequence of evolution of modern birds and their link with mammals and reptiles. The student could be given the most primitive of the species and the most highly developed and asked to reconstruct some of the characteristics of types which were evolved between the earliest and latest forms.

The study of rock-layers led to the study of the fossils found in them. Although most plant and animal bodies eventually decay, the remains of some have been luckily preserved as fossils. Fossils may be partial or entire skeletons, a footprint, the outline of a body, or even of body tissues. Or, sometimes, a whole animal or plant may be preserved intact, as in amber. The study of the fossil record of life in the past is called Palaeontology and has given us a picture of the plants and animals that existed in the earth's long history. The picture shows that during geological time life gradually changed, or evolved, becoming more varied and more highly organized. In this book we shall study the evolution of life. If evolution is true, fossil history will reveal a branching plan for the advance of life, with each branch showing a gradual improvement for its particular mode of existence.

In some comparatively recent groups such as the horse the fossil record is nearly complete. In older rocks, the record is naturally not so complete. But it is enough to indicate a branching advance like the one illustrated, with reptiles branching off from amphibians; and then the reptile line itself branching into many lines, including reptiles and birds.

Modern birds still lay large-yolked shelled eggs like reptiles, but they are warm-blooded, they have feathers instead of scales (except on their legs) and jaws without teeth, but covered with a horny beak. Their fore-limbs have been turned into wings, the tail has become shortened to serve as a steering organ in flight, and the part of the brain controlling balance, the cerebellum, is very big.

Two lucky finds have shown us an intermediate stage in the evolution of birds from reptiles, which has been christened *Archaeopteryx*. The Solenhofen slate in Germany is used for making lithographs. It is a fine-grained solidified clay, originally laid down in shallow fresh water in Jurassic times. About 150 million years ago, two *Archaeopteryx*, about the size of a large crow, fell into the mud and their bones and feathers were beautifully preserved in the clay. In 1861, one was discovered by workmen quarrying the slate; another was found in 1872. These toothed half-reptilian birds must be very close to the ancestor of all modern birds. Archaeopteryx is a fossil link between two great groups of animals. But sometimes we find such links in so-called "living fossils", which have managed to survive with little change for many millions of years. One such is the Duck-billed Platypus *Ornithorhynchus* from the Australian region. It is definitely a mammal because it has hair and is warm-blooded and suckles its young with milk. But it lays eggs like a reptile and its skeleton shows many reptilian features. It is a survivor of a type half-way between a reptile and a modern mammal which has managed to survive in the Australian region for 70 million years or more, because it was isolated from competition with the more efficient higher mammals.

Perhaps the simplest proof that evolution has occurred is the fact that animals leading very different kinds of lives are constructed on the same general plan. For instance, air-breathing vertebrates typically have two pairs of limbs, and the skeleton of the forelimb consists of one bone in the upper arm, two in the lower arm, several small bones in the wrist, and a set of digits and fingers. The skeleton of your arm and hand is very like that of a lizard. In bats, the long fore-limb is a wing, and its leathery membrane is supported by the enormously elongated second to fifth digits, while the first digit or thumb is free and has a claw for holding on with. In birds' wings the same general plan is there, but the bones of the wrist and hand have been reduced in number, shortened, and fixed together to provide a strong base for the feathers. In whales the fore-limb is a short finlike flipper, used as a stabilizer; but inside it the skeleton shows the same plan of five finger-bones, and though the upper arm is extremely short and embedded in the body, it still has the typical single bone.

Why should organs which look so different and have such different purposes as handling, crawling, flying, and swimming all be constructed on the same general plan? The only answer is that they have all evolved from one original stock. The ancestral plan has been kept, but has been altered in detail to fit the animals for their particular way of life.

Fish, amphibians, reptiles, birds and mammals are all built on the same general plan, the vertebrate or backboned plan. They are all related by common descent from one original ancestor. Insects, centipedes, spiders, scorpions and crustaceans are also all built on a common plan, the arthropod or jointed-limb plan, but this is quite different from the vertebrate plan.

This is because they are all descended from a different ancestor. You yourself when you were a young embryo were very like the embryos of lizards, rabbits, chickens, dogfish, and other vertebrates. The only reasonable explanation is that we vertebrates are all related by common descent.

At a certain stage in your development, you had a small but definite tail, just like the embryo of a rabbit or a dog. This can only mean that man once passed through a tailed stage in his evolution.

Even more extraordinary is the fact that we and all other land vertebrates show a fish-like plan of construction in early embryonic life, with a fish-like heart, gill-slits, and pattern of blood-vessels. This only makes sense if we, as well as all other mammals, birds and reptiles, have gradually evolved from some kind of fish.

Vestigial organs provide more evidence. Vestigial organs are mere rudiments, and are of no use to their possessors. The most obvious example comes from whales. Externally, whales show no trace of hind-limbs; but inside the body are the vestiges of a hind-limb skeleton—for instance, the vestige of a hip-girdle with the vestige of a thighbone attached to it. If we believe that whales were specially created, these vestiges are nonsensical. But if whales have evolved from land mammals, their presence is natural and full of meaning. The tiny hairs on our bodies are vestiges of the time when our ancestors were as hairy as apes.

Embryology gives us the most striking proof of evolution. Many animals which are extremely different as adults are hard to tell apart as embryos. The next proofs we shall present come from what man has done to organisms. Long before recorded history, probably around 7000 B.C., man began domesticating animals and plants, like dogs and junglefowl and cabbages and wheat, and breeding them for his own purposes. In the process they have been changed enormously. Take the horse, for example. In human hands, the original single species of wild horse has produced breeds of many sorts and sizes, from the huge powerful cart-horse to the Shetland pony and the racehorse. Man, in fact, has caused artificial evolution by selective breeding. He has selected the variations found in plants and animals which seemed most suitable (for the purpose he had in mind) and bred from these, and so produced types quite different from anything found in nature.

Dogs supply perhaps the most striking evidence for artificial evolution. Think of St. Bernards, Toy Terriers, Bulldogs, Chows, Pointers, Pekinese, and Greyhounds, all quite different from anything found in wild wolves or jackals, and many of them quite incapable of surviving in nature.

Man has also selected for what gives him pleasure. Garden flowers like tulips and roses are all products of artificial evolution, very different from their wild ancestors. And this artificial evolution is still going on. The roses of Elizabethan times were very inferior to those of today; and now modern methods of selective breeding are giving us new varieties of all sorts of plants every year.

The facts about domesticated animals and plants show that they have changed during their history. But how do the changes originate? Sometimes we know the precise origin of a domestic variety. The Ancon breed of sheep had very short legs. This condition arose suddenly in one ram on a Massachusetts farm in 1791. The local farmers selected this character because the sheep could not jump over the local stone fences, and so a distinctive breed was established.

A sudden change like this in the inherited characters of an animal or plant we call a *mutation*. Today we can produce mutations artificially by X-rays and various chemical treatments.

Most mutations have only small effects, but they do change the character of the organism, often unfavourably, but sometimes favourably.

So mutations provide the raw material of change,

and selection can then pick out and combine the most suitable ones.

(Julian Huxley, *The Wonderful World of Life*, pp. 9–15)

The story of evolution required much painstaking work in extrapolating and filling in the gaps with facts, sequencing the species and relating them to a common origin. Learners should see in this selection that evolution is a progression that moves forward through successful evolvement. The learner should see that one can extrapolate from what is known of Darwin's natural selection theory to hypothesize that many variations of a species must have been produced. However, only those well adapted to the changing environment survived, had offspring, and passed on their variations.

Judging

In trade books there is an abundance of examples of science content which can be used to promote the growth of the cognitive ability of judging. The five examples given, from diverse areas of science, are well within the conceptual levels of most middle and upper grade children. In the first example, taken from a trade book on Stonehenge, the ancient architectural mystery on Salisbury Plain in England, judging in the form of making choices among probabilities is demonstrated.

But I would like to put forward this opinion.
The Stonehenge sun-moon alignments were created and elaborated for two, possibly three, reasons: they made a calendar, particularly useful to tell the time for planting crops; they helped to create and maintain priestly power, by enabling the priest to call out the multitude to see the spectacular risings and settings of the sun and moon, most especially the midsummer sunrise over the heel stone and midwinter sunset through

the great trilithon, and possibly they served as an intellectual game.

To amplify a little on those three supposed reasons, let me state that it is well known that methods for determining the times of planting were of most vital concern to primitive men. Those times are hard to detect. One can't count backwards from the fine warm days, one must use some other means. And what better means could there be for following the seasons than observation of those most regular and predictable recurring objects, the heavenly bodies? Even in classic times there were still elaborate sets of instructions to help farmers to time their planting by celestial phenomena. Discussing the "deepe question" of the "fit time and season of sowing corne," Pliny declared, "this would bee handled and considered upon with exceeding great care and regard; as depending for the most part of Astronomie. . . ." Doubtless there are today many farmers who time their planting by the sky.

As for the value of Stonehenge as a priestly power-enhancer, it seems quite possible that the man who could call the people to see the god of day or night appear or disappear between those mighty arches and over that distant horizon would attract to himself some of the aura of deity. Indeed, the whole people who possessed such a monument and temple must have felt lifted up.

The other possible reason for the astronomical ingenuity and contrivance of Stonehenge is, I must admit, my own invention. I think that those Stonehengers were true ancestors of ours. I think that the men who designed its various parts, and perhaps even some of the men who helped build those parts, enjoyed the mental exercise above and beyond the call of duty. I think that when they had solved the problem of the alignments efficiently but unspectacularly, as they had in Stonehenge I, they couldn't let the matter rest. They had to set themselves more challenges, and try for more difficult, rewarding, and spectacular solutions, partly for the greater glory of God, but partly for the joy of man, the thinking animal. I wonder if some day authority will establish a connection between the spirit which animated the Stonehenge builders and that which inspired the creators of the Parthenon, and the Gothic cathedrals, and the first space craft to go to Mars.

In any case, for whatever reasons those Stonehenge builders built as they did, their final, completed creation was a marvel. As intricately aligned as an interlocking series of astronomical observing instruments (which indeed it was) and yet architecturally perfectly simple, in function subtle and elaborate, in appearance stark, imposing, awesome, Stonehenge was a thing of surpassing ingenuity of design, variety of usefulness and grandeur—in concept and construction an eighth wonder of the ancient world.

The seven classic wonders of the world were the pyramids, as a group, (or the Great Pyramid), the Hanging Gardens of Babylon, the statue of Zeus at Olympia, the temple of Diana at Ephesus, the mausoleum at Halicarnassus, the Colossus of Rhodes, and the Pharos lighthouse, at Alexandria. With the exception of the more perishable parts of the Babylonian gardens and the colossus—supposedly a 280-foot figure of brass—all of those wonders would seem to have been of stone. Yet surely in none of them was stone itself so skillfully used to record the fruits of intellectual endeavor in an emotion-inspiring temple as in the great monument on Salisbury Plain.

> (Gerald S. Hawkins, *Stonehenge Decoded*,
> pp. 117–18)

The teacher may want to assist the learner in exploring the choices of the author by a question similar to the following: What reasons does Mr. Hawkins give for the existence of Stonehenge?

Hawkins hypothesized that Stonehenge was an astronomical structure. He fed the relevant data into a computer which confirmed his hypothesis. In this selection, he tells why he made the decision to investigate Stonehenge. This is an example of judgment in making choices. The learner should discover that Hawkins chose to investigate this phenomenon because he found this problem a challenge.

In a passage from *Exploring Chemistry* a problem is suggested concerning the use and disappearance of seafood. A teacher could have the learner analyze the problem through a question of this nature: What is happening to the world's fish and seafood supply? Once the problem has been analyzed—the scarcity of some of sea life used for food—the learner can be led to check on the accuracy of the assertion through other sources. In this case more current periodicals and newspapers could be used.

> The world's fish and supply of other sea foods, if not carefully controlled, can be exhausted easily. Already along the Maine coast lobsters are no longer as plentiful as they were a short ten years ago. Clams are even scarcer. As the demand for these sea foods has increased, many fishermen sell or eat many of the young undersized lobsters and clams instead of returning them to the sea as the law requires. While this may not be the major cause of the Maine lobster and clam shortage, it certainly is a contributing cause. But Bonner and other scientists are looking to different sea creatures—algae to come to man's rescue. Algae are microscopic organisms you often see as a green scum floating on the surface of a lake or pond. Since these creatures are an extremely rich protein source, Bonner's idea is to breed a domesticated animal that would live on algae and convert them to meat.

(Roy A. Gallant, *Exploring Chemistry*, p. 114)

The accompanying paragraphs on new alternatives to accepted foods offer further opportunities to using judgment skills in erecting criteria, and deciding among alternatives.

Another food expert, Britain's Ralph Whitlock, is also looking to protein-rich plants to help solve the world's food problem. His plan calls for such oddities as sunflower cookies, nettle soup, pea-vine ice cream, rye-grass juice, and clover canapés. To develop such foods, he says, will require man's most imaginative inventive efforts. To date there is no machine that can cheaply do a large scale job of grinding protein-rich plant leaves into edible foods the way livestock can. Such a machine would first have to squeeze protein juices out of leaves, then somehow convert them to a powder that could be kept on the kitchen shelf.

According to Whitlock, the tropics is one area of the world where millions of people are protein starved, yet in their regions of lush vegetation they are surrounded by protein. If they had "protessors," protein processing machines now being made in England, they could grind banana tree leaves, sugar cane, and weeds into protein-rich food. The day such machines are perfected and can operate on a large scale wasteful protein gobbling cattle and hogs may become curios which future generations will see only in zoos.

On hearing such "farfetched" ideas many people shake their heads and say that they'll *never* drink rye-grass juice, eat pea-vine ice cream, or other such concoctions. "Imagine the awful taste," they moan. Well, taste isn't quite what it seems to be. With a little effort we can change our tastes for food as we can change our tastes for music and paintings and end up liking a new type food as well as one we have known for years. Hundreds of soldiers returned from Japan after the war eating raw fish and seaweed and liking them. But taste in new kinds of food need not be the obstacle it appears to be. Today chemists can duplicate nearly any flavor we know. So once they begin grinding up plant roots and leaves into a mashed potato consistency they will also be able to give the roots a potato or even a squash flavor. The chemist today is a modern miracle worker.

Although some of these ideas may sound foreign to

us now they may well be our only way of solving the food problem which becomes greater every day. According to Bonner, we have reached such a point in our unbalanced technology today that we are finding it easier to produce a television set than it is to produce a pork chop. But he says that there is really no important limit on what we can attain in the way of food resources if we look beyond our present systems for answers. New systems, however, will require such energies and equipment as we have never before mustered—or even dreamed of.

(*Ibid.*, pp. 114–15)

For example, how will they decide whether to try new foods? What are the alternatives to rejecting new foods? On what basis will they make their decisions? What standards will they use? These and comparable questions will lead learners in using judging skills.

A somewhat different aspect of judging can be explored through the use of selections on the introduction of a revolutionary new idea.

In 1661, Boyle published a book, *The Sceptical Chemist*, which shook the already shaky foundations of 17th century chemistry. In it he exploded the earth, air, fire, and water "elements" which had held sway since Aristotle's time—nearly two thousand years earlier. Boyle said that only four so-called elements could not even begin to account for all the chemical changes we observe in nature. And he set out to offer a new explanation of *elements*. He did this by melting first gold and then silver. Then he mixed them with other metals to make alloys. He examined them again. Gold and silver always remain gold and silver, he said. When mixed with other metals, or burned, they do not produce earth, air, or water. They always remain the same. My gold and silver are true elements, he said. By "elements," he explained, he meant "certain primitive and simple bodies which, not being made of any other bodies or of one another, are the ingredients of

which all those called perfectly mixed bodies are immediately compounded, and into which they are ultimately resolved."

(*Ibid.*, p. 56)

Emphasis in the discussion of this selection should be
placed on the enormity of a decision to publish a book
exploding an idea that had been accepted for two thousand years. On the whole we tend to like best those
ideas which we now hold and feel comfortable with.
The impact of this attitude on judging the worth of
ideas has historically shaped the acceptance of scientific
findings. Understanding the emotional elements that
color our judgment in these cases is a salient objective
in the education of all learners for a rapidly changing
world.

Another passage which carries out the same idea and
presents an excellent illustration of some of the problems in judging such questions as the nature of our
criteria for truth, comes from a book on astronomy.

Aristotle's astronomy is little more than a summary
of the major ideas of philosophers who lived before
him. Like Pythagoras, he believed that the Sun, planets, and stars were round, not flat. But he taught his
students that the Earth did not revolve about the Sun.
We will see later on how much faith men put in Aristotle's ideas.

In a way it's strange that only ten years after Aristotle's death Aristarchus (310 to 230 B.C.) challenged
one of his major ideas about the solar system. Aristarchus insisted that Aristotle was wrong in saying that
the Earth did not revolve about the Sun. The Sun,
Aristarchus believed, was motionless and the Earth
and other planets revolved about it. He even attempted
to measure the Sun's distance but missed it by a wide
mark.

For the next four hundred and fifty years there were
few important new ideas about the Sun and stars. Not

until about 140 A.D., when Ptolemy, an Alexandrian astronomer and mathematician, appeared on the scene do we find excitement brewing. Ptolemy was important for two reasons. First, like Aristotle, he reviewed nearly all work in astronomy done before his time. Then he summarized it in a large book entitled the *Almagest* (which means *greatest*). Second, Ptolemy's word on affairs of astronomy became the final word. The Church and scholars alike frowned on anyone who challenged Ptolemy's map of the solar system in which the Sun played only a minor role.

The Earth, said Ptolemy, is the largest of all heavenly bodies. It is fixed in space. By this he meant that it did not rotate. If the Earth rotated, Ptolemy reasoned, birds would have their perches whipped out from under them. His map of the solar system showed the Moon circling Earth. Next came Mercury also circling Earth, then Venus, the Sun, Mars, Jupiter, and Saturn. In Ptolemy's plan the Sun was little more than a rather bright "planet" circling the Earth as the fourth most distant object in the heavens.

Nearly fifteen hundred years passed before anyone challenged Ptolemy's solar system. The man to do the challenging was Nicholas Copernicus, a Polish scientist and officer of the Church. When Copernicus, who lived from 1473 to 1543, announced that Ptolemy, together with Aristotle and other great men of the past, were wrong, he set the academic world in a tizzy. How could the great men of the past be wrong? university professors asked. And who is this man Copernicus with his high and mighty theory? Such was the reaction to Copernicus' book *On the Revolutions of the Heavenly Spheres*. In it he contradicted Ptolemy by saying that the earth rotates and so accounts for day and night. And that the Sun, not the Earth, is the center of our solar system. As innocent as this last idea sounds, it became the most explosive bomb in the history of astronomy.

Realizing the trouble such an idea would cause, one of Copernicus' friends wrote at the beginning of his book: "This is written to present NOT a scientific fact, but a playful fancy". But there was little need to protect Copernicus. A few days after his great work was published he died. But a Sun-centered solar system was about to be born.

Among the enlightened people to see the value of Copernicus' theory was a scientist named Galileo Galilei, who lived from 1564 to 1642. Although Galileo believed in Corpernicus' Sun-centered solar system, he had no evidence to show that Copernicus was correct —that is, not until the telescope was invented. When Galileo heard of Hans Lippershey's work with lenses he became interested. And by about 1610 he had built a telescope which revealed to him wonders never before seen or imagined by man. Here, Galileo realized, was evidence to show that Copernicus was right, that all planets circle the Sun, not the Earth.

Galileo's telescope showed him clearly that Venus was circling the Sun. And, like the Moon, it went through phases. Also, he discovered that the planet Jupiter had four moons circling it. Here, before his very eyes, was a miniature model of the solar system. Jupiter represented the Sun, and its moons represented the planets. If the stuffy scholars who criticized Copernicus would look through the telescope they would see that Ptolemy was wrong. But when Galileo announced what he saw, many scholars laughed at him and even refused to look through his telescope. Some of them did look but said that they saw nothing important. Still others said that Galileo had bewitched his telescope.

Church authorities had told him "that he must neither hold, defend, nor teach (his) opinion in any way whatsoever." Galileo was a condemned man for holding to the truth. While some leading Church figures and a few scholars supported Galileo's views, he was nevertheless arrested and tried for his "crime." In court he was forced to deny that the Earth circled the Sun and he was made to promise that he would never again teach the doctrine since it contradicted the Scriptures, Ptolemy, and Aristotle. If philosophers can turn over in their graves, Aristotle certainly must have during Galileo's trial. The last eight years of Galileo's life (he was seventy at the time of the trial) were spent under "house arrest." In his declining years he was nearly blind, supposedly from not protecting his eyes during the years he studied the Sun through his telescope.

(Roy A. Gallant, *Exploring the Sun*, pp. 21–24)

Extended discussion of ways people have judged scientific findings, how we arrive at a suitable criterion for acceptance of a scientific finding, is a high-level functional scholarship skill that has broad application in every area of human experience. The learner may be led to analyze the two different methods used in this passage, and discuss the reasons which led to the eventual acceptance of one. Learners can be guided in the search for other historical examples similar to these and may obtain information and practice in using the tools and procedures used in scientific method.

The following example illustrates how students can, after reading a passage and questioning a basic proposition, be led to replicate the experiment to see if they obtain the same results, and consequently establish the truthfulness of the proposition.

Torricelli discovered that the 34½ foot column of water was simply the most that could be supported by the atmosphere; and that the pressure exercised by the column of water was exactly the same as that of the atmosphere. He realised, too, that the pressure of the atmosphere changed a little with different weather conditions. In 1643 he devised his famous barometer, substituting for water a column of mercury about 30 inches high which, he found, was also supported by the normal pressure of the atmosphere. In 1648, the French scientist, Blaise Pascal, got his brother-in-law to measure the pressure with a Torricellian barometer at the top and bottom of a mountain, thus giving the first proof of the differences in air pressure at different heights.

In Germany, in 1654, the Mayor of the town of Magdeburg, Otto von Guericke, gave a most convincing demonstration of the pressure of the atmosphere. He made two large, strong, hollow, metal hemispheres, which fitted together with an airtight joint and washer; and from these spheres he extracted as much air as possible with the efficient air-pump he had invented. He then attached teams of horses to each hemisphere and found that no less than eight pairs were needed to pull the spheres apart, which they did with a considerable explosion, as air rushed in to replace the vacuum. Not long after von Guericke's experiment, in 1662, Robert Boyle discovered the law named after him, namely, that the volume of a gas is inversely proportional to the pressure. He thought of air as tiny particles in restless motion, which is not far from the truth as we now understand it.

(James Fisher, *The Wonderful World of the Air*, p. 37)

Both of these experiments are easily done in class. The first requires only a thirty-six-inch tube open at one end, and a bowl of mercury. The second can be done with two plungers. In these experiments the focus should be on the judging of a proposition, not the spectacular reaction of the experimental materials. The building of acceptable open criteria is essential in the scientific method. The above and similar passages in other trade books provide opportunities to work with the skills needed in this crucial area.

Judgment is the highest type of cognition and requires mastery of the previous four categories. In order to render a judgment one must understand the concept involved, be able to utilize it, and discriminate and chain ideas into some kind of conceptual scheme or pattern. Only then can one establish standards, consider alternatives, and make decisions.

Judgment is an area of cognitive abilities that all citizens in a democracy must exercise—yet it is the one most neglected in our schools. The ability to make objective, carefully thought-out decisions does not come automatically with the twenty-first birthday. It comes only with a great deal of practice from primary grades on.

Gladys S. Kleinman

CHAPTER V

DEVELOPING COGNITIVE ABILITIES WITH MATHEMATICS TRADE BOOKS

With the current curricular interest in improved cognitive functioning, the mathematics curriculum has assumed an important role. Not only is an understanding of mathematics essential for everyday living, but it also is becoming an essential key to advanced scholarship in the sciences and social sciences. To aid the learner in developing a competency that is based on understanding rather than simple manipulative skill has become a major goal of all mathematics curricula.

Crucial to developing proficiency in mathematics is practice in using the tools of mathematics and the ability to apply them in different situations. Trade books offer many excellent opportunities to develop proficiency in many skills. Using the framework of broad areas of cognitive abilities, the teacher can direct the learners to use trade book materials in a manner that supplements the mathematical understandings that constitute the functional scholarship skills of the discipline.

Before launching into the illustrative materials, a word of warning on a current misconception on the teaching of mathematics is in order. Since mathematics is a formal logical system, there is great danger that teachers who attempt to teach contemporary mathematics in the elementary school will become overly formal in their approach. A strictly formal approach should be avoided. This does not mean that children should not be taught to develop deductive techniques in deriving conclusions. Children should be led to discover relationships and patterns, and to formulate generalizations, but they may express these generalizations in language that is suitable to them rather than in the language of strict mathematical precision.

It takes time and maturity to refine mathematical ideas into the mathematician's sophisticated terms. The discovery of mathematical ideas should be an enjoyable experience to children. The attachment of numbers to represent sets of objects, the relationship of these numbers, the ease with which numbers can be compared and manipulated in contrast to their original objects—all these processes are within the young learners' grasp of experience. They can be made more usable and achieve greater flexibility as the teacher heightens the learners' awareness through practice with a variety of materials.

EARLY GRADES

The introduction to the concept and uses of number can be begun at a very early age. Growing awareness of the importance of mathematics in our society and the close scrutiny that all mathematics programs are now undergoing have resulted in an increased concern about the arithmetic programs in kindergarten and Grades 1 and 2. Since there is little in the way of actual arithmetical materials for kindergarten and primary grades, the classroom teacher must seek activities where numbers are used. Correct mathematical concepts can be learned in early grades through the use of well-chosen trade books which use numbers in various ways as they are needed in the natural context of the story.

The number program for kindergarten should provide the young learner with many opportunities to count, to draw marks to show "how many," to learn to distinguish size (greater than, less than), shapes, and measures (day, week, month, year, cups, etc.). Children should be afforded number experiences as an integral part of the regular kindergarten program, but such instruction consists of direct and specific attempts by the teacher to help pupils get an idea of the numbers involved in day-by-day activities. While specific kindergarten number experiences will vary from program to program—depending upon the projects under way and the literature used—there will be, for the most part, a general core of number experiences from the areas of arithmetic presented in the list below. Using these areas of arithmetic, examples are given of trade book materials and how they can be related to the areas of cognitive abilities.

Counting Used to Identify Which One

Teachers of the early grades frequently read aloud fables which offer abundant opportunities to explore number concepts within a cognitive framework. In the well-loved and familiar story of *Chicken-Little,* the very fundamental concept of ordinal (counting used to identify which one) can be used. Ordinal writing, attaching numbers to objects to ensure a logical pattern and aid in memory and manipulation, is a basic chaining concept involving sequencing. Using the above illustration, the teacher would ask, "Which animal did Chicken-Little meet first?" "Which one did she meet next?" In the second question the learner would be brought to see that the next animal becomes the *second* animal. "Which one did she meet next?" becomes the third animal and on through the sequence. The learner can be brought to grasp the relationship of these animals to Chicken-Little as the story can be chained together through their positioning by ordinal numbers.

In the story of *The Little Red Hen,* it is readily apparent that the same areas of chaining abilities can be pursued:

There once were five friends who lived together in a small hen house. A PIG who slept in a puddle outside in the front yard. A CAT, who slept where there was room to curl. A DUCK who just wanted to swim in his own little pond. A DOG, who was always roaming away from home, anyway. And the little RED HEN.

The red hen did all the work inside and outside the little hen house. Outside she scratched for food. One day she found some grains of wheat and decided to plant them. So that her four friends would hear she cackled loudly, "Who will help me plant this wheat?"

"Not I," said the pig, who was lying in a mud puddle.

"Not I," meowed the cat, who had one eye open and one eye shut.

"Not I," quacked the duck as he ducked into the pond.

"Not I," said the dog. "I'm busy chasing a cat."

"Then I will plant the wheat," clucked the little red hen, "for there's no time to lose!" And she did!

Soon the wheat was grown and ready to harvest. "Who will help me harvest the wheat?" asked the little red hen.

"Not I," yawned the cat, "I'm too sleepy."

"Not I," grunted the pig. "I'm late for my morning snooze."

"Not I," yapped the dog. "I'm busy chasing rabbits."

"Not I," said the duck as he waddled toward the wading pond.

"Very well, then, I will," said the little red hen. And she *did!*

After the wheat was harvested, the little red hen asked, "Who will take this wheat to the miller?"

"Not I," said the pig. "I'm too sleepy."

"Not I," barked the dog. "I'm leaving to chase a squirrel."

"Not I," meowed the cat. "I need another cat nap."

"Not I," quacked the duck. "My feathers are not dry."

Soon the little red hen returned with the flour and made a batch of cookies. "Who will eat my cookies?" she clucked.

"I will!" purred the cat, who was wide awake.

"I will!" said the dog, who suddenly had no place to go.

"I will!" said the pig, who was all ready with a napkin.

"I will!" said the duck. "I'll soon be dry."

"Well," said the little red hen, "I found the grains of wheat. I planted them. I harvested the grain and carried the flour. Then I baked the cookies. Here's what I shall do with them. I shall eat them all myself!" *And she did!*

(*The Little Red Hen,* retold and illustrated by Tony Palazzo, unpaged)

Once the learners begin to see the pattern of chaining in the sequencing of ordinal numbers, the story of *The Little Red Hen* can be used to promote the utilization of the concept. In this example the learners would be attaching ordinal numbers to the animals in the order that the little red hen encountered them: first came the pig (one), then the cat (two), the duck followed (three), and finally the dog (four).

A further area of cognitive abilities which can be developed with trade books containing mathematical content is the area of understanding abilities where numbers can be used as names of objects to identify or describe. Again, this is a fundamental concept in arithmetic which is crucial to understanding the formal system of mathematics.

Use of Number Names to Identify or to Describe

Using the trade book *The Three Little Kittens*, the teacher can assist young learners in comprehending the author's use of the number three as well as attaching the ordinal numbers 1, 2, 3 to the kittens.

> Three little kittens
>   lost their mittens
> and they began to cry.
> Oh Mother dear, we sadly fear
> that we have lost our mittens!
> Lost your mittens!
> You naughty kittens—
>   then you shall have no pie!
> Meow, meow, meow, meow—
>   then you shall have no pie!
>
> The three little kittens
>   found their mittens—
> and they began to sing.
> Oh Mother dear,
>   see here
>   see here—
>   we have found our mittens—
> What, found your mittens—
> you good little kittens!
> Then you shall have some pie!
> Purr, purr, purr, purr—
>   then you shall have some pie!
>
> The three little kittens
> put on their mittens
> and soon ate up the pie:
> Oh Mother dear, we greatly fear
> that we have soiled our mittens.
> Soiled your mittens—
> you naughty kittens!

Then they began to sigh.
Sigh, sigh, sigh, sigh—
then they began to sigh.

The three little kittens
washed their mittens
and hung them up to dry;
Oh Mother dear,
look here, look here.
See, we have washed our mittens!
Washed your mittens!
You clever kittens—
but I smell a rat close by.
Hush, hush—
meow, meow—
We smell a rat close by!

(*The Three Little Kittens,* retold and
illustrated by Tony Palazzo, unpaged)

Using the illustrations that accompany the text, the
learner can explore the fact that giving the kittens
numbers facilitates talking about them and their plight.
The basic understanding ability—that objects can be
identified by numbers and that such a process facilitates
handling our experience as well as objects is easily
demonstrated in street addresses, with coat racks, and
so forth, all within the young learners' experience.

Counting to Find How Many

This kind of counting is used in all situations where
the amount must be expressed with numbers, and is
crucial in the ability to discriminate quantities. Using
the content from fables such as *The Three Little
Kittens,* and *The Little Red Hen,* the learner can be led
to practice discriminating abilities through such questions as "How many animals are there in the story?
Are there more animals in the story of *The Three Little*

Kittens than in the story of *The Little Red Hen?* How can we find out?" In these examples very rudimentary addition and subtraction is involved as the learners discriminate between the numbers involved.

Rudimentary arithmetic skills are also involved in seeking the solution to the question, "How many mittens are there in the story of *The Three Little Kittens?*" Since kittens only seem to wear mittens on their front paws there are three sets of two mittens each and learners discover that $3 \times 2 = 6$. In the latter process the learners can be led to discover that numbers may be chained together in different sequences—for example, by 2's—without teaching them the formal system of mutiplication.

Rote Counting

Being able to chain arithmetical processes in rapid fashion is one facet of command of basic processes. Ordinarily the act of counting is not engaged in for its own end, but rather to give a person information for another purpose. Therefore, as a process, the learner needs much practice in chaining of numbers, knowing ordinal number sequence. And it is clear that rote practice, if it is not to become deadly and defeating, must involve the same skill in a number of contexts of interest to the learner. Trade books offer a myriad of opportunities to the teacher of the early grades through rhymes and jingles as well as stories.

> 1 2 3 4
> Mary at the cottage door.
>
> 5 6 7 8
> Eating cherries off a plate.
>
> 9 10 11 12
> Peasants often ditches delve.

12's a dozen 13 14
Little boys with kites are sporting.

15 16 17
Betty is a May Day Queen.

18 19 20 and 1
Girls may play when work is done.

(*The Giant Nursery Book*,
selected and illustrated by
Tony Palazzo, pp. 64–65)

Chaining abilities of sequencing, mentioned before, or variants of interpolation and extrapolation can be practiced by leaving out sections or endings and having the learner fill in the missing information, which is underlined. The learners can look at the illustrations for assistance.

It's wintertime on Brown Cow Farm. The animals are all inside the big brown barn. Outside, the barnyard is piled high with cold white snow. There is snow on the barn roof too, and long shiny icicles hang from the eaves. High up on the roof top is a weather-vane cow showing that the cold north wind is blowing, but inside the big barn, where the animals are, it is snug and warm.

There is one big brown horse in a big box stall. A big shiny brown horse with a long black tail and a wavy black mane. Farmer Brown feeds her oats and hay and brushes her and combs her mane.

There are two brown hound dogs that sleep in the hay, two brown hound dogs with long brown ears. They wag their tails and sniff the air.

There are three cats that live in the barn. They drink white milk and catch brown rats and sleep in the hay-loft up near the eaves. . . .

There are ten brown cows on Brown Cow Farm. Ten brown cows with curly horns, and tails with tassels at the ends.

(Dahlov Ipcar, *Brown Cow Farm*, unpaged)

Use of Indefinite Quantitative Terms

Young learners generally have some knowledge of indefinite quantitative (big, bigger) as opposed to definite quantitative (40 people, 8 horses, 3 pigs) representation of properties. For understanding, however, they often need experience and much practice with indefinite quantitative terms: long-short, small-large, fast-slow, few-many, more-less. In these basic cognitive areas of discriminating, numerous opportunities can be given the young learner to explore and expand his quantitative knowledge.

The three bears always went for a walk before breakfast. There was a big Papa bear, a not-so-big Mama bear, and a wee small Baby bear. One day they had a visitor, a tired hungry visitor called Goldilocks. There was no one at home, so she walked in. The very first thing she saw was the three chairs. A big Papa chair, a not-so-big Mama chair, and a wee small Baby chair! After she tried the big chair, and the not-so-big chair, she flopped into the wee small chair. She flopped so hard that she broke the wee small chair into wee pieces. There, on the floor were three bowls of food. A big bowl, a not-so-big bowl, and a wee small bowl. After she ate all the food in the wee small bowl, she became sleepy and climbed upstairs to take a nap. The very first things she saw were three beds, a big Papa bed, a not-so-big Mama bed, and a wee small Baby bed. She curled herself into the wee small bed (although she barely fit) and slept and slept and slept! Then the three bears came home from their morning walk. "SOMEONE HAS BEEN SITTING IN MY CHAIR!" growled the big Papa bear.

"SOMEONE HAS BEEN SITTING IN MY NOT-SO-BIG CHAIR," cried the not-so-big Mama bear.

"Someone has been sitting in my wee small chair," said the wee small bear in his wee small voice, "and it's *all broken*."

Then they saw the bowls of food. "SOMEONE HAS BEEN TASTING MY FOOD!" growled the very big Papa bear in his very big voice.

"SOMEONE HAS BEEN TASTING MY FOOD!" cried the not-so-big Mama bear in her not-so-big voice.

"And someone has eaten up all my food!" whimpered wee small Baby bear.

All the noise downstairs awakened Goldilocks. She leaped out of the wee small bed and out of the window and ran and ran and ran far, far away. AND . . . to this day the three bears never knew who came to visit them, nor who had sat in their chairs, slept in their beds, or tasted their food. (*Only Goldilocks knows.*)

(*Goldilocks and the Three Bears,* retold and illustrated by Tony Palazzo, unpaged)

Through dramatizing the story and adhering to the characterization of the bears, the learners would gain personal experience with quantitative sizing—a smaller child for the middle-size bear, a larger child for the big bear, the smallest child being the smallest bear. Indefinite quantitative comparisons are found in stories such as the following and the teacher can build others where these qualities are involved, as in the following selection which is accompanied by illustrations:

Once, long ago, God told Noah that it was going to rain for forty days and forty nights, until everything on earth was covered with water.

"Build an ark of wood," God told Noah. "Build it with many rooms and a window and a door. When it is finished, go on the Ark with your wife and your sons. With you take two of every kind of beast and bird that lives on earth." Noah and his three sons, Shem, Ham and Japheth, built the Ark. They made it strong enough to keep all the birds and animals safe during the flood. Then Noah took enough food on the Ark for everybody to eat. He took hay for horses and cows, meat for dogs and cats, nuts and seeds for

squirrels and mice. He took food for himself and his
wife and his sons, and their wives, too.

And now the animals came two by two . . . big and
little, fat and thin and medium. The ANTEATER and
the ALLIGATOR . . . are the Ark's first boarders.
The BUFFALO is a great shaggy beast . . . who
takes up much room! CATS come of all kinds . . .
Persian, alley, Siamese, and tabby. . . . Mrs. Noah
thought the Buffalo were big . . . but ELEPHANTS
are bigger.

(Willard Goodman, *Noah's Ark ABC*, pp. 4–13,
18–19)

Number as a Property of Matching Sets

One of the most important concepts in the modern
approach to the understanding of mathematics is the
concept of set. A set is a collection of objects which
are grouped together. In mathematics the concept is
basic to the theoretical system where objects can be
arbitrarily grouped together for a logical reason rather
than some common characteristic of identifiable reality.
In short, the elements of a set need not be alike and
one can safely mix apples and pears and have them in
the same set. Identifying sets requires both understanding and discriminating abilities. Trade books provide a
broad area of data where children can search for sets.

At a very elementary level children can discriminate
sets from sections of simple stories as in the following:

Tommy has a dog. Sally has a cat. They take good
care of them. The dog likes bones. The cat likes milk.

The Littles have an automobile. They are going for
a drive. Tommy sits in front with his father. Sally sits
in back with her mother.

(Lois Lenski, *The Little Family*, unpaged)

If the learners look at the illustrations which accompany the text of the first example, they can make a set of Tommy and his dog, and a second set of Sally and her cat, or another pair of sets of Tommy and Sally and the dog and cat. Further, the learner can be assisted to make a set of all the objects in the picture.

Once having understood the idea of sets, the learner can utilize his knowledge in the case in which the Little family is pictured in an automobile. Again a series of sets can be formed which are similar to the original illustration, Father and Tommy, Mother and Sally, Father and Mother, Tommy and Sally, the entire family, even the entire family and automobile. Utilizing the basic understanding, the search for sets can be extended to less similar materials, as in the following introduction from a story with accompanying illustrations of the tiger family.

> Once there was a tiger, a little striped tiger. He was striped with stripes, beautiful black and gold stripes, from the top of his head to the tip of his tail.
>
> He was just a baby tiger, and he lived in a cave in the jungle with his mother and his father and his brother and his sister. And they were all of them striped with stripes as stripey as they could be.

(Dahlov Ipcar, *Stripes and Spots,* unpaged)

Or another example of simple sets which learners can easily form is contained in the book *The New Pet.* A series of fine illustrations accompany the following text, depicting Dick and Judy at the described tasks:

> So Dick and Judy had to wait for their new pet. Dick and Judy were very good while their mother was away. They were very good because they knew how to take care of themselves and how to help their grandmother.
>
> Judy and Dick cleared the table after meals.
>
> They picked up their toys and hung up their clothes and helped keep the little red house tidy and neat.

One day they helped their grandmother make a warm little bed for the new baby to sleep in.

(Marjorie Flack, *The New Pet*, unpaged)

At a more complex level for more mature readers a story about a circus offers many interesting opportunities to form sets. A teacher might want to select a passage from a book and have the learners form as many sets as they could from the descriptions.

It was a small clown suit/and two small clown shoes. Pete jumped up/and jumped down/and laughed and laughed and laughed/because NOW he could be a small clown/and do his small clown tricks/for all the people/who came to see the circus.
Pete gave his father a big hug/and a big kiss./
He gave his mother a big hug/and a big kiss./
He hugged his small clown suit/and his small clown shoes./
He said, "Mother, may I put them on now?"/
But Mother said, "No,/wait till after lunch."/
So Pete put his suit and his shoes/right in the middle of his bed/and went to see the Circus Animals/and the Circus People./
And when he got to them he said to/the Lion in his cage/
and the Big cats in their cages/
and the Giraffe with his tall neck/
and the Fat Lady/
and the Thin Man/
and the Horse Lady and her Horse/
and the Tightrope Man/
and the Circus Man/
and Tim the Circus Man's son, . . .

(Nancy Faulkner, *Small Clown*, pp. 14–23)

To illustrate that the area of utilizing abilities on the forming of sets can be practiced with vastly different materials is seen in the following example.

Dunder was kept in a pen and shed of his own on the far side of the barn.

Yonie had helped Pop, but he had never taken care of Dunder by himself as Ammon always had. He knew he must speak quietly to the great beast. He knew how to use the staff that Pop kept handy, too, and how to attach it to the ring in the bull's nose. So he felt safe, even though Dunder was so big and fierce.

The summer was really over. The hay was in the barn and the harvest gathered. But it had turned very warm again. Yonie's shirt was damp from the heat, and his yellow hair clung to his forehead. He wished he could stop work and go wading in the creek. The Little Conestoga ran through the meadow, and Yonie knew how cool it would be in the shade of the willow tree on its bank. He dropped the bucket he was carrying and started toward the creek. Then he remembered his promise to Pop—and Pop's promise to him. He picked up the bucket and went to pump more water for the rest of the animals and the chickens.

"Ach, vell," he told himself, "I can douse good, once, when I get the chores done."

He grunted as he lifted the heavy pail out of the trough. The water spilled a little onto his bare feet. It felt good and made clean patterns where it washed off the dust. He carried the bucket as full as he could. The chicken pans had to be filled, the calves needed a drink, the pigs had to be fed, and there was still the water to carry in for Granny.

When Yonie had filled the pans in the chicken yard, he made sure to lock the chicken house door. He knew the eggs had been gathered, so he didn't bother to look inside again.

He picked up the buckets in a hurry to water the calves and then stopped. Was that an airplane he heard? He couldn't see it but now he remembered that Granny wanted the round-wood for the fire.

"Rount-wood gives a hot fire," she had said, "and supper makes soon."

So Yonie went to the woodpile to get it. He could see Nancy under the big tree happily playing with her doll.

He started to gather the wood, and again came the deep purr of an airplane. This time he was sure. It might even be a new kind. He dropped the wood and ran to the corner of the house where he could see better.

(Marguerite de Angeli, *Yonie Wondernose,* un-paged)

It is necessary to use materials that are more complex than and different from the material in which the concept was originally learned, in order to develop the ability to utilize the concept.

A second conceptual process basic to set theory is matching of sets. In the process of matching, the elements of sets are paired with the elements of a second set. When there is an exact matching of the elements of two sets, we say there is a one-to-one correspondence between the two sets. For example, there is a one-to-one correspondence between our set of hands and our set of feet. Many sets are matched in one-to-one correspondence in the primary classrooms when each child is matched with one sheet of paper, a bottle of milk, a chair in the reading circle, pairs of boots, a coat or gloves, or both.

When the elements of one set can be matched exactly with the elements of another set we say that all the sets that are so matched have a common property. And all the sets that have the common property of matching each other are assigned the same number. *Goldilocks and the Three Bears* is an excellent story for this kind of "matching" of sets of objects, since there are several matching sets involved in the story, such as, a chair for each bear, a bowl of porridge for each, and a bed for each. Children can develop their powers of discriminating by such questions as "What is the only thing that is the same about the different sets of objects?" The manyness of the sets, that is, the only thing these sets have in common, is the property of size or number (threeness). The three pigs can be matched with the three bears which can be matched with the three little kittens, etc.

What about sets that do not match? Suppose all of the elements of one set have been paired with the elements of a second set, and the second set contains some unmatched elements. The second set has more elements than the first set, and the first set has fewer elements than the second set. By matching the elements of various sets, children learn about "more than" and "less than," greater and lesser. This can be refined a little more by having children match two sets whose difference is one. Thus, they practice discriminating that five is one more than four, four is one more than three, three is one more than two, etc. They can learn that there is an order to numbers. Also, the sequential order of numbers and the relation between numbers become apparent.

The superior convenience of using numbers, both in everyday activities and in literature, helps pupils get the import of the numbers used. By matching the elements of various sets the child learns about number as the property of a collection of matching sets, about one-to-one correspondence, and the number names associated with the different kinds of sets or groupings. A basic understanding of the real meaning of number which underlies the theoretical system of mathematics is enhanced.

In Grades 2 and 3, elements of the formal operations on numbers are an important part of the mathematics program. The fundamental concepts of addition and subtraction can be begun at the first grade level, however, by the use of sets of objects and the adding on or taking away of members of the set and counting to see how many are then in the set. In the story of *The Three Little Kittens,* the students can be asked to consider how many animals there are if the mother is counted in the set. Thus the students discover that $3 + 1 = 4$. In the story of *The Little Red Hen* the total number of animals is five, but if the red hen is removed from the set there are only four left. So children are led to generalize that $5 - 1 = 4$. The total number of characters in *Goldilocks and the Three Bears* is four; however, if Goldilocks is removed from the set of characters, there are only three in the set of characters. Thus students can generalize that $4 - 1 = 3$. Many more such illustrations exist in these and other trade books.

Since mathematics is a formal system with its own self-contained logic, the elementary school teacher is faced with the very difficult task of teaching mathematics in such a way that children learn the basic concepts in mathematics. Providing a classroom atmosphere where children are given many opportunities to discover these meanings for themselves is the best path to developing cognitive abilities of understanding as well as utilization. Informal learning situations using trade books with mathematical content provides for individual differences, challenging the very capable pupils and at the same time not frustrating the slower learners. For parallel to the concern for building a solid basis for further mathematics through the elementary school program is the concern for the child's development as a learner. Greater efforts must be made to make mathematics meaningful and interesting in the early grades.

UPPER ELEMENTARY AND JUNIOR HIGH SCHOOL

The upper elementary and junior high school program focuses on the utilization of basic processes and developing further understanding of mathematical systems.

The learner at this level receives further insights into fundamental constructs which underlie mathematical systems. For modern mathematics is concerned with systems and their interpretation as representative models or various aspects of the physical universe, or both. One of the most important relationships in the emphasis on systems and models at the secondary level is the understanding that algebraic and geometric systems may be interpreted as aspects of the same data.

Some Examples of Introducing Mathematical Systems

Algebra is often associated with sets of numbers and unspecified representatives of these sets, such as the familiar x and y. Geometry is often associated with sets of points. The important understanding to be cultivated here is the relationship that can be established between these two systems. Associated with the geometry of points on the line there is an algebra of the coordinate x of the points on the line. And associated with plane geometry there is an algebra of the coordinates of the points $\xrightarrow{y}x$ considered as ordered pairs of numbers (x,y). Therefore, algebra and geometry may both be used to study either sets of numbers or sets of points.

The assigning of numbers to points has lately been

receiving attention as one of the major ideas in the development of mathematics. While the detailed study of coordinate geometry is reserved for senior high school, the elements of analytical geometry are rapidly finding their place in the upper elementary grades. These are being taught to students as they analyze the how and why of scale drawings. In the trade book *The Secret of the Simple Code* the concepts of coordinate geometry and analytical geometry are used. As the learner studies the story and attempts to break the code he can be directed to understanding and utilizing some of the methods of the mathematical systems in geometry.

The following selection illustrates how an understanding of advanced concepts can be communicated to the learner in the middle grades.

The professor took the four slips of paper and a large rectangular folder from his pocket and put them on the footrest of the chair. "Now," he said, lining up the small slips and speaking with precision as if he were in a classroom, "you all remember how these read—in the order you found them—N2, B10, K6, F3, G9, C4, and H5. All week I've tried to make some sense out of the pesky things and couldn't. I've had some experience in breaking codes and I used every trick in the book. None of them worked. Then this very morning while I was getting dressed, I had occasion to look at this." He tapped the folded rectangle. "Not, mind you, in connection with our problem. I wasn't even thinking . . ."

"*Professor!*" Abby interrupted, "what is that thing? If you don't tell us I—I'll purely *scream.*"

"Gently, Abby girl. I'm coming to it."

The professor unfolded the rectangle with tantalizing slowness while the others leaned forward, their bodies tensed, as if they expected the thing—whatever it was—to explode. When the professor finally spread the large, unfolded paper across the footrest the three of them slumped back, their disappointment showing clearly. "Why," Paul put words to all their thoughts, "it's just a kind of old *map!*"

"Exactly!" The professor beamed on them. "It's a large scale map of the area around here. It shows everything to be seen for about ten miles around the inn. See, the inn is just here." He pointed to a symbol in the center of the map, a tiny picture of a house such as a child might draw, and waited as if he expected some comment.

Abby and Paul said, "Oh." Luke said nothing but his eyes had lit up as if someone had put a candle behind them. He got to his knees and leaned closer to the footrest and stared at the many different symbols that covered the network of black lines on the white paper.

"Now," the professor went on. "Look here. And here." He pointed to the margin of the map. "See there are letters along two sides of the paper and numbers along the other two."

All three of his listeners nodded.

"As I looked at the map this morning, I had an idea. You see, anybody can get a map like this one, showing the main features of any country. It had occurred to me that the numbers and letters on our messages were somehow familiar. Once I looked at the map here I knew why they had seemed so. Now watch. Let's begin with the first one of our mysterious papers. Take N2."

He ran one finger from the N on the side margin, another from the 2 on the top until his fingers met. "See the little sign here?" He pointed to two tiny crossed shovels. "That means a mine. Now let's look at the other papers."

(Nancy Faulkner, *The Secret of the Simple Code*, pp. 119–20)

Once the understanding of coordinate geometry is grasped, the learner could reproduce a similar map from the above description. Then he could be encouraged to utilize this knowledge on other maps and graphs. From extensive utilization the major principle that from two known points axes can be drawn to find a third point evolves, and another cornerstone is added to the foundation of a mathematical system.

Thus, a story can be used to test and strengthen students' understanding and utilization abilities and advance the development of functional scholarship skills useful in future mathematics. In this specific case of coordinates, a scheme of assigning numbers or pairs of letters or numbers or both to points or locations, the fundamental has wide application in map making, presenting of data on graphs, and other related areas where two knowns can define a relationship or location of a third unknown.

In connection with this topic, *The Wonderful World of Mathematics* by Lancelot Hogben offers further interesting examples concerning the development of the method of graphing with coordinates. Examples of the various uses of coordinates which would not occur to the learner also provide further chances to utilize the understanding in another context.

> During the sixteenth and seventeenth centuries, navigators began to plot the day-to-day position of their ships on maps marked with lines of latitude and longitude. A connecting line drawn through all these points gave the navigator a convenient summary of the voyage.
>
> Mathematicians were already trying out much the same technique to represent figures by paths which a moving point traces on the sort of grid we now call a graph. If we make such a grid with vertical lines to show time and horizontal lines to show distance, we can easily plot Achilles' race with the tortoise. One line shows where the tortoise starts and how fast it runs. The point where the lines cross shows where Achilles overtakes the tortoise.

> (Lancelot Hogben, *The Wonderful World of Mathematics*, p. 58)

Learners might be asked to list various applications

of this method of graphing information within their daily experiences by using a grid system to draw a local map of their community, locating specific points, or by using two types of data, as in putting the numbers of units of a given commodity such as automobiles on one line (y axis) and the years of production on the bottom line (x axis). Then by joining the points for the years of production the reader can easily see the up-and-down flow of production. Many other similar applications of coordinates can be explored.

Most students fare better in their study of intuitive geometry than they do in mathematics in general. There are two reasons for this phenomenon. One reason is that geometry does not necessarily have to be related to the past study of arithmetic, in which many students have already encountered frustration. Secondly, diagrams help students see relationships among points, lines, and planes—the objects being studied. However, if we are to hope for any transfer of learning, classroom experiences will have to contribute toward the development of cognitive learning. A special project might be required of all students in the class. This could consist of the construction of a model, a report on some library research in areas where geometric concepts are used, or a report on an extension of an individual's knowledge of mathematics beyond the requirements of the course.

Verbal Problems

In the middle grades learners confront a variety of verbal problems as they develop more proficiency in the utilization of basic processes. These verbal problems typically involve distance, rate, time, units of measure and their translation into equivalent measures in other systems, or the approximate nature of a number obtained in the measurement of some quantity, or both.

The ability to discriminate among several sets of data is important in solving verbal problems. First the learner must develop a systematic way of viewing the problem at hand, then analyze the problem for the important data given, and finally organize the information to be able to transform it into the symbolic language of mathematics. Since most practical problems involving mathematics do not come in ready-made equations or even in common units, meeting problems in an open-ended context promotes flexibility in utilization of mathematics skills.

Some excellent open-ended mathematical problems can be obtained from trade book materials, as in the following example, where the need for standard units based on a different system than children are accustomed to is explained.

Airplanes were flying so fast now that men were beginning to compute their speed in a new way. Miles per hour didn't tell the whole story any more, so scientists devised a system of Mach comparisons. A Mach number represents the ratio of the speed of an airplane to the speed of sound in the air. It is not an absolute number, such as ten miles per hour, because the speed of sound is greater at high temperatures than at low temperatures, and the higher above the earth you go, the lower the temperature becomes. At sea level, at about 60 degrees temperature, sound travels at 750 miles an hour. But at 40,000 feet, where the temperature is 70 degrees below zero, the speed of sound drops almost a hundred miles an hour.

The speed of sound is the important fact, for when an airplane approaches that speed it comes to what is called the *sonic barrier*. That is an increase in resistance or *drag,* caused by mixtures of pressures known as *shock waves*. When an airplane approaches the speed of sound the drag increases very greatly, and the shock waves are so heavy that they will tear an airplane apart if it is not properly designed to pass the sound barrier. But past the sound barrier, the shock waves decrease just as greatly, and resistance to acceleration decreases as well.

Since the sonic barrier was the important point in airplane design, it also became the basis for determining the speed of the new kind of airplanes.

So Major Yeager measured the speed of the X-1 in terms of Mach. The new fighter planes of the U.S. Air Force were now traveling at Mach .75. Yeager had already flown the X-1 at Mach .94, officially, and he may even have come closer to Mach 1, which is the speed of sound. But he had not passed the sonic barrier, as far as he knew. This day was the important day.

The B-29 cleared with the Muroc field control tower, and took off, bearing its strange little airplane. The X-1 was carried by the bomber on take-off so it would not have to waste precious rocket fuel in taking off and climbing to the rarefied air where the tests would be made.

The bomber climbed to 5000 feet, and Yeager moved painfully back to the bomb bay, then climbed down the ladder to the X-1 and got in. He adjusted his seat, put on oxygen, checked the cabin for pressurization—because that was all-important to his survival at high altitude and high speed.

The bomber went up to 15,000 feet, then to 20,000 feet. Then, at a signal, the X-1 dropped away from the big plane, and Yeager began firing the rockets that would send him to tremendous speed.

He climbed to 35,000 feet, then to 40,000 feet, and leveled off at Mach .96. The Mach needle moved to .98, then suddenly jerked, and jumped completely off the scale. Yeager had broken the sound barrier!

A few months later another plane, the X-2, exploded, killing its pilot. Then came the X-3, the X-5 and others, all of them traveling faster than Mach 1. It was not long before Mach 2 was reached, and that meant airplanes were now traveling at 1600 and 1700 miles per hour—twice the speed of sound. The whole world of aviation had changed by 1953 when Major Yeager flew the X-1A at Mach 2.

(Edwin P. Hoyt, *Heroes of the Skies*, pp. 140–42)

The understanding that can be developed from this passage is the need to move from a fixed system of miles per hour to a system related to the sonic barrier. Since the sonic barrier is influenced by temperature the learner should understand the relationship of temperature to elevation above the earth. In this passage the learner is introduced to the idea of conversion in a very meaningful sense and how one system of measurement in a given set of circumstances needs to be converted to make it more useful. The passage offers opportunity for the learner to convert Machs to miles per hour at different levels and to see that the Mach is not a fixed constant measure. The teacher might wish to have the learner develop some conversion tables of miles per hour into Machs at different altitude levels.

Another type of mathematical problem which has become prominent in the space age due to supersonic speeds is discussed in this passage on reaction time.

Because man is not a creature of speed, nature did not equip him to cope with the speeds brought on by the automobile age, and now by the jet and rocket age. Like the pilot who flew through the B-47 formation, the *reaction time* of all of us is too slow to guard us against the hidden dangers of high speed. George simply could not see the other bombers and make a decision to maneuver his plane out of the way fast enough. By "reaction time" the flight surgeon means the length of time it takes to yank your thumb back after you have hit it with a hammer, or how long it takes a driver to stamp on the brake pedal of his car or swerve out of the way when another car pops out of a blind driveway.

Every day, at football, baseball, or crossing a busy street, most of us are in situations requiring quick reaction. Automatically we "know" when to swing at the pitched ball, or quicken our steps as we scoot into a rapidly turning revolving door. But few of us realize the complex process that enables us to react. Consider for a moment an automobile driver who sees something out of the corner of his eye. It may be a piece of paper blown by the wind, or it may be a child chasing a ball into the street. Before he acts, the driver must correctly identify the object. To do this he must turn his eyes toward it. This takes a fraction of a second, during which time the car has moved closer to the object. The image printed on the retina of the eye sends a message along the optic nerve to the brain which "decides" what the object is. If it is a child, then the brain must make a decision to act—slam on the brakes or swerve out of the way. Another fraction of a second has passed. The car has moved still closer to the child. Next, the brain must send its decision through the nerves of the arms and legs to tell the hands and feet to act. Another fraction of a second and the car is still moving. The final step is the length of time it takes to stop the car. The greater the speed, the greater the danger.

Unhappily, our reaction time cannot be speeded up at will. Because a situation demands super-fast decisions and action does not mean that we can speed up our reaction time. All messages travel along the nerves at a fairly constant speed of 230 feet a second, or 155 miles an hour. (This is far slower than a message traveling along telegraph wires.) Your reaction time also depends on your health and whether or not you are tired. An alert person can respond more quickly to a stimulus than someone who is tired.

While the automobile incident gives us a working definition of reaction time and decision making, it does not describe the strange situations our slow bodies can cause during high-speed flight. Say that a pilot of a rocket plane is flying at 2000 miles an hour. Suddenly he sees another plane, also traveling at 2000 miles an hour, heading straight toward him. The average pilot takes three-tenths of a second to see an object. It takes this long for the image of the object to be flashed onto the retina and sent to the brain where "sight" takes place. In those three-tenths of a second each plane has traveled 880 feet. In other words, if you were one of the pilots you would see the other plane where it was *three-tenths of a second ago*—not where it is at the moment. So it would be 880 feet closer to you than your eyes told you it was. Also your own plane would have traveled 880 feet, closing the gap between you and the other plane by a total of 1760 feet. Now if you were an alert pilot it could take you about two seconds to make a decision to dive, climb, or turn out of the way to avoid a collision. In those two seconds your plane and the other one have narrowed the gap by an additional 11,732 feet, or 2.2 miles! There's no need to go on. You could not see another fighter plane heading straight for you *more* than two miles away. And by the time you did see it you would not have time to decide what to do to avoid a collision. Within the two seconds required for a decision you would have met head on.

(Roy A. Gallant, *Man's Reach into Space*, pp. 48–49)

This passage presents a series of possible relationships to be explored involving the dimensions of time, distance, rate of speed. Also the learner is given a striking demonstration of the practical use of mathematics in the space age.

Another dimension of mathematics and their use in air safety is provided in this chart from a study on pilot ejections from airplanes.

In this brief chart the learner is introduced to simple statistics in comparing occurrences and postulating relationships on the basis of the frequency of the occurrence. For example, having the learner examine the

TOTAL NUMBER OF EJECTIONS: 2502

Number of Ejections	What Happened	Per Cent
1257	No injury	50
450	Death	18
396	Minor injuries	16
399	Major injuries	16

ALTITUDES OF THE 2502 EJECTIONS

Altitude (in feet)	Number of Ejections	Deaths	Per cent of Ejections Fatal
0 to 1000	379	214	56
1000–2000	298	45	15
2000–3000	186	19	10
3000–5000	305	13	4
5000–10,000	533	20	4
10,000–20,000	497	30	6
20,000 plus	207	21	10
unknown	97	88	91

(*Ibid.*, p. 116)

per-cent-of-ejections-fatal column and the altitude column, the relationship of the two variables altitude and fatalities becomes quite clear. The learner might wish to speculate on the reason for the unusual relationship (curvilinear) before searching the text for the answer.

Both of the above references contain numerous other samples where conversion, use of standard measures, and ratios can be examined and used in a meaningful context.

Another trade book which explains the origin of some standard units of measure also describes how some of these measures were used.

During the century that followed Watt's inventions, steam power rapidly changed the whole way of life in the Western world. Industry moved away from the country cottage into the factories of huge industrial cities which sprang up near coalfields, where fuel for steam-engines was cheap and plentiful. Smoking funnels replaced white sails along the world's sea-routes. The clip-clop of the coach horse died out on the highway and made way for the rattle of steam locomotives carrying freight and passengers along the new railroads. Such rapid increase in the use of steam power was at first largely due to the way in which Watt and his business partner, Boulton, were able to convince customers of the usefulness and cheapness of the engines they made. They found by experiment that a strong horse can raise a 150-lb. weight, suspended over a pulley, 220 feet in one minute. If one of their engines could raise ten times that weight through the same distance in one minute, they classed it as a ten horse-power model. The customer could then compare the cost of buying fuel for such an engine with the cost of providing keep for ten horses, and usually he found that it would pay him, in the long run, to lease the engine.

It may seem strange that horse-power became a standard unit of power-measure just at the moment when horses were losing their importance in industry, but the reason is not hard to find.

Learners should have an opportunity at this point to discuss the reason and compare their reasons with one which is explained in the text:

New kinds of measurement are more easy to understand if based on older ones we already use. When improved oil lamps and gas lamps were taking the place of candles at the beginning of the new industrial age, the illumination they gave was at first measured in candle-power.

In the time of Watt, all steam-engines worked at the same pressure. It was thus possible to estimate the horse-power of an engine from the size of its cylinder. As design became more varied, indicators or steam gauges came into use to measure the pressure of steam generated in the cylinder in pounds per square inch.

Many units of measure we use today would have puzzled the engineers and scientists of Watt's time. When we speak of volts and amperes in connection with electricity, or therms and calories in connection with heat, we are using language of precise measurement devised to meet the needs of the age of power.

(Lancelot Hogben, *The Wonderful World of Mathematics,* pp. 62–63)

From these definitions and explanations, the learners can be encouraged to develop utilization abilities by applying the information on horsepower to practical problems. How much weight would a 120-horsepower automobile engine move 220 feet in a minute? How many horsepower does a jet airliner 707 generate? Or a learner can be encouraged to make up a series of problems from the information to be worked by other members of the class.

The ability to convert many types of standard units is essential to intelligent consuming as well as traveling and speed. Once the understanding of these units is established, the abilities of utilization of these units in many problem situations is essential if the learner is going to be able to transfer his understanding from one context to another.

Business Arithmetic

The subject matter of the middle grades and junior high school includes the arithmetic used in business and finance. Such topics as interest on savings, charges for borrowing money, the cost of buying on installment, sales and income taxes, insurance, and social security are all taught at this level, as well as in classes considered general mathematics classes in the high school. Such books as *Wall Street* can provide opportunities for utilization to the young learner, who is isolated from the business world and rarely has an opportunity for firsthand experience of how it functions. After having read such a story, students can be asked to report to the class. This practice will give the learner a chance to make an inventory of the facts; this is one of the discriminating abilities discussed in an earlier section.

The learner should not have a difficult time in selecting the main ideas from the following passage from *Wall Street*:

The modern corporation is patterned on the old merchants' trade company, but it is infinitely bigger and more complicated. The London Company of Virginia was owned by a few hundred men. It spent a million dollars to establish a settlement in the New World. The American Telephone and Telegraph Company has 1,307,000 shareholders and its plants and equipment are valued at $14,000,000,000.

Raising capital for American Telephone and Telegraph and its fellow giants has become a business in itself. In place of the merchant, there is the financier, the investment banker, the stockbroker. In their hands, a new kind of trading developed—the buying and selling of shares in industry.

To understand how this works, let's imagine that you want to start a lemonade stand. This is to be a superstand, open every weekend all summer long. A real business.

Your mother groans. "I know you made a dollar and a half in one afternoon last year, but think of what it cost me in lemons and sugar and broken glasses. Don't count on me for your supplies!"

Perhaps John's mother or Joan's will have shorter memories. But Mrs. Brown reminds you of a borrowed pitcher that was returned without a handle, and Mrs. Smith needs the bridge table that you counted on for a stand.

"I can see we're going to have to finance this our-
selves, . . ."

(Dorothy Sterling, *Wall Street: The Story of the
Stock Exchange,* pp. 19–23)

The story continues with a description of how a
stock market functions.

[Middlemen] make it possible for buyers to buy and
sellers to sell. They represent traders in Chicago, in
Alabama, in California and Maine.

Just as you can go to a market to buy a pound of
hamburger or a dozen oranges, so you can go to a
market to buy shares in a corporation that manufac-
tures television sets or mines uranium. This is the
securities market, which, when it is organized under
one roof and closely regulated by law and custom, is
called a *stock exchange.*

(*Ibid.*)

Some excellent passages from the same book which
contain arithmetic problems as well as the story of the
market can be used to develop utilization abilities.

Back in Andrew Jackson's day there were few investors who lived outside New York or the major
cities along the East Coast. If you were a Chicagoan
wishing to buy stocks or bonds you would probably
travel to New York to make your purchase. Otherwise weeks might elapse between the time you wrote
to your broker to ask for current prices and he received your order to buy or sell. Weeks in which the
stock in which you were interested might have doubled
in price or dropped to a disastrous low. Suppose Erie
Canal was selling for $30 when your broker read your
inquiry, for $35 when you received his answer, for
$40 when your order finally reached him. One hun-
dred shares of stock would cost you $1,000 more than
you anticipated!

Time means money in the stock market, and time
must be measured not only in weeks and days but in

minutes and seconds. Before the Exchange could become a national market place it had to find ways for speedy communication. Investors in New York were informed of changes in stock prices by a crew of messengers known as *pad-shovers*. All during trading hours these young men collected figures from the Exchange and then ran from one brokerage office to another, shouting out the latest prices.

A more elaborate system was worked out to send messages to Philadelphia financiers. While mail was still traveling by stagecoach, the New York Stock & Exchange Board manned a series of stations on hills and ridges across the state of New Jersey. Each station was equipped with semaphore signals for sending messages and telescopes as an aid in receiving them. Information about stock prices could be wigwagged in as short a time as ten minutes from New York to Philadelphia. The telegraph put the semaphore out of business in 1844, . . .

(Ibid., p. 83)

Among the useful passages to test understanding abilities is the one on pricing.

The First, High, Low, and Last figures give a blow-by-blow account of BAT's selling prices for the day. The first sale was made at $12.75, the last at $12.87½. During trading hours it rose as high as $13 and dropped as low as $12.50.

The final column in the table, Net Change, compares BAT's last price yesterday and today. Yesterday, BAT closed at $13, today at $12.87½. The net change, therefore, was $-⅛$.

If you are reading a large metropolitan newspaper, you will find similar stock tables for the transactions on the American Exchange, the Toronto and Montreal exchanges, and for the New York Stock Exchange's bond market. You will also notice a table titled "Over-the-Counter Securities." All securities which are not bought and sold on the exchanges are spoken of as being traded *over-the-counter*. The expression goes back to colonial days, when stocks were sold, like tea or beaver skins, over the counters of merchants or private bankers.

Bank and insurance-company stocks, government and municipal bonds are traded over the counter. So are the stocks of corporations whose businesses are too new or too small to be listed on an exchange (Lemonade, Inc., for example) and the stocks of companies whose directors, for one reason or another, do not want them listed on an exchange. The over-the-counter market is a large one—how large, no one knows exactly. But it is a safe guess that its total sales are more than the combined totals of all the exchanges.

(Ibid., p. 118)

To test for correct understanding of the material in the text, one might ask what the $-\frac{1}{8}$ means in the paragraph above. The difference in price is $12\frac{1}{2}\cent$; why does the $-\frac{1}{8}$ mean the same thing? This type of example can be used fruitfully when students are considering the topic "Signed Numbers," since the positive sign $(+)$ and the negative sign $(-)$ are used to represent increase and decrease in price, thus providing good examples with which to test for understanding and utilization.

And in addition to discovering how the world of finance and business functions, students are afforded an opportunity to read interesting material which they can analyze. They can practice and develop powers of discriminating, and the teacher can also use the same material for construction of verbal problems involving mathematical solutions.

Some of the understandings that can be expected from a thorough investigation of the material in *Wall Street* are:

(1) How the stock market functions and its role in the economics of our country and the world

(2) The historical development of the Exchange, including the effect of better communications on its growth, and how it in turn affected the growth of big business in America

(3) The importance of mathematics in business, especially the need for efficient and accurate methods of carrying out computations. Students will surely be more strongly motivated to learn the basic skills needed for solving arithmetic problems when they are given an opportunity to see how these skills are used in life situations

(4) Relationships to other subject areas such as social studies

Scientific Notation and Approximate Numbers

In the middle grades students are also taught to work with large numbers; approximating and rounding-off skills are developed. For instance, judging abilities are involved in this procedure where a student must decide how to round the number 348 to the nearest hundred. The answer is 300. Such a problem presents difficulty for students since 48 seems a large amount to drop off. A number which is arrived at through approximating is, of course, useful in certain areas where accuracy is not of prime importance. Some students are also taught how to work more efficiently with large numbers—they are taught to use scientific notation, a skill needed and used most frequently by the physicist and engineer. The physicist finds scientific notation extremely helpful in computations involving very large numbers ($10,000,000 = 10^7$) or very small quantities ($.000027 = 2.7 \times 10^{-5}$). Some interesting examples where very large numbers are used may be extracted from a trade book such as *Man's Reach into Space*. The numbers used in the passages which follow are rounded off, and are good examples of the use of approximate answers rather than exact answers.

Case 3: In September 1956, Captain Milburn G. Apt flew Bell's famous X-2 rocket plane at a record speed of 2260 miles an hour—three and a half times the speed of sound. The early part of Apt's flight went like clockwork. First, he and his midget plane were dropped from the B-29 "mother ship" that carried them to launching altitude. Free of the ponderous bird, Apt cut in the rockets, climbed to 70,000 feet, and nosed over to level flight. Next he pushed the throttle wide open for his speed run. The X-2 leaped ahead, breezing past Lieutenant Colonel Frank K. Everest's earlier speed of 1900 miles an hour.

Case 4: In August 1957, Air Force Lieutenant Colonel David G. Simons was sealed into a metal capsule and lifted by balloon to 102,000 feet—more than nineteen miles above the earth. The altitude Colonel Simons reached is not alone important. But the fact that he spent thirty-two hours in a sealed cabin—completely cut off from outside air—high in the atmosphere is important.

. . . At 50,000 feet, however, even pressure breathing cannot keep you alive. At this altitude the atmospheric pressure is only 1.69 pounds a square inch. And it so happens that the pressure of the waste gases the body tissues pour into the lungs is also 1.69 pounds a square inch. What this means is that there is simply no more room in the lungs for incoming oxygen. This condition is called *anoxia,* which means that the body tissues are not getting any oxygen. Above 50,000 feet, then, no matter how much pure oxygen you try to breathe you simply cannot stay alive. What you need is a pressurized cabin or pressure suit.

A healthy person in good physical condition can hold off oxygen starvation a few seconds longer than an unhealthy person. But healthy or not, we all need oxygen; without it we would die. You could expect to react to hypoxia the following ways if you were not wearing an oxygen mask. (Remember, the higher you go, the less atmospheric pressure there is. And the less pressure, the quicker oxygen starvation will come about):

From 8000 to 10,000 feet for more than four hours you would begin to feel tired all over and sluggish. This feeling would remain as long as you stayed at this altitude.

From 10,000 to 15,000 feet for two hours you would begin to feel tired and sleepy. You would develop a headache and show poor judgment in your work.

From 15,000 to 18,000 feet for one half hour you would have a false sense of well-being and would become overconfident in whatever you were doing. If you were working arithmetic problems you would make many more mistakes and would find it difficult to concentrate. Also, your memory would begin to fail you. Your vision would blur and you would find that you had unsteady muscle control. And if you were in poor physical condition you would become unconscious.

Higher than 18,000 feet all of these symptoms would come on more quickly. In addition, you would not be able to think a problem through. You would find yourself gripped by fits of laughing and crying over nothing in particular.

At 26,000 feet you would lose consciousness in four to six minutes; at 30,000 feet, in one to two minutes; at 38,000 feet, in thirty seconds; above 50,000 feet, in ten to twelve seconds.

(Roy A. Gallant, *Man's Reach into Space*, pp. 8, 10, 32–33)

From the above materials learners may be expected to develop understanding which will answer the questions: When are approximate numbers used? What instrument is used to measure altitude? Is this kind of measurement considered an example of direct measure or of indirect measure? What kind of graph would be used to show this information? This material also provides appropriate data for students to practice making graphs. In fact, in the same book, a fine graph is used to give information concerning altitude records for manned flight.

Learners could also be asked to write the various numbers in scientific notation, i.e., 26,000 feet = 2.6×10^4, to provide practice in the use of this method of writing large numbers.

Cognitive Abilities in Mathematics and Student Interests

If students are given opportunities to see the relationship between their primary interests (art, science, astronomy, etc.) and mathematics, they begin to be more serious students in mathematics. Through development of utilization abilities both of their areas of interest will benefit. Several excellent trade books are available for students for this kind of independent research. *The ABC's of Astronomy* by Roy A. Gallant is an interesting book that reveals the use of mathematics in the study of astronomy.

Altitude:
The angular height of a body above the horizon. For example, a star has an *altitude* of 30° when the angle between the star, observer, and horizon is 30°. [A very clear diagram accompanies this definition.]

(Roy A. Gallant, *ABC's of Astronomy*, p. 9)

This definition can be related to the definition of *angle of elevation* and *angle of depression* which students will encounter in the early study of trigonometry and geometry.

Angular Distance:
The distance between two objects measured by an

angle. The *angular distance* between two stars, for example, could be found if you project a line to star A and another line to star B. The angle formed at your position becomes the *angular distance*.

(Ibid.)

An excellent diagram accompanies this definition also. Students can also find related problems of coordinate geometry where we sometimes must draw projections to the coordinate axes in order to measure length or distance. In discovering the use of mathematics in astronomy, the student is provided with an opportunity to use a spectrum of cognitive abilities to solve the same kinds of problems in the study of astronomy as those presented to him in the mathematics classroom. Students can be helped to deepen understanding and utilization of their knowledge of mathematics through projects with trade books of the type in the foregoing examples. Chaining of the relationships between systems in mathematics is also a valuable by-product of the open-ended problems presented.

Mature students can also be assisted toward understanding that mathematics and science are related to a total pattern of activity in a period of time by gaining some insight into the social setting of the development of these subjects. The history of mathematics can become part of the understanding of living. *The Wonderful World of Mathematics* by Lancelot Hogben provides students with an opportunity to develop their cognitive abilities, especially in building understanding of topics in mathematics through information on their historic setting and development.

On pages 10 and 11 in *The Wonderful World of Mathematics,* one finds a discussion of several ancient systems of numeration. Basic to all the systems that are presented are two properties that are also used in our decimal system of numeration, namely the repetition of basic symbols and the additive property. As a good practice in discriminating abilities students could be asked to read about the various number systems and then compare them to find what properties they have in common and what properties make them different from each other. It would then be worthwhile to compare these ancient systems with the system which we use at the present time. They would then discover that our system is more advanced and efficient for calculation because of the property which we call place-value, where the value a digit represents, as in the case of 1 in the numerals 1, 10, or 100, depends on the place of the digit within the numeral. Students might also be asked to reason out why these old systems did not have place-value. The analysis will be aimed at eliciting the understanding that the concept of place-value depends upon the use of zero for the cardinal number of the empty set and such a symbol is not present in the ancient systems of numeration presented by Hogben.

In the same book one finds a description concerning the use of shadow reckoning by the ancient Egyptians. The following is an example of a thought-provoking passage on use of natural phenomena to develop a formal system of mathematics:

> In finding direction and measuring time, the Egyptian had only the same clues as the hunters and food-gatherers of a bygone age: the rising and setting positions of sun, moon and stars, the shadow of the sun by day and the rotation of starclusters around the Pole Star at night. Years of careful recording, however, enabled the Egyptian to make far better use of these clues. The early hunter looking at the long shadow cast by a tree could say at best: It is still early morning. The Egyptian, with a sun-clock which measured the length of a shadow falling on a marked strip

of wood, could look at the shadow and say: The second hour of morning is at hand.

> (Lancelot Hogben, *The Wonderful World of Mathematics*, p. 19)

The teacher might use this paragraph as an opening into the topic of proportion and such problems as: Find the height of a tree which casts a shadow 4 feet long at the same time of day that a 5-foot pole casts a shadow 2 feet long. How did shadow reckoning help the Egyptians determine the time of day? Do we apply the same principle to the solution of the first problem? Here the learners would have an opportunity to develop their powers of discriminating.

An excellent passage which can be used to teach learners how to *extrapolate,* one of the forms of chaining described in Chapter I, is presented below.

> It seems likely that the priests of those days had discovered a way of using square tables which enabled them to multiply any two numbers together without using the abacus. Here, for example, is how they would multiply 102 by 96.
>
> Step 1   Add 102 to 96 and divide the result by 2 to find the average 99
> Step 2   Take 96 from 102; divide the result by 2, to find half the difference between the two numbers . . 3
> Step 3   Look up in the table the square of 99 and you at once see it is 9801
> Step 4   Look up in the table the square of 3 and you at once see it is 9
> Step 5   Take 9 from 9801 and you find the correct answer 9792
>
> If we understand this method, we can multiply any two numbers together in the same way.

> (*Ibid.,* p. 23)

Students with a little practice should not find it difficult to reconstruct the method, apply it to other examples, and, finally, generalize that when we multiply one number by another, the result is always equal to the square of their average minus the square of half the difference between them. However, it would be a very unusually gifted student who will be able to explain why this method works, or why this method of multiplication is not widespread. The process of chaining would be used in the thinking out of answers to why and how this algorithm (a rule of procedure) for multiplication works. Students might begin by comparing this algorithm with the procedure they have been taught to use to discover whether there is any relationship. This lead might be fruitless and students should be led to recognize that a fresh start might be made by looking at the problem as repeated addition rather than as a multiplication problem. Thus students start with a given set of evidence, a fixed method or pattern, and a need to relate this information to previously learned concepts.

In relation to multiplication algorithms, an interesting book by Ann Cutler called *Instant Math* might be provided for those students who have mastered one rule of procedure and are capable of using shortcut methods with understanding. Various multiplication short cuts are presented in this little book which might prove worthy of use by gifted students who would study these short cuts to see if they can explain why they work. Such a book would provide enrichment material in the mathematics classroom and practice in several cognitive areas.

Anne S. Grossman

CHAPTER VI

SOCIAL DEMANDS AND INSTRUCTIONAL PROCESSES

"Stand up and read the next paragraph," commanded the teacher. The pupil dutifully stood and read in a rapid flowing monotone. Other students were peering at their textbooks, following the reader with some small degree of concentration, for only the teacher knew who was going to be next. Pupil number nine ended the story by reading the last paragraph, books automatically closed and a recitation followed.

"Who was the main character? Class!"

"Nathan," the class responded.

"Where did he live? Class!"

"Texas," the class responded in unison.

A few more factual questions addressed to individual members was followed by a "thought question": "Did you like this story?"

The answers seemed to be following a routine, always prefaced with an "I liked the story because. . . ."

". . . it was about a boy our age."

". . . I learned something new."

". . . it had animals in it."

Having delivered themselves of what had become an educational litany, the students' attention was directed to a new activity with a mechanical pronouncement: "Spelling next." Spelling consisted of having students stand on command and spell words from a previously assigned word list. The correct spellings were rewarded with a smile or nod, the incorrect spellings found the student being admonished to be more persistent in his study. After thirty minutes of oral spelling the fifth grade—class of 1916—turned their attention to arithmetic.

Arithmetic instruction resembled spelling and reading. "Repeat the table of fours, Harry."

Harry droned, "Four times one is four. Four times two is eight," up to and including four times twelve.

Memory work, recall of specific information, emphasis on a few basic skills, and oral participation under teacher direction characterized the elementary classroom of fifty years ago. This is in sharp contrast indeed to good elementary classroom instruction today, where one finds students engaged in a variety of activities, the teacher teaching individual children or small groups, and the children seemingly engaged in more spontaneous child-initiated tasks.

If, however, one should try to explain the differences in classroom functioning by studying the specific classrooms and their activities, one would find it difficult. Why do the contrasting teaching styles differ so markedly? Why is it believed that the content should be varied for children in the present classroom in contrast to the homogeneity of fifty years ago?

Understanding of the way a school functions and the purposes it seeks to fulfill cannot be found exclusively in the classroom. In general the classroom practices derive their meaning from the larger context of society—what it desires of its future citizens, what it intends to become, to what extent it sees formal education as contributing to over-all purposes. Any lag between the school's educational practices and society's expectations has been a focal point in examining educational practice and judging whether it is adequate or obsolete.

While the sage's observation of several thousand years ago, that men cannot agree on what children should learn, is still true today, the educational concern over greater educational achievement is probably at an all-time high. For as the country has come to place its trust in formal education to keep the society functioning, the question of whether education is living up to expectations becomes more urgent. As urgency increases, so does the prominence of instructional issues, for the instructional process is at the core of education.

There has always been a certain amount of tension between the school and its critics because of demands that instruction solve certain perceived social problems and the assumed lag in the school's response. Keeping this tension within manageable bounds has always been a concern of thoughtful educators. Inevitably, though, instructional changes are generally made in response to societal demands, and the sharper and more insistent the demands, the greater the changes.

The history of our schools reflects educational change undertaken in response to societal crisis. Historical examples can be multiplied.

The need for attention to agriculture and mechanical arts induced direct governmental intervention in the setting up of land-grant colleges. Faced with a foreign enemy who seemed to possess superior technological skills, the federal government brought funds to bear on developing and staffing vocational programs and in the latest instance science, mathematics, foreign language, and guidance programs. Other less spectacular, but significant, instances of public pressure to replace irrelevant subject matter with a more practical curriculum are commonplace details in the history of American education. One conclusion seems obvious: as social problems and pressures, whatever their source, accumulate, they eventually influence the public's demands on the schools. Consequently, an important phase of any curriculum development is the analysis of society and projection of trends. Nevertheless, this rational approach to curriculum-making is of relatively recent vintage and there is still some resistance among educators to viewing instruction as part of a total system that sees the school as part of society.

There is still a pronounced tendency among some educators to ignore historical issues as instruments of educational change and rely on time alone to resolve instructional issues. They believe that somehow problems are outgrown by schools rather than actively resolved. One cannot escape the feeling that radiates from some educators that social changes come and go but the schools lumber on. As one educator remarked to the author when queried on her reaction to a recent widely publicized research study, "I think it best not to pay any attention to these things, but rather to go into your classroom and teach." If this tendency to ignore outside influences on instruction is at all widespread, and one would like to believe that it was more a matter of cultural lag than deliberate negligence, the present state of public concern for schools and their direct contribution to societal problems is at a low ebb. But for most people, the radically heightened perception of the school's contribution to society has overridden the assumption that schools can stand aside from the society.

At a time when schools fulfilled rather limited formal functions, which not infrequently had little to do with contemporary life and problems, much of the learning needed to cope with the real world came from direct experience and "on-the-job-living." Social change has sharply realigned the focus and expectancies of formal schooling. Moreover, the overriding instructional issues are a product of this realignment.

In the redefinition of the task of education the prominent tendency has been to give students an education that promotes direct involvement with societal problems as contrasted with merely transmitting some basic skills and knowledge. The new expectation that education will be an active social force dictates that the school produce a student who can identify problems, analyze problems, reconstruct knowledge, and produce knowledge. In addition, the tasks of the school and the student are greatly compounded by the wealth of new knowledge which is being accumulated in every discipline.

The Problem of Knowledge Expansion

Available knowledge, it is said, doubles every ten years, defying any individual's ability to synthesize and master the total of any of the recognized disciplines. The current instructional problems in education, which seem at first glance to be hydra-headed, thus spring from two main sources: (1) the new demands placed on the school for direct knowledge about and direct intervention in the organized complexities of our contemporary world, and (2) the enormous growth of new knowledge.

As any quick perusal of school and educational budgets at local, state, and national levels will indicate, our commitments as a society to education and the development of intellectual resources to keep our society afloat are enormous. One expert, in assessing this commitment, finds that the total has moved from an estimated 51 billion dollars in 1956 to over 100 billion dollars in 1966, an increase unrivaled by any other sector of the economy. With the willingness to make such commitments come added pressures and demands for effective instruction culminating in greater cognitive development, and ultimately more effective solutions to social problems.

The reorganization of the disciplines with an eye to an earlier introduction of basic concepts has been the most conspicuous development in the vast curricular changes of this decade. If students are anticipating higher ranges of achievement in a given subject, it then seems only logical that instruction in the specific skills and processes begin earlier in the school program. New curricula, new methods of instruction, and new materials are all part of this pattern. Each innovation increases the demands on students—more reading, more writing, more time in labs thinking like scientists—all aimed at upgrading the cognitive ability of the future citizen.

There is one very real problem with the new curriculum and its demands on the student. It springs from casting much of the subject reorganization along the lines of a logical arrangement of the material and ignoring the cognitive functioning of the student. In many cases the main purpose of curriculum reorganization, as the student sees it, is to make him learn more without giving him much assistance in improving his *methods* of learning.

Demands that students develop their cognitive functioning to new levels unattained by previous generations cannot be satisfied by simply requiring students to commit more time to their schoolwork. Already, in the more academic schools, the student's waking hours are devoted exclusively to schoolwork, necessitating a work week which is staggering when compared to the work week of other age groups in the population.

Under these circumstances rebellion becomes a prominent by-product of youth's experience, as some occurrences on our college campuses so well attest.

Not infrequently discouragement and a sense of personal futility settles on the student as he is faced with an increasingly overwhelming mountain of knowledge. It is becoming steadily clearer that the problem of the knowledge explosion and the attendant need for mastery cannot be met simply through increasing the time students devote to the educational task and reorganizing the materials studied.

An Alternative to Complete Knowledge

Another approach that is receiving attention consists of using psychological research in identifying the cognitive skills to give assistance to ordering and mastering knowledge in subject disciplines. If cognitive skills in identifying, ordering, and mastering knowledge and its application to problems can be isolated, organized, and developed, then the perennial historical problem plaguing the school—attempting to teach all the significant knowledge—becomes less overpowering to both pupil and teacher. The main task involved is the identification of areas of cognitive abilities and specifying the functional scholarship skills involved in analysis, selection, organization, and utilization of knowledge on a given task.

Several solutions are beginning to emerge and more will be forthcoming with the impetus of massive research and development funds, using methods which have proved effective in industry and science. One of these approaches—using written materials to develop cognitive abilities—is the central topic of this book.

The application of knowledge further compounds the task of educator and student alike. Few problems which are met in the reality of social contexts lend themselves to solution by direct application of memorized materials. In the instance of using basic arithmetic to total a shopping bill in a supermarket, the task soon becomes complicated as the consumer grapples with two cans purchased on a three-for-eighty-nine-cent offer, six-cents-off specials, and other "bargains." Research studies demonstrate that few consumers can begin to cope with the arithmetic problems of comparing weights and prices to arrive at true cost per unit quantity.

Yet in this last process all the operations involved are contained in the basic processes of arithmetic: addition, subtraction, multiplication, and division. In comparison to other types of social problems—fighting air pollution, ordering traffic, providing adequate housing, and governing our cities, to mention but a few —the application of mathematics in a supermarket has a direct reality and limited intangibles. Nevertheless, in practically all instances of application, the process is still some distance removed from the knowledge as directly learned and hence is not directly transferred.

Using knowledge in different situations presupposes the ability to analyze relationships, uncover common processes, and bring to bear appropriate specific knowledge which is needed to effect solutions. Insofar as the intangibles grow in a problem, the untangling of relationships becomes more abstract and requires a surer command of the symbolic processes of language.

In understanding power relationships within the federal government, the usual procedure is to confront the learner with a diagram of the three branches of government. These are labeled the Executive, the Judicial, and the Legislative branches. From the formal diagram in shorthand fashion he learns the following power relationships: the Executive branch enforces the laws, the Judicial judges the laws, and the Legislative makes the laws. Yet as he watches the President's State of the Union Message on television he hears the President say, "I'm going to send a bill to Congress . . ."

The facts are that the relationships of these branches do not lend themselves to description adequately or even accurately to diagrammatics. A diagram in this case would be an ikon, a diagrammatic representation of the symbolic idea of the branches of government. To describe properly the subtleties of relationships, the thinking process must leave ikons and move to the more abstract level and manipulate symbols. Thus, facility in the thinking process is highly correlated with ability to use symbols.

Our current educational efforts with a heavy emphasis on language are in keeping with the intangible type of problem and the symbolic style of approach needed—for our problems increasingly do not lend themselves to analysis as direct experience. Those situations that do are largely dealt with on a reflex level: unlocking the mailbox, punching the elevator button, or opening the apartment door. But the ones which grasp our conscious attention or cause an uneasiness in our lives, generally are fraught with intangible assessments which cause one to need to evolve principles and test inferences. As our lives have become more involved with personal relationships and jobs that have no directly experienced product, the intangibles in the problem situations grow. At present there seem to be several obvious solutions available to the schools.

The Nondirected Approach—Retreatism

One authority, speaking recently about the problems of identity in American culture and mass media's role in culture, cites the huge demand for simple formula, pat situational comedy, and drama on television. Mr. Average American, forced to navigate in

everyday life on a sea of problems which resist easy
face-to-face appraisal, being fraught with abstract intangibles, finds solace in a television fantasy. This
fantasy, if not very intellectually demanding, does give
the comfort of limited confusion on alignment of personal relationships and clear-cut, directly solvable
problems.

If there is any characteristic which has persevered
in popular television drama it is the sharp delineation
of good and evil and the ultimate triumph of the good.
This is a strong contrast indeed to many current issues and contemporary social reality. Moreover, much
as we may cry out for a respite from a world that
keeps presenting us with problems which seem to
have in common only their ability to baffle us with
intangibles and complexities, it is too much to expect
any abrupt change when we examine the evidence
from many scientific and social investigations.

It may be of more than passing significance that
the writers of television scenarios have been moved
to seek their setting in a fictionalized West remote in
time and obscure in factual detail, or, if bowing to
the contemporary, to circumscribe the action in a
house or fenced-in neighborhood which seems to be
unrelated to most Americans' world and quite isolated
from any of the broader community's social problems.
In the face of the difficulty of application of knowledge because of the intangibles with which modern
living and its problems are riddled, retreat from reality
becomes a favorite recreation.

It has been suggested that such a response to complexity makes a mockery of the belief that the American citizen can handle the power to make judgments
on political, social, and economic issues involving his
life. Removal of social issues from direct accessibility
to individual experience, with retention of ultimate
political control by the voter, is the outstanding char-

acteristic of contemporary American political life. Whether we can bridge this gap by educating for a higher level of application of intelligence to abstract issues is probably the central issue in the present-day attempt to produce an alert public-spirited citizenry.

Which Road Shall We Take?

In examining the way the citizen should be educated for effective participation, several possibilities are discernible. The recent experience of a Germany in which extreme emphasis on technical and specialized education of a high order glossed over moral issues scarcely needs re-examination; it is one road which most Americans would reject out-of-hand.

A second possible direction, and one that seems more nearly within the realm of possibility for American schools, is the early separation of students into separate tracks where different groups are taught at different levels of abstraction. This is the educational practice in many European countries, where it has come under critical scrutiny. Early separation has the consequence of establishing several classes of citizens. Over several generations the class lines harden and communication as well as social mobility is limited.

Whatever might be said for this latter approach, it represents a drastic change in the educational commitment of America. Previous curricular arrangements have largely subscribed in theory, if not in practice, to an open system which tries to alter environmental differences and provide many alternate routes to earning a livelihood and becoming a participating citizen. A scheme of separated class education ignores the plan of general education whereby all American students have common experiences and develop a common commitment to democratic ideals.

A third approach, one which has enthusiastic exponents, is the use of technical and mechanical devices to speed up the process of learning, to reduce the time lag in bringing new knowledge into the classroom, and to short-cut the retraining of staff. Several good explanations of such devices and materials are available, giving detailed information on the programing and use of these media, for which reason specific information on these procedures will be omitted here. However, the question whether these devices (more specifically, television, programed learning, and computers) will replace more traditional modes of education needs to be explored.

Programed instruction, with the assistance of a wide press popularizing and heralding it as a radical departure and brilliant innovation, moved into the educational scene in the late 1950s. The basic technique underlying the most popular type of programing, that of presenting an immediate reward for the correct response, was not new. It had been dormant as an experimental classroom procedure for many years, inasmuch as it had not had widespread application to education.

What is now conceded to be an unfortunate sequence in the development of the medium, even by its supporters, was the promotion of the hardware aspects of the new development, emphasizing teaching machines, in advance of the designing of adequate programs. Classroom testing soon demonstrated the relationship of program to teaching machine. This was analogous to the relationship of a painting by an acknowledged master and its frame, the latter in each case being only of relatively minor importance—a support for the primary medium.

Meanwhile, programs with carefully arranged sequences, identifiable ranges of objectives, and personally structured rewards were exceedingly slow in developing. Early enthusiasm waned as the optimistic predictions of rapid learning in skill areas and quick assimilation of general information failed to materialize.

Also contributing to the disappointment was a harsh reality which has been the shoal on which many an education innovation has foundered in the past. Students have a highly individualized approach to learning which one single program, developed for all, could neither foresee nor adequately provide. Work still proceeds in this area, without many of the extravagant claims of its early enthusiasts, but discussion of its complete replacement of other written materials has receded.

The career of educational television as a medium for use directly in the classroom has, in broad terms, paralleled that of programed learning. An initial wave of enthusiasm coupled with broad claims created a flurry of excitement among the lay public and susceptible educators. Before demonstrations had evidenced its strengths and limitations, extravagant claims were made for its potential as a means of solving the persistent teacher shortage and upgrading the classroom curriculum.

The staggering expense of the initial steps in establishing educational television caused many a public school system to pause before plunging into a broad-scale program. Nevertheless, heavy foundation support soon started series of programs in several parts of the country. One comprehensive attempt included large areas of six states and an estimated school population of several million.

Again the old curricular problems which had arisen to harass programed instruction manifested themselves, along with others which were peculiar to the medium. There were limitations to television teaching. If the material for instruction did not lend itself to visual presentation, in many cases there resulted a presentation characterized as "a talking textbook with a blackboard."

The theory that a good teacher in a classroom of thirty could, through television, spread his influence to thousands and millions of remote students also frequently collapsed under testing. The sensitivity of a good teacher to feedback in the classroom was absent in the television studio and impossible with such a vast audience. Again that plague of curriculum innovators, the lack of flexibility, manifested itself. Where learning, as in foreign languages, was heavily dependent upon the logical arrangement of subject matter and succeeding steps were predicated upon the mastery of the preceding, the audience rapidly dwindled as students lost the continuity and were unable to keep pace.

Furthermore, the assumption of the total superiority of the visual presentation of ideas needed considerable refinement. The concepts and principles of experience which rely heavily upon symbolic language aren't always capable of being replicated in pictures or objects without considerable distortion of the idea. Research on cognition demonstrates that thinking moves rapidly from representative images of the real object, ikons, to the symbol for the object in order to gain greater flexibility in thinking.

Educational television began in a spirit of adventure, which flagged as the student audience felt its impersonality and remoteness. These weaknesses, along with a failure to correlate and parallel the instruction of the classroom teacher, have chastened the medium's early proponents and sharply defined the place of the medium as one more supportive tool in the total instructional program in the classroom. Other criticisms were based on the exclusive preoccupation with factual materials in programed learning and television. They stressed the limited range of application inherent in the manner of presentation of materials, and the resulting narrow range of transfer of learnings. With the subsequent delimitation of the approaches to learning offered by these media, and the need for much broader critical research, the hopes for radical breakthroughs with these media have waned and their use as ancillary but significant tools in the classroom has become accepted.

A characteristic which has been noted by critics of the American scene has been the propensity to turn human problems into technical problems and to apply mechanical, statistical solutions. Any general criticism such as this leaves large gaps for attack and one would have to detail the specifics before accepting this criticism as valid. However, an indication of that propensity, if it be a propensity, is the application of computer technology to the classic problems in a multitude of areas.

It was only a matter of time before instructional problems would undergo rigorous computer experimentation. Considerable experimentation and demonstration has been under way, principally outside the public school classroom. The potential for computer technology in the classroom appears to be vast enough to give spectacular assistance with analysis and direct intervention in the classic problems of learning.

Up to the present, work has been handicapped by the heavy expense involved in using computers and the need for trained staff. A merger of the curriculum experts who have a specialized knowledge of curriculum design problems, child development, and learning, with the personnel who have highly specialized expertise in computer technology has been slow in coming.

Several advanced projects are under way which, if they fulfill current hopes, may provide a major breakthrough in instruction. Nevertheless, the shortage of personnel to program and use the computer adequately as a learning aid will still be a major obstacle for the foreseeable future, and it is likely that, if advances are made in computer instruction which make it feasible for classroom use, the roadblock of retraining personnel remains for many years. Even then, given this optimistic assessment of our most flexible and creative innovation since 1940, repeated experimentation and demonstration will doubtless uncover limitations which will narrow its application, much as was done with television and programed learning.

The versatility of the computer and its ability to imitate many of the processes of the human mind offer both frustration and hope. Meanwhile, other practices more readily adoptable in the classroom must carry the burden of providing the education that equips American children to cope with immediate and long-range problems. At present, the unknowns in the field of instruction far surpass the knowns and, except in the broadest of terms, make projections of its future direction risky.

Each of these burgeoning instructional innovations poses a host of issues. These issues involve, principally, ways to develop the intellectual abilities and functional scholarship skills needed to master the new society which already confronts us. It is becoming increasingly clear that traditional instructional approaches of "read, recite, and test," of "read, write, and repeat," of nondirected reading do not provide the new cognitive patterns needed. And direct assistance from electronic aids is not in the offing. Are there procedures and materials of instruction that can be utilized in the present-day classroom, which do not require extensive retraining of teachers yet suggest ways to develop high-level cognitive skills?

Improving Cognitive Functioning

Extensive research in instructional practice and the psychology of cognition has caused investigators to identify broad areas of cognitive abilities. These parallel the functional scholarship skills, which are useful in fostering learning at many levels. Since learning at every level involves using abilities to manipulate symbols, it is productive to develop these abilities through written materials.

In the instance of the cognitive ability to discriminate superordinate (more inclusive) ideas from subordinate (less inclusive) ideas, cultivation can begin at an early age by having students select the generalization and its supporting facts, or separate generalizations, on the basis of inclusiveness. The same functional scholarship skill is brought into play at a far more complex level in the behavioral sciences when scholars build models employing a few selective generalizations which will bring complex phenomena into the realm of predictability. As an example, the model of social class status, which has been widely utilized by sociologists, employs generalizations about education, income, and types of residence to explain and predict a variety of attitudes and behavior. These range from voting behavior to child-rearing practices. While the development of areas of cognitive abilities can be done with numerous types of written materials, trade books offer some advantages over other written materials, such as textbooks. The orientation of development of areas of cognitive abilities to functional scholarship skills requires the activities of the learner to be similar at the different levels of learning, varying only in complexity and abstraction. Whereas the presentation of information in trade books is not directed to as specific a purpose, it is, consequently, more likely to confront the learner with a task similar to that met in higher levels of scholarship.

By contrast, textbooks are generally more focused, less open in their presentation, more tightly organized, and frequently quite explicit in giving guidance on the interpretation of facts and generalizations. The structuring of the materials by the learner into a cognitive map that is clear, ordered, and related to previously learned information has been a distinctive feature of the new curriculum developments. Using written materials to promote development of cognitive abilities poses some instructional issues which must be resolved by the classroom teacher, for the instructional processes imply some changes in the learner-teacher relationship.

Maurice J. Eash

CHAPTER VII

SOME INSTRUCTIONAL ISSUES IN THE USES OF WRITTEN MATERIALS

A story circulating among educators has a teacher reporting to her new assignment in an ultramodern school. When she asks the principal for her supplies to begin the year, he hands her a screwdriver, an oil can, and a slip of paper containing the telephone number of an electrician. Notably absent are any books or written materials. The story is apocryphal, at least for the present, but there is enough public discussion of recent work on modes of instruction which depart from traditional practice to cause one to question the use of written materials. Are written materials on their way out? Or is it a matter of revising methods of *using* written materials? How can written materials be used effectively? These are some of the questions that will be considered in the examination of three instructional issues which follows.

These issues were selected in view of (1) the use of written materials under the imperatives of education as an active agent in societal problems, and (2) the proliferation of knowledge, which requires far greater ability to order and organize content as well as posing persistent problems in thoroughness in mastery and use of content.

1. *Are written materials outmoded as primary instructional tools in the classroom and to be superseded by other modes of instruction?*

The last decade has seen the development of a number of electronic devices which are used in the organization as well as in the presentation of material and which were widely heralded as innovations that threatened more conventional instructional methods with obsolescence. After the initial excitement wore off and serious inquiry was started on the strengths and weaknesses of electronic approaches, limitations were discovered. Although electronic devices had demonstrable values as aids, evidence seems to indicate they are not going to totally replace modes of instruction in which written materials play a central role. By comparison written material demonstrated greater flexibility in meeting individual differences, in pacing of learning, and in allowing students to deal with a broader range of stimuli, to check one set of stimuli with another, to look at the presenter's organization, and to question critically a total idea in the light of background materials.

One of the greatest challenges to programed learning has been in meeting these criteria of flexibility, all which can be provided for by open-ended written materials made available to every child. Whether the child responds to open-ended written material along these lines is a matter of teaching. Nevertheless, the possibilities are inherent in the nature and structure of the material, especially where trade books are used.

A second advantage of written materials as opposed to certain types of electronic presentation of information (films and filmstrips) is the early movement of learning from a direct representation of images in thinking to a symbolic use of experience. The latter stage in thinking offers far more flexibility than the former in manipulating the content of experience.

Learning moves very quickly from dealing with things as directly perceived to abstractions and symbols. For example, while a very small child may relate *chair* to his chair, only with more experience does he learn to use a symbolic concept of chairness to any object that has similar common properties. Presenting direct images in place of the symbolism becomes a slow process and may in some cases slow learning rather than enhance it. "A picture is worth a thousand words" is not a consistently accurate statement once the child has achieved the use of symbolic language. The reading process wholly dependent upon symbols and symbolic thought therefore becomes in many instances more efficient in transmitting concepts than direct-image approaches, which are used by other media.

The higher the stage of learning in any discipline, the less likely it is that direct images can be used. Even the diagrammatic explanations are usually representations of the abstract in an attempt to simplify, through reducing the complex to a representational image. For example, in depicting the dollar drain of the United States economy, arrows are drawn on a map between the United States and other countries on which are printed the sums spent on imports and exports by each country. A complex process involving very sophisticated reasoning on monetary policy, the gold standard, geopolitics, and a myriad of other economic issues is labeled but certainly not explained. In what is perhaps a more common instructional procedure, we are (or should be) well aware, when we depict graphically the water cycle in a science lesson, that we are by-passing complicated but essential processes—ones which defy our representational attempts to describe them as direct images.

Written materials have often been described as abstract and not related to direct experience. Admittedly this is true—and herein lies their strength. For learning of any depth soon moves to the level of abstraction and the thinking process at higher levels uses the symbolic rather than direct representational images in its dealing with the world, thus making written materials a more real component of thinking than direct-image presentation.

The argument for written materials may be carried to another level. When it comes to presenting information efficiently, a good book well written, whereby the individual reader can make his own adjustment to the material, is difficult to replace. A comparative study on the learning of information through programed materials and the putting of the same materials into a well-written narrative style found the latter producing more learning in a fraction of the time.

It is also significant to note that with the growth in electronic presentation of materials we are also getting a corresponding growth in demand for written material. Newspaper, book, and library circulations are at an all-time high. The television presentation of a book has been known to produce runs on the book as viewers wish to satisfy the glow of imagination, which can only be done through the printed word where each reader produces his own interpretations.

In any of the numerous studies on the unemployed we find low reading skills to be one of the most common characteristics in the inability to find and hold a job. On the grounds of employability, among others, it is probable that written materials and their contribution to learning will continue to grow in importance and that they will remain central in the instructional process. Other media of instruction—television, programed learning, and films—seem to become aids and enhance the place of written material. The correspondence of written materials to the symbolic process in thinking makes it a formidable contributor to the thinking process. This must be developed to handle higher levels of symbolic and abstract thinking, which increasingly characterize work at all job levels.

2. *Should written materials (books, magazines, and so forth) be used in a classroom to help students accumulate knowledge or to reconstruct knowledge?*

An obvious position on the above issue is a middle ground. It should do both. Before acceptance of this position, one needs to examine desired educational outcomes, which can only be validated with respect to the way a person should function in a given social context. Let us examine briefly the position that would have written materials being read and defended on the basis that students are building a background for future use in a discipline.

The storage theory of knowledge is a venerable theory which has permeated the schoolroom and the instructional practices for many centuries. Contained within the theory is the assumption that the schoolroom is the preparation for some future life and that the materials of education are to be absorbed and stored. Then at some future time, when information in the different disciplines has been mastered, this information, which constitutes education, could be applied to problems. The accumulative stage then is one where materials are read primarily for retention and stored for later use.

Much of the use of written material in the classroom, both textbooks and trade books, has been geared to information accumulation only. The former are frequently used with exercises on recall of materials, while the latter are read with superficial attention given to plot, characters, and episodes in the book. If the trade book is of a factual nature, then a rough recounting of facts is seen as the primary responsibility.

One of the major criticisms of the accumulative

approach to the use of instructional materials is its failure to have correspondence to any model of the development of cognitive styles in children. Cognitive styles do not come from the shuffling of random facts, leaving organization to chance. A second criticism arises from the proliferation of knowledge.

Not only is the day past when the individual can master all the information available in a given subject area, but he may even have to meet the problem of having mastered obsolete knowledge which may handicap him in problem-solving. Thus, emphasis on the information accumulation process can pose a very real threat. Furthermore, to accumulate knowledge without organization and system is a wasteful way of learning as well as a distinct hazard in applying old solutions to new problems.

Other recent findings on the structure of knowledge offer leads to the use of written materials in the classroom which put the accumulation process into a systematic framework of cognitive organization, thus providing the child a way to manage a vast amount of information and to avoid the dilemmas of obsolescence. The learner effects a reconstruction of knowledge in the process of learning. He analyzes, orders, and organizes the information with which he deals. This structure-of-knowledge approach which both emphasizes the basic principles of knowledge in the disciplines and builds techniques of discovery and use of knowledge is at the heart of the reconstruction process.

Written materials such as textbooks, trade books, and magazines should be read with emphasis on observing structural processes, inference, comparison, building of generalizations, use of evidence, development of conclusions, and other cognitive skills. Leaving a residue of key ideas with power to generate other ideas, they will then leave the student with reconstructed knowledge useful in application and without the confusion of disjointed facts.

The secret of the application of knowledge has been the ability to analyze the context in which the problem occurs and to reconstruct information from other contexts to fit. The sculptor needs a mental conceptual framework with which to approach the block of marble in order to come out with a work of art. No sculptor starts chipping away aimlessly, accidently discovering relationships which coalesce into a finished form. Aimless accumulation of knowledge without attention to structural properties is a wasteful approach to learning and one which can be avoided if some basic cognitive skills are recognized and used in guiding children in using written materials.

The processes in reconstruction of knowledge *can* be taught. In the investigations of mental development of children it is clear that they do go through stages in their abilities to conceptualize and handle information. For some time it was thought that the processes of cognitive development, combining opposites, moving from thought processes based on perceptions and action to hypothesis casting, moving from pre-causal thinking to the ability to understand causality, were a function of teaching in helping children to move through the stages of cognitive development.

While it is true that the different stages have to be acquired (i.e., that a child cannot move directly into seeing causal relationships without doing considerable pre-causal exploration), the child's cognitive processes are not completely at the mercy of physical developmental stages. Direct teaching can move the child through the stages at a much faster pace. It is clear then, that systematic instruction in the structure of knowledge using identifiable approaches to cognitive abilities can aid a child in the development of the ability to reconstruct knowledge. This is a process which is essential to transforming the student from a learner into a thinker, one in which written materials can play a significant role.

The older accumulative process which left discovery of basic generalizations and the processes of analyzing, ordering, and reconstructing knowledge to chance must be abandoned as wasteful and inefficient. Getting on with the task of helping children develop the ability to reconstruct knowledge into useful forms is one of the most pressing instructional issues of our time. ⌋

3. *Should classroom instruction using written materials emphasize active critical participation of the student or noncritical acceptance and absorption?*

The passivity of instruction in schools has been recognized and decried. Most of the new curriculum innovations have addressed themselves to the problem of broadening student participation in the learning process. One approach in learning materials has been to furnish the student with more materials, some even contradictory to each other, and have the student reconcile disparities. Others have used incomplete tasks and problems which require the student to develop the problem as well as formulate solutions. What is behind this approach is a psychological assumption which stresses that maximum learning keeps the learner involved in the task. Written materials, used with an organized approach, can lead to active participation which gains commitment and motivation. To move the learner from the role of one acted upon to actor is a goal of many of the new curricula.

The serious consequences of nonparticipation carry over into other areas of life. Retreat from active engagement, withdrawal from complexities, escape into fantasy, have been noted as growing trends in the American culture. When the major portion of education has centered on noncritical acceptance and emphasized absorption of material as its processes, little opportunity is afforded for learning skills of effective participation which are transferable to adult life. More specifically, dependence upon outside direction, spoon-feeding of instruction, inability to identify problems, and one-sided approaches to answers are characteristics of American college students and have been noted as contributory to the high drop-out rate in college. These students, acting on their own, lack the independent scholarship skills needed for functioning in a college environment.

Functional scholarship skills that are developed through written materials in a variety of situations to assist in transfer of learning, and that become integral to the mental habits of the learner, are crucial in a society which demands high levels of education. The functional scholarship skills involved in analyzing written materials, making comparisons, deriving subtle meanings, selecting consistent evidence, all are part of a cognitive approach which is developed over a time with the active participation of the learner. The passive approach may give the learner some content, but the operations and processes so essential to independent learning are glossed over.

There is a similarity between mental functioning of the human being and the processes of a computer. The computer differs from other machines in that it is able to profit from its own output, make corrections and adjustment in the input, and change the process. The autonomous student who is able to function as an independent scholar has the same capacity to evaluate his learning products. In order to regulate one's learning in line with previously defined goals, the learner needs to be able to instruct himself as the result of his own feedback. Working with written materials is the primary style of learning at higher levels of education and the basic skills of functional scholarship, including analysis of feedback, can be incorporated into the elementary classroom program.

Finally, the most cogent argument for the active participation of the learner in all classroom instruction, including those which use written materials, revolves around the personality of the individual. As the learner sees himself through active confrontation with his experience he becomes more able to exercise conscious choice on all levels of decision-making. It has been said that the dearth of appraisal of personal experience makes one a prisoner of impulse and emotion.

In the confrontation process the use of written materials provides a broad range of experience against which a student can, if guided, juxtapose his own personal experience. Moreover, in the juxtaposing of experience the student can select the range at which he feels secure, and does not need to expose his weaknesses publicly. Active participation at the level of examination of emotions is an educational quest at its deepest level. In these experiences the fantasy, speculation, and provisional tries which are present in any personality in the making find a testing ground; conflicts are resolved and the self begins to emerge more clearly. A sense of identity and self-respect are at the very heart of the achieving process. Confrontation of experience through the learner's active participation with written materials is a requisite part of the learning process in the classroom.

Written materials pose both a problem and a hope to the classroom instructional program. The very abundance of information published and deemed essential to competence in each subject confronts both teacher and learner with an almost impossible task. Knowledge that the public's expectations for direct intervention by education into serious social problems places an additional burden of responsibility on both teacher and learner. Therefore, a curriculum stressing cognitive development takes on a new significance and moves into the central focus of the educational picture. So, too, the time-honored processes of instruction are coming under critical scrutiny as newer ways of organizing, sequencing, and presenting information are investigated.

Written materials of all types have been the principal tool in the classroom instructional program since the advent of the printing press. Results of research on cognition indicate that these materials still have a central role to play. However, this role must be recast and a greater interrelationship must be achieved between the various levels of instruction. The cognitive functions which must be developed are of one piece. They differ in complexity and abstraction but not in function.

Written materials, it has been said, can be replaced as the main tools of the instructional process. The traditional uses are indeed ripe for re-examination, as the previous discussion suggests. However, the characteristics that are unique to written materials and have historically secured their place in the curriculum still seem to be valid. The task of developing the cognitive processes through written materials is just beginning. It is a task whose accomplishment is vital to the successful producing of citizens able to contribute to their personal and social welfare, a state which increasingly hinges upon the understanding and management of organized complexities.

Maurice J. Eash

LIST OF BOOKS MENTIONED IN THIS VOLUME

Anderson, M. D. *Through the Microscope: Man Looks at an Unseen World.*

Barclay, Isabel. *Worlds without End: Exploration from 2000 Years B.C. to Today.*

Bauer, Helen. *California Indian Days.*

Bauer, Helen. *California Rancho Days.*

Berke, Ernest. *The North American Indians.*

Commager, Henry Steele. *Crusaders for Freedom.*

Cutler, Ann. *Instant Math.*

d'Aulaire, Ingri and Edgar Parin. *Benjamin Franklin.*

d'Aulaire, Ingri and Edgar Parin. *Buffalo Bill.*

d'Aulaire, Ingri and Edgar Parin. *Leif the Lucky.*

de Angeli, Marguerite. *Yonie Wondernose.*

Eberle, Irmengarde. *A Chipmunk Lives Here.*

Elting, Mary. *The Lollypop Factory and Lots of Others.*

Evans, Pauline Rush (ed.). *The Best Book of Horse Stories.*

Evans, Pauline Rush (ed.). *The Best Book of Mystery Stories.*

Faulkner, Nancy. *The Secret of the Simple Code.*

Faulkner, Nancy. *Small Clown.*

Ferris, Helen (ed.). *Favorite Poems Old and New.*

Finger, Charles J. *Tales from Silver Lands.*

Finlayson, Ann. *A Summer to Remember.*

Fisher, James. *The Wonderful World of the Air.*

Flack, Marjorie. *The New Pet.*

Flack, Marjorie. *Tim Tadpole and the Great Bullfrog.*

Gallant, Roy A. *ABC's of Astronomy.*

Gallant, Roy A. *Exploring Chemistry.*

Gallant, Roy A. *Exploring the Planets.*

Gallant, Roy A. *Exploring the Sun.*

Gallant, Roy A. *Man's Reach into Space.*

Gilbert, Miriam. *Shy Girl: The Story of Eleanor Roosevelt, First Lady of the World.*

Goodman, Willard. *Noah's Ark ABC.*

Gottlieb, William P. *Jets and Rockets and How They Work.*

Gottlieb, William P. *Space Flight and How It Works.*

Grimm, Jakob and Wilhelm. *Grimm's Fairy Tales.*

Gruenberg, Sidonie Matsner (ed.). *Let's Hear a Story.*

Gruenberg, Sidonie Matsner (ed.). *Let's Read More Stories.*

Gruenberg, Sidonie Matsner. *The Wonderful Story of How You Were Born.*

Hammond, Penny. *My Skyscraper City: A Child's View of New York.*

Hansen, Harry. *The Story of Illinois.*

Harvey, Tad. *The Quest of Archimedes.*

Hawkins, Gerald S. *Stonehenge Decoded.*

Heavilin, Jay. *Fast Ball Pitcher.*

Hinchman, Jane. *A Talent for Trouble.*

Hofmann, Melita. *A Trip to the Pond.*

Hogben, Lancelot. *The Wonderful World of Mathematics.*

Hollander, John, and Bloom, Harold (eds.). *The Wind and the Rain.*

Hoyt, Edwin P. *Heroes of the Skies.*

Huxley, Julian S. *The Wonderful World of Life.*

Ipcar, Dahlov. *Brown Cow Farm.*

Ipcar, Dahlov. *Stripes and Spots.*

Ipcar, Dahlov. *Wild and Tame Animals.*

Irving, Washington. *Rip Van Winkle and Other Stories.*

Kenworthy, Leonard S. *Profile of Kenya.*

Kenworthy, Leonard S. *Profile of Nigeria.*

Kessler, Ethel and Leonard. *All Aboard the Train.*

Kessler, Ethel and Leonard. *Big Red Bus.*

Kipling, Rudyard. *The Jungle Book* (1931 ed.).

Lauber, Patricia. *The Quest of Louis Pasteur.*

Lee, Laurie, and Lambert, David. *The Wonderful World of Transportation.*

Lenski, Lois. *The Little Family.*

Lewis, Janet. *Keiko's Bubble.*

Mabie, Hamilton Wright (ed.). *Myths Every Child Should Know*.

McCracken, Harold. *The Winning of the West*.

MacDonald, Golden. *The Little Island*.

O'Neill, Mary. *Hailstones and Halibut Bones*.

O'Neill, Mary. *People I'd Like to Keep*.

Palazzo, Tony. *The Giant Playtime Nursery Book*.

Palazzo, Tony. *Goldilocks and the Three Bears*.

Palazzo, Tony. *Three Little Kittens*.

Palazzo, Tony. *The Little Red Hen*.

Pease, Howard. *Mystery on Telegraph Hill*.

Perry, George Sessions. *The Story of Texas*.

Pinney, Roy. *Animals, Inc.*

Pratt, Fletcher. *The Civil War*.

Roosevelt, Eleanor, and Ferris, Helen. *Partners: The United Nations and Youth*.

Selsam, Millicent E. *Exploring the Animal Kingdom*.

Selsam, Millicent E. *The Quest of Captain Cook*.

Simon, Tony. *North Pole: The Story of Robert E. Peary*.

Smaus, Jewel Spangler, and Spangler, Charles B. *America's First Spaceman*.

Steiner, Charlotte. *Birthdays Are for Everyone*.

Sterling, Dorothy. *Freedom Train: The Story of Harriet Tubman*.

Sterling, Dorothy. *Insects and the Homes They Build*.

Sterling, Dorothy. *Wall Street: The Story of the Stock Exchange*.

Stirling, Nora. *Up from the Sea: The Story of Salvage Operations*.

Swift, Jonathan. *Gulliver's Travels*.

Swinton, William E. *The Wonderful World of Prehistoric Animals*.

Turnbull, Colin. *The Forest People*.

Twain, Mark. *The Adventures of Tom Sawyer*.

West, Jerry. *The Happy Hollisters Series*.

White, Robb. *Candy*.

White, Robb. *Torpedo Run*.

INDEX